The Achievement of
WILLIAM STYRON

edited by

Robert K. Morris & Irving Malin

Cop. a

The University of Georgia Press
Athens

Library of Congress Catalog Card Number: 74–75942
International Standard Book Number: 0–8203–0351–8

The University of Georgia Press, Athens 30602

Set in 11 on 13 pt. Monticello type
Printed in the United States of America

Acknowledgments

Excerpts from the work of William Styron are reprinted with the kind permission of Random House and Bobbs-Merrill. Acknowledgments are also made to the following who have granted permission for the reprinting of copyrighted material from the periodicals and books that are here listed:

"Notes on a Southern Writer in Our Time" by Louis D. Rubin, Jr., originally appeared as chapter 8, "William Styron: Notes on a Southern Writer in Our Time," in his *The Faraway Country: Writers of the Modern South* (Seattle: University of Washington Press, 1963).

"*The Confessions of Nat Turner* and the Burden of the Past" by George Core originally appeared in the *Southern Literary Journal* (Spring 1970).

"History, Politics, and Literature: The Myth of Nat Turner" by Seymour L. Gross and Eileen Bender originally appeared in the *American Quarterly* (October 1971).

"William Styron: A Bibliography" by Jackson R. Bryer updates and supplements previous listings by Harold W. Schneider in *Critique* (Summer 1960); David D. Galloway in *The Absurd Hero in American Fiction* (Austin: University of Texas Press, 1966); August J. Nigro in *William Styron*, edited by Melvin J. Friedman and Nigro (Paris: Lettres modernes, 1967); and Bryer and Marc Newman in *William Styron's "The Confessions of Nat Turner"—A Critical Handbook*, edited by Melvin J. Friedman and Irving Malin (Belmont, Calif.: Wadsworth, 1970).

The editors wish to thank William Styron for his granting the two interviews published in this collection.

Table of Contents

Abbreviations

ROBERT K. MORRIS & IRVING MALIN

Vision and Value: The Achievement of William Styron

Not quite a quarter of a century has passed since the heroine of a remarkable first novel flung herself and a dubious heritage from the twelfth story of a dingy Harlem tenement, shocking a silent and almost unshockable generation, and rocketing a young southern writer to fame. Peyton Loftis was the fated, tragic girl; *Lie Down in Darkness* the novel; and the writer William Styron: an expatriate intellectual from Virginia's Tidewater, to whom it must have seemed unlikely (though not undeserved) that his novel of southern generations would have spoken so eloquently to the entire generation of the fifties, and that his own place among important contemporary writers should have been so quickly secured.

It was, of course, something other than chance that accounted for Styron's immediate popularity, indeed notoriety; for he had labored over the book with conflicting emotions for nearly five years, honing each sentence to such perfection that his paragraphs could defend themselves by their cutting edge alone. But there was no denying chance had a good deal to do with it. Styron had caught in a precise and lucky way the spirit of time and place. The postwar world sagged with weariness, disbelief, acedia, and guilt. Naturally prepared to find its own conscience trapped in the psychic rifts of one like Peyton—possessed and dispossessed, haunted, alienated, desolate—it was equally willing to universalize the neuroses destroying the Loftises: to see their "nothingness" both as moral sanction and symbol for what remained for so many after Belsen and Buchenwald, Hiroshima and Nagasaki and Dresden. Everything about *Lie Down in Darkness*—whose very title spoke of the metaphysical uncertainty of eternal certainties—

proved that the sins of the fathers (both nouns damning whether capitalized or not) had been visited on the children; and showed it by way of instinct and art. For Styron seemed to be grappling with the big problems of the ethos: seeking to make more explicable and coherent what was easily absurd and incoherent; striving to unravel the gross and unreasonable confusion attending the change and destruction that operated in one small part of the South, but, spreading tentaclelike, were becoming symptomatic of America as a whole.

What we can see today, twenty-five years later, is that *Lie Down in Darkness* was not only in part a parable of and for the fifties, not only in part an incantatory prophecy of middle-class confusion and breakup in the New South following hard upon the breakdown of the Old, but paradigmatic of the fictional world Styron was to recreate in subsequent novels. That world, as he articulated in a letter to the *Paris Review* in 1953, was one of "disorder, defeat, despair," in which men and women search for "love, joy, hope—qualities which, as in the act of life itself, are best when they have to be struggled for, and are not commonly come by with much ease."[1] In the best way that writers "repeat" themselves in order to fathom and expand as profoundly as they can those very ideas that have initially committed them to art, so Styron continually drives his protagonists to the very edge of the abyss; lets them peer into deep, empty, nihilistic spaces before, in tragic recognition of themselves, they pull back, renewed, to carry on their search, or ecstatically transformed embrace their death. Such a theme—metaphysical, existential, overwhelming—is by no means original. Modern man's encounter with the abyss—his confrontation with being and nothingness, his agonizing over free will, his apprehensive acceptance of fear and trembling, his search for his soul—has, in one way or another since Dostoevski, been at the center of the modern novel. And no one would rest claims for Styron's originality or importance or achievement on this all-too solid, if worn, surface.

What makes him unique is that he has created characters who, despite their realization of the abyss, are willing out of the sense of an ultimate motive and purpose in life to challenge it. This is much of the reason why Peyton commits suicide, why Cass Kinsolving plunges into the gaping hell of Sambuco, and Nat Turner into the horrendous, inevitable blood bath in Southampton County, why Captain Mannix and Private Magruder persist in their small, marvelous, unnoticed martyrdoms! To be sure, much of this movement comes from sheer drive and energy alone. Styron's people are compulsive, intense, made of a human fiber both elastic and tough. It comes as well because in some ideal way each does aspire to "love, joy, hope," does (in Frederick J. Hoffman's words) "struggle just to *assert* one's humanness, to get over the barriers of understanding, to clear one's personality of obsessions."[2] But they are not impelled by intellectual, physical, even emotional kinesis alone. They are equally galvanized by a higher intuition, by the belief that the abyss, all too ready to claim and damn them, can be transcended, and some "impossible state"[3] (where pride, dignity, nobility become the final measure of man) achieved. Their quest is for nothing less than a kind of grail: buried within the darker divisions of a world of conflicting change and lost value, to which they are drawn by its fitful incandescence, as by their own burning, ecstatic, and often tragic visions.

To speak, first of all, of vision in Styron's characters is to realize at the outset a formidable play of perceptions among them: ranging from the realist to the mystic, from the supernormal to the lunatic, from the secular to the divine, from the private to the apocalyptic. It is to realize further that any and all such visions are spun out of a novelist who himself happens to tack close to being considered a "visionary": one, as Northrop Frye has defined the type elsewhere, "who creates a higher spiritual world in which the objects of perception in this one have become transfigured and charged with a new intensity of symbolism."[4] Unlike other visionary writers, though, who depart from parabolic or abstract figures of reality (we think of Dante and Milton, Blake and Yeats), Styron creates his personae's visions from metaphors of reality. His characters' yearning for the "impossible state," for (on their terms) a finer, more desirable world, even for some glorious surcease from the anxieties and pressures of this one, are always built

[3]

upon what is concrete, mundane, ordinary: as though their symbolic imagination need root itself in the solid stuff of life.

Styron's visionary esthetic emerges almost entire in his first novel. The Loftises' progress through private purgatories to attain some ultimate, untroubled heaven where mind and spirit and body are at peace proves a series of doomed encounters with a reality each tries to shape according to his own distorted, disoriented, self-serving and self-seeking yet solipsistically "true" vision. But such journeys become more. In Milton Loftis one senses something other than the merely fallen, aging, middle-class male at climacteric who seeks, but never finds, refuge and salvation in adultery and alcohol. Beyond the stereotype looms an archetype: that of the failed quester who has hoped to transform a common mistress into a divine Beatrice, and drink into the ambrosia that preserves to the last the dregs of mortality, shields him against age, despair, loss, inadequacy, pain, failure, and impotence; the quester who has found life a depressing recurrence of half-open doors through which he followed a dream, hoping to open the final door and look upon a beatitude instead, as he does, of peering into the horror and nothingness.

Like Milton, Helen is equally the victim and agent of her fate. Her effete, sentimentalized religion (the obvious foil to the vitalistic faith of La Ruth) is no less a dangerous construct of reality and of living in the world than her husband's sex and drink. She too hoped, through transcendental longing, for a "timeless, unaltered" state in which to knit crippling despair into wholeness. But if Milton is pulled down by his materialism and sensuality, Helen is damned by her obsessive piety and Puritanism: by her having traded this life for one of spiritual emasculation. Like certain fanatics who lose touch with the flesh-and-blood world, Helen treads the fragile line between mystic and catatonic.

And there is the incomprehensibleness and complexity of Peyton herself, whose neurotic, inspired madness and hallucinatory excess lead her to an end that is, as much as a reaction to her parents' conflicts, the consequence of their (and Sir Thomas Browne's) insights that life irretrievably slips away, evanesces. Peyton's hypersensitivity to love, hope, and joy, and her rejection of the cold, cheerless mechanisms making life run on as best it can, bespeak a prelapsarian idealism. But her answer to life is no truer than Milton's or Helen's. Her suicide, while partially a tragic expiation by doomed youth of sins committed by its fathers, at the same time evades all responsibility for harnessing one's strengths—instead of agonizing over one's weaknesses—and working for stability and order. It takes neither intelligence nor guts to surrender to chaos; in retrospect, her death has perhaps more retaliative than retributive value. Indeed, her final vision—anti-mechanistic, falsely liberating, purgative, death-yearning—accompanying her fall from the highest rung of perverted innocence and her flight from paradise through a wilderness of tangled literary allusions, has almost no place in Styron's later work. Had she, in her final soliloquy, her *Liebestod*, brooded upon Camus rather than upon Aeschylus and Dante and the Bible, she might have understood that embracing the cosmos is meaningless without first having gained mastery over one's self. For as Styron implies, the holocaust at Hiroshima and Nagasaki enacted synchronously with Peyton's suicide should give the lie to our ever taking the random, unthinking cosmos as anything but hostile. In the most important way, their failure to conceive man's inward, latent power—the power leading to his ability to endure—permits the easy submission to fate by the three protagonists of *Lie Down in Darkness*. The lack of stoicism allows the self to be swallowed up by fate, victory in death, and nothingness.

Just how primary the affirmation of self is to Styron becomes apparent in his next novel, where the vision of recovery preempts this vision of extinction. Death gives the impetus and occasion to both books; but where the funeral in *Lie Down in Darkness* travels an inexorable route to pessimism and a kind of suspended nihilism (we are left at the end, however ambiguously, with the stoicism of the Negroes), the eight corpses strewn about the Carolina countryside at the opening of *The Long March*—transmitting an anonymous, but imagistically as potent a sense of capricious destruction as the single crushed body of Peyton Loftis—are calculated foils to the life-affirming purpose and sense of survival harbored in the themes and shaping vision of that novel.

It is Culver, the central intelligence of *The Long March*, who establishes from the first the novel's concern with vision. He ordains those subjective inventions of reality shared among the trio comprising himself, Mannix, and Templeton: inventions, however disparate and conflicting, that are psychologically and morally necessary for any one who believes life is a matter of design rather than accident. Consequently, *The Long March* becomes—after the grim, offstage misfiring of mortar shells—a series of small, resonating human explosions set off by charged psyches and volatile imagination. The world of the novel is scarcely rendered objectively at all, but through its progressive transfigurations of reality by each of its three principal actors.

When, for example, Culver stares at the "slick nude litter of intestine and shattered blue bones, among which forks and spoons peeked out like so many pathetic metal flowers," he transfigures the particular scene as well as the total setting of the novel by at once mediating and juxtaposing its two planes: the grim regimentation of barracks life and forced marches, and the world of nature whose order has been disturbed and violated. Even in the underplayed simile we find a jarring irony—one finds something almost identical in Henry Reed's magnificent poem, "Naming of Parts" —on the use (or misuse) of such vision. What we learn from *Lie Down in Darkness* is that the transfiguration of reality not only heightens the real world but makes it more tolerable to contemplate; what we learn from *The Long March* is that the passion of Styron's characters to transform the ordinary enables them to see things more clearly, and, however erroneously, more cohesively. This is much less of a paradox than it seems. Even so deadly and inimical an artifact as Templeton's .38 becomes for him a totem which substantiates his identity and helps transform *his* world. By owning this "emblematic prerogative"—an extension of himself, one of those concrete metaphors of reality alluded to above— he demonstrates to himself that he is "authority." As Templeton shapes his quite literal revolver into a symbol of existence, so Mannix shapes Templeton and the march into mythic quanta of fiend and trial to which he as the rebel hero must give battle.

This is by no means all *The Long March* has to say. But once we see how the various themes of *Lie Down in Darkness* have been heightened (and even defined) through visions induced by alcohol, religion, neuroses, and how through natural and mythic orderings of experience such visions have swelled to touch on additional themes of "will" and "power," we may better understand how Styron's material crescendoes and fuses in his next two novels, *Set This House on Fire* and *The Confessions of Nat Turner*: the one dealing with the artist's, the other with the revolutionary's vision.

Suggesting that Styron is writer qua visionary is not to imply either directly or indirectly that his work shows a preponderance of content over form. The content of art qualitatively inheres because of the form imposed upon it: the "fancy" of the artist, the "aggregating or associative vision" as Coleridge (who has never been bettered in the esthetics of the creative principle) called it, is only completed through the act of "imagination" or "shaping vision." Exactly to what degree any artist must absorb the stuff of reality—the fixed objects of the real world that become his vision— before transmuting that vision into art, is a problem he must face sooner or later in his creative evolution; generally, with a writer, the problem itself provides a theme to be written about. Styron sought to face it (among other things) in *Set This House on Fire*, to question the force and responsibility of artistic visions as they tamper with life: not as Mann or Joyce or even Hesse did through surrogates of mature or ab ovo genius, but through three fallible visions by "artists" of sorts who themselves are subjected to tampering by life.

The first of such is Cass Kinsolving, a *peintre manqué* who views the world in bizarre, nightmarish ways, and who is dangerously overwhelmed by such visions, be they "good" or "bad." Here, for example, is one of the "good" visions: an epiphany of Paris:

> It wasn't just the *scene*, you see—it was the sense, the bleeding *essence* of the thing. It was as if I had been given for an instant the capacity to understand not just beauty itself by its outward signs, but the other—the elseness in beauty; this continuity of beauty in the scheme of all life which triumphs even to the point of taking in sordidness and shabbiness and ugliness, which goes

[7]

on and on and on, and of which this was only a moment, I guess, divinely crystallized. (SHF, p. 257)

And here is one of the "bad": not an autistic inspiration, this time, but one of a plethora of recurring

> wild Manichean dreams, dreams that told him that God was not even a lie, but worse, that He was weaker even than the evil he created and allowed to reside in the soul of man, that God Himself was doomed, and the landscape of heaven was not gold and singing but a space of terror which stretched in darkness from horizon to horizon. (SHF, pp. 275–276)

Here, and throughout the novel, Cass's visions—alternatingly beatific and apocalyptic—are almost textbook examples of his sublimating the art that fails to get put down on canvas and a budding schizophrenia exacerbated by drink and illness. Such visions support, on several counts, his Dostoevskian plunge into sin and damnation (one recalls in *The Brothers Karamazov* Dmitri's paradoxical reconciliation of the Madonna and Sodom) before the Dantean ascension through grace to salvation. Yet while the novel is concerned with Cass's redemption, with his phoenixlike rise from a wrecked bone-house near consumed by literal and symbolic fires, it does more than spontaneously generate an eschatology from the dunghill of psychopathology. Despite the novel's "Christian" overlay—the epigraph from Donne, however gloomy and portentous, nevertheless augurs resurrection—Cass's "aggregating visions" have not readied him for last or otherworldly things; rather, his fanciful, privileged *Augenblicke* have returned him to the things of this world. That Cass comes by way of these eternal moments to reject the fatal, narcissistic longings of mystic, martyr, potential suicide, shows how even the imagination of a failed painter can reshape the imperfections of life in something like (as he calls it at the very end of the novel) ecstasy.

There is, in quite a different vein, the vision of Mason Flagg who transfigures reality through his own peculiar artistry: sex. "Sex," he sees, combining his idée fixe into Krafft-Ebing objectivity and de Sade delirium "is the last frontier." He wants an eternal "exploration of sex," one which will enable him to get free of his body and his oppressive feelings of oncoming impotence and weakness. But Mason as an artist—he claims that sex at its greatest is "nurtured and refined like any other high art"—fails to thrive either on vision or experience; he is too conscious or too *self*-conscious to mature in the throes of one or the other. Unlike Cass, who is overpowered by his visions to the point that each endows him with a "presentiment of selflessness," Mason is always in control: a *mechanical* man who manipulates any sensation to further perfect the lie that ultimately destroys him.

If, as would appear from this discussion thus far, Styron has so structured *Set This House on Fire* to suggest that through one kind of vision his protagonist is saved, and through another his antagonist is damned, then somewhere in the scheme of things we must account for the novel's third significant vision: that of its narrator, Peter Leverett. To say simply, as too many have, that Peter is the man between, impoverishes the book's taxonomies. Clearly, Peter—square, normal, cool, solid, *l'homme moyen sensuel*—is a mediator of sorts; he comes to us initially as a bundle of fragile sensibilities which, like so many iron filings, are alternately attracted and repelled by the magnetism of Cass and of Mason. Yet just as clearly Peter is more than an absorbed, poetic shuttlecock. Like the Marlowe of *Heart of Darkness* whose rawness has been refined, his ego purged in the black vortex of Africa and Kurtz's hell, Peter struggles to cut through the chaos and illusion of personalities (his own included) and detail the fantasies, aberrancies, truths, lies into an intelligible, if not always explicable, pattern: what, in fact, by way of theme and structure, becomes the novel's design.

Unless we should, perversely, insist on reading *Set This House on Fire* (as one might read Ford's *The Good Soldier*) as some incredibly tenuous and ironic byplay among author, narrator, and reader, then we must trust Peter to exercise the "shaping vision" of the novel. His imagination comes as close to being Styron's artistic voice as Cass's articulation of visions comes to being his spiritual one. It is probably even safer and less suspect to conjecture the former. To a degree greater than *Lie Down in Darkness* and only slightly less than *The Confessions of Nat Turner*, *Set This House on Fire* imposes the present upon the past, experience—in the Blakean sense of the term—upon innocence. Almost from the beginning of the novel, the intensity of Peter's perceptions, and the magnitude, are established in a striking way as he recalls a pond in which he almost drowned when a boy, his furtive returns there despite the incident, and its "obliteration," its "stupendous unmaking" to accommodate a suburban development:

> For now everything about the place . . . seemed to be informed by a sense of mysteriousness and brevity. . . . Here there had been taken away from me that child's notion that I would live forever; here I had learned the fragility not so much as of my own as of all being, and for that reason if it seemed a cruel scary place it also possessed a new and fathomable beauty. . . . in that stillness . . . I shivered with the knowledge of mortality. . . . Yet here on the identical spot, years later . . . everything was gone. Not just altered or changed or modified, not just a place whose outlines may have shifted and blurred . . . but were still recognizable, dependable, fixed—my marsh had vanished, a puff into thin air, and nothing of it remained. (SHF, p. 17)

Yet beyond mere nostalgia, beyond a set piece of purple narrative, beyond the fantasia on the theme of ubi sunt, Peter's remembrance inspires the more urgent reflection on the devastating possibilities of the past interacting with the present:

> Perhaps one of the reasons we Americans are so exceptionally nervous and driven is that our past is effaced almost before it is made present; in our search for old avatars to contemplate we find only ghosts, whispers, shadows: almost nothing remains for us to feel or see, or to absorb our longings. . . . Estranged from myself and from my time, dwelling neither in the destroyed past nor in the fantastic and incomprehensible present, I knew that I must find the answer to at least several things before taking hold of myself. (SHF, pp. 18–19)

Here, antecedent to everything that happens in the novel, is almost its logical coda. For if the past cannot be recaptured, nor the present returned to the past, then the human imagination must, like the artistic vision itself, try to reconcile both phases of irredeemable time: must try, as Peter's imagination does, to understand life shorn of its "illusions and innocence." By acknowledging the "destroyed past" and the "fantastic and incomprehensible present," but by refusing to be enslaved by them, Peter fuses the visions of Cass and Mason—and surpasses them. The narrator, like the novelist, transfigures and shapes experience to understand his continuous and changing world, and ultimately to see it "steadily and whole."

Through such a synthesis of author and narrator's voice in *Set This House on Fire*, Styron enlarges its visionary mode. *The Confessions of Nat Turner* pushes voice and vision still further. As critical (both over and under) reactions attest, the novel is Styron's most notorious experiment; generally it is acknowledged an incredible success; it may be to date his finest achievement. Styron has gotten inside a black mind, not *the* white one; he has deserted the expatriate world of middle-class sophisticates to reconstruct the antebellum ethos through the eyes of an inspired revolutionary; and he has turned aside from esthetic or psychological speculations on time to treat it obsessionally, intuitively, symbolically, even four-dimensionally. Time in *The Confessions* —synergetic with space—flows on two levels at once, the horizontal and the vertical, and carries Nat with it. Unlike Peter, he is not merely intellectually enslaved by past and present; he is literally enslaved by them. The literal, however, leaps into the metaphysical. For as Nat tries to escape finite time—that is, historicity and the shameful history of his people—he converges toward a point and instant in infinite time. Styron's "meditation on history"—the culmination and most complex of his transfigurative patterns—becomes as well a meditation on timelessness.

The Confessions transforms the potentially lethal interplay of past and present—so keenly felt by Peyton and Peter—into the centrifuge of the future. As Styron's previous novels flow toward the anticipated awareness and epiphany, this novel, defying anticipation, startles us at the opening with a glimpse of Revelation, only just as suddenly to move backward through time. No longer will epigraphs from Sir Thomas Browne or John Donne—both meditations, broodings on eternity—serve to frame the temporal scheme. Now the novel must create—must *become*—its own metaphor for eternity. In part, Styron achieves this through his exacting choice of superscription. John 21:4 is summoned out of Isaiah

[11]

26:21: the Christian belief in the final judgment at the end of an age supersedes with quiet vengeance and nostalgia for transient, ephemeral, sinful man the Judaic belief in periodic judgments at times of historic crises. History (Isaiah) and apocalypse (John) are welded in a single vision, as fearful as it is benign.

But the true art of *The Confessions* rests on the primacy and fluidity of the vision itself, flowing through a human vessel who is grand, though not grand enough to contain all of it, yet who has come the closest of any of Styron's creations to embodying the eternal moment in the mundane. It is for this reason that the beginning of a novel treating a man, a revolutionary, the major link in the new-forged consciousness of a race, holds eternity in the balance: for this reason that Genesis mirrors forth Judgment Day. Nat has judged, has been judged, and will, after enduring the judgment of his society, be called to the final judgment by his God. Judgment is the omega of existence toward which Nat has been yearning without being able to fathom or articulate it. Presentiments come to him only by way of a strange, recurrent dream filled with cliffs and seas and mazes. The dream is a "contemplation of a great mystery" that he is still unable, even on the eve of his execution, to discover. It is, of course, a vision of the apocalypse, wrapped up with his own death and resurrection and the call of the Lord: all only fulfilled shortly before the Southampton massacre in his most terrifying vision of the black destroying angel, the image of the holocaust to precede apocalypse.

Styron, however, has done more than impose the apocalyptic on the historic. In Nat, he has given us historic man's encounter with apocalypse, while paradoxically freeing him from the shackles of history. *The Confessions* is a novel of man's becoming and completion in time: of a life plunging linearly toward an end, changing the world as it does so, and controverting in its gallop toward apocalypse the archetypal entrapment in grinding, historical cycles. Nat shatters the cycle that seems overwhelming and ineluctable, and escapes to "freedom" through rebellion. And as with all revolutionaries—particularly with mystical, prophetic, religious revolutionaries—it scarcely matters whether the vision creates the age, or whether the spirit of the age generates the vision. It is a symbiotic, coalescing force catapulting the undistinguished, the obscure to a fame that may be as tragic as it is great; yet the phenomenon of such greatness is its inability to be otherwise. Nat—like the "young Luther" of a study that strongly influenced *The Confessions*—accedes to the acme of Erik Erickson's eight stages of man, where ego integrity champions over despair:

> Although aware of the relativity of all the various life styles which have given meaning to human striving, the possessor of [ego] integrity is ready to defend the dignity of his own life style against all physical and economic threats. For he knows that an individual life is the accidental coincidence of but one life cycle with but one segment of history; and that for him all human integrity stands or falls with the one style of integrity of which he partakes. The style of integrity developed by his culture or civilization thus becomes the "patrimony of his soul," the seal of his moral paternity of himself. . . . In such final consolidation, death loses its sting.[3]

Where, but to apotheosis, could such a vision lead Nat Turner!

The Confessions is, as we mentioned above, the culmination of the transfiguration patterns in Styron's other fictions. In an astounding way, the novel is Styron's declaration of the power of the human imagination to rebel against a world enslaving it, to make over through the act of creation such a world in its own image, and, just as inexorably, to go on to destroy itself and all that it created. The South could never be the same after Nat Turner's rebellion; and in a similar way our feelings about the South could never be the same after *The Confessions*. One may (like Cass Kinsolving)return from the abyss and begin anew; one cannot, after a vision of the apocalypse, return (if return one does) without experiencing some significant transformation.

And yet *The Confessions*, so charged with image and vision, raises disturbing and fundamental questions about Styron as visionary novelist. What, in the particular sense, is one left with after the singular, painful, final vision of Nat's has been recorded? What can we take away additionally from all of Styron's work after the numerous and numinous visions have been collated? Have we, that is, throughout all his novels and his single play anything apart from the visions themselves?

Before answering these questions, we should like to carry the consideration of the visionary novelist a bit further. Modern literature's invasion by the apocalypse, and the American novelist's particular (though not exclusive) acquiescence to it, have made it progressively more difficult to wrest from the intense fictions of writers like James Purdy, Thomas Pynchon, Joseph Heller, and John Barth social or metaphysical values that only several decades earlier were at least apodictic in the apocalyptic world of crumbling centers and windswept wastelands. Lawrence could evoke his dark, savage gods; Yeats could look to the ether for his "widening gyres"; and Eliot could eventually claim that in the end was his beginning. Now we only wait for the end. As Frank Kermode has pointed out in his brilliant study, the "sense of an ending" has progressively become the conditioned response of writers who have come to distrust the temporal, historic framework, *chronos*, and must consequently seek inspiration from the mythic superstructures, *kairos*. Apocalypse has superseded Henry Adams's dynamo as the integrating archetype of our disintegration.

One may rightly ask what sense there is in attempting to define values in a world so clearly tending toward entropy, or in seeking oases of permanence beyond the borders of wastelands where novelists have sent weary heroes hungering after illusive beasts of revelation and corroded grails; and where, as an inevitable consequence, many ill-caparisoned critics have gone in quest of the questers. One may answer no sense at all. Perhaps there may be relief, if no comfort, in steeling ourselves for ultimate hopelessness: buying tickets of admission to watch the approaching spin-off; and, as corollary to this, perhaps the critical imagination, in its desire to expose, refine, explain, should not dare vie with the apocalyptic one.

On the other hand, even with apocalypse imminent and immanent, one may feel that the quest after values, though dubious and vain, is preferable to paralysis. There is, too, the nagging suspicion that however poetic and revelatory and fierce and deterministic the apocalyptic imagination is, it begs a rather basic question about apocalypse: for once it *is*, we are *not*. Putting aside for a moment the perdurability of the human spirit—since Polly-anna generally seems to wither before Cassandra—we would call attention to the cartoon in which in the first panel an Elijah-type sports a sandwich board reading "The World Will End Tomor-row" and in which in the second panel, nothing has been changed save the phrase, now reading: "The World Ended Yesterday." We do not offer the analogy to blur a vision that has produced some of the most original and vital literature of the past decade: merely to suggest that equally original and vital fiction has also come by way of alternatives. We have, of course, Styron's work in mind. And that element of his work in particular which em-braces the apocalyptic vision surrendering to its hysteria and con-fusion and nihilism. New values may spring fully armed from old ones. But those of Styron's characters who find some measure of love and hope and joy do so not by ascending a growing mountain of corpses thrust up by the past, but by hewing holds in whatever is concrete, stable, viable in the present.

Admittedly it might seem disastrous to determine from Styron's first novel that anything viable could emerge from the world as he then felt and knew it. *Lie Down in Darkness* reflects almost perfect disintegration. As in *King Lear* "nothing" cracks open a world and a universe; "nothing" echoes through the widening death-rictus of an ethos; almost complete in rendering personal despair, the novel is even more complete in catching the resonances of communal negation. Class fails; love fails; sex fails; religion fails; tradition fails; psychotherapy fails; history fails—or rather suc-ceeds in effecting the great holocaustal synthesis of all negations at Hiroshima. Even the Negroes' exultant cry after Daddy Faith is a whimper lost amidst the agonizing cry of Milton and Helen's "nothing," amidst "the whistle, roar, gigantic sound . . . like the clatter of the opening of everlasting gates and doors" as the train rushes north into the eternal blackness of "oncoming night."

But—as we suggested above in discussing the visionary aspects of the novel—such total negation was ancillary to a young novel-ist's sweeping away all debris of a culture he could, would no longer accept. *Lie Down in Darkness* seems opulent in disclaim-

[15]

ing any values whatever, in its generational inbreeding of melancholia, introversion, hysteria, neuroses, Puritanism, sin, and guilt. All this, we say, seems clear enough. Yet by way of paradox—a paradox that Styron was reasonably unaware of at twenty-five when he wrote *Lie Down in Darkness*—the novel, for all its despair, goads us into sloughing off our stifled sensibilities, liberating ourselves from the paralysis, shaking ourselves free of narcissistic brooding over how lost and damned we are, and beginning reassessment of ourselves somewhere—anywhere. By showing his generation where he felt it went wrong, Styron was indicating how it might go right. We spoke of *Lie Down in Darkness* as part parable; and it is just possible its moral is this, a faint hopeful light encroaching on the dark center of irony and ambiguity.

There is, however, a still further reading of the novel that expands its contexts somewhat. At its most general, the book has been taken as a tragedy enacted within three circles of meaning—private, domestic, social—all calculated to enclose and destroy the principal actors. In view of Styron's subsequent fictions, we are less inclined to see these circles linking, so much as overlaying each other—forming a cohesive, multifaceted *relievo* of the institutional or collective mind of the New South. Such a mind, at its most enfeebled, can be no more than a mute barrier to change and progress; at its most dangerous it can set in motion profligate forces to engineer its own humiliation, defeat, and self-destruction.

Because it is immune, indeed resistant to new problems, because it is conditioned to solve old problems only through ritualistic, aimless gestures, the world of the Loftises and Cartwrights and Carrs falls away at both center and peripheries; the sap dries up; the roots wither; the stock atrophies. Styron's white, middle-class, Protestant South is almost exclusively a choked world of the collective—country clubs, churches, fraternity and cocktail parties, socials and smokers—where being alone even for a moment becomes synonymous with loneliness, and where this loneliness immediately summons some crutch like drink or sex or God as support against anxiety and fear. To live within a framework where one scarcely knows oneself until it is too late is to be damned; yet to escape from it (as Peyton thinks she can) is to be equally damned. For in *Lie Down in Darkness* the collective mind is not endemic to the South. Harry's clique of northern liberal-progressive-intellectuals operates differently, but no less depressingly. Peyton is trapped—trapped just as the South is—between tradition and change; in this way she adumbrates Styron's future heroes, is linked to Cass and Mannix and Nat Turner: individuals questing for truth, longing for perfection and completion, who must escape the organized, rigid, ritualistic snares of the collective mind.

Or do battle with them: which in this way makes Styron's heroes rare in contemporary American fiction. They are not in the grain of those naive picaros who bungle their quests and end up as violated innocents. Styron's questers are rebels, though less out of choice than occasion and necessity. For to rebel is to endure, just as to endure is to rebel: a syllogism we offer without any design of mad tea party logomachy or solipsism or tautology, but as an entire construct of values that provides the Styron hero a reason of being as well as a reason for being. Those like Cass and Mannix who are lucky—if being alive at the end of a novel constitutes luck—may "last" as well as "endure." But Styron seldom guarantees much value beyond the self-defining act of rebellion.

This at least appears to be the case in his two treatments of the theme within military settings: *The Long March* and *In the Clap Shack*.[6] Styron wrote these works twenty years apart; one is a psychological novel, the other a stage comedy; yet their focus and conclusion (in places even their tone) are consistent enough to suggest his continuing fascination with the irrationality spawned by this particular breed of the collective mind. In one sense, these works are his most compressed studies of an institution trying to usurp identity by imposing conformity on the individual: attempting, that is, to absorb personal values in collective ones.

Yet like other of Styron's collectives, the United States Marines is not overtly hostile; it is an entity beyond feeling or involvement, and perhaps this is what makes it—and organizations like it—more monstrous. It creates, by the very nature of its collective existence as opposed to private existence a world outlook (such as we would find in the New South of *Lie Down in Darkness*, the Old in *The Confessions*, the expatriate world in *Set This House on Fire*) that can scarcely fathom anyone's desiring to go against it. What such organizations—incredibly inured, it would seem, to history and to meditations upon history—fail to learn is that the more they would impress obedience and anonymity on the individual, the more they would demand his surrender, the more forcefully he rebels.

As for the rebellion in the two works at hand, it is valued as more than quixotic tilts at power or emblems of power or a chain of endless command. Reason dictates that bucking the system is unreasonable; yet intuition makes demands beyond reason. Mannix and Magruder refuse to be stripped of the remnants of value left them, or to be desensitized to their belief in themselves as more than rank and serial number. Each rebels to affirm an identity in the face of an encroaching paranoia, symbolized in *The Long March* by the chaotic figure of Templeton, and *In the Clap Shack* by the comically monomaniacal Budwinkle. One should recall that *The Long March* was written in 1953: considerably before tremors of paranoia (sounded, for example, in *The Naked and the Dead* and *Invisible Man*) swelled into the literary shock wave exploited with considerable brilliance by writers like Heller and Purdy, and so recently elevated to genius by Pynchon in *Gravity's Rainbow*. Styron's novella anticipates what is by now a nearly universal suspicion: that our rampant paranoia is scarcely an orderly deviation from "norms," but a logical response to conditioning under systems that have surpassed in ambiguity those perfect, though inexplicable worlds of Gogol and Kafka.

Templeton's delusions of grandeur are volatile and potentially tragic; but ironically it is the persecuted Mannix who, as war hero, is responsible for sustaining the glory of the corps that fires men like Templeton on. In another, only explicitly comic way, Magruder's hypochondria has already prepared the ground for the psychosomatic burrowing which in turn tunnels into the paranoid maze. We are, Styron suggests, haunted by the bizarre ghosts and grotesque fancies we ourselves have created. Thus, though visions and illusions might momentarily sustain our metaphysical health, they are in the long run just as surely responsible for our metaphysical ills. Being so divided, so—more profoundly than the cant sense of the word admits—insecure, we cannot affirm values without first understanding what they are. Our fear of what we might discover prevents us from knowing or defining ourselves, yet the fear of nondiscovery paralyzes us further still. To be forced to crisis—as Mannix in the gung-ho march, as Magruder with his falsely diagnosed syphilis—is perhaps the sole means of unearthing the values we have, through one means or another, buried with our humanity.

It is this awaited impulse to find what is quintessentially human in all of us that makes the quest in Styron valuable in itself. Its object is almost without importance; to endure in it is all. Were it otherwise, it would be difficult to assess values in a novel like *Set This House on Fire* which is almost pure quest, and in which the act of questing performs its own art of healing, transforms what is fragmented into what is whole. The search to know and explore oneself is not, however, carried on in isolation—the book shows how impossible isolation is; Port Warwick and Sambuco are, as states of the mind, one and the same place—but in terms of people, and, most emphatically in the novel, in terms of avatars.

For *Set This House on Fire* marks a departure from Styron's creating character of pure Being, since without regeneration of the self, Being has very little value at all. Rather, it is a novel of Becoming, of emergence out of a past that has shaped us, and which we must learn to reshape instead of reject. The book reaches out to embrace nothing less than America itself: not the America of the jingoist or sentimentalist, but the America creative and destructive of our personalities and psyches, formulative of our feelings of love and hate toward her. The novel is both challenge and response to our culture. It is elliptical about many things, but almost transparent in its moral assertion of what it means to flee blindly or scrap mechanically the visible manifestations of our roots and origins. Thomas Wolfe said we were all lost in America; Styron says we are probably more lost anywhere else. To find America is to find the parts of ourselves we have lost. Thus a novel ostensibly concerned with expatriation becomes one of repatriation. It is not only Cass's continuing quest, but his continual questioning, his dialogue of self and self, self and soul—a dialogue in

[19]

which Peter shares, and in which Mason, cinematically frozen in his static mask, does not share—that defines his, as well as the book's, Becoming.

The way stations reflecting Cass's progress from frantic visionary to one ready to wrestle with doubtful values and ambiguities about America are raised in much of his dialogue, though we think the substance of his change can be gathered from three short quotations. The first comes as a response to Poppy's question "Oh *why* are you so anti-U.S.A.?"

> Because it's the land where the soul gets poisoned out of pure ugliness. It's because in the U.S.A. everything looks like a side street near the bus station in Poughkeepsie, New York. . . . It's because whenever I think of stateside I can't picture nothing else but a side street in Poughkeepsie, New York, where I got lost one night when I came to see you, and whenever I think of it I get consumed with such despair over its sheer ugliness that I feel great waves of anguish rolling over me. . . . Whatever I've said in—in *mitigation* of the horror America afflicts me with, strike it out. Strike it out! I was just being sentimental. (SHF, p. 282)

The second is reflected in his journal entry, some hundred pages later:

> And I suppose its true, some twisted connection or crossed up circuit between love & hate in me is the secret of it all, . . . I am my own soul diviner & I do not hope to dredge up out of the depths anything but that which would momentarily solace me. And the blame is my own to bear. So that whenever I dream as I have done of old Uncle standing there as my own executioner I do not place the horror in his hands. . . . It's not old Uncle's fault any more than it was Cape Gloucester. . . . Nor when I look into my heart of hearts is it the U.S. I can blame at all though many times I would like to & do, a bleeding expatriate that would put a bowery bum to shame. Because though say even somebody like Poppy don't know it there are times when just the thought of one single pine tree at home, in the sand, & a negro church in a grove I knew as a boy & the sound of the negroes singing In Bright Mansions Above (?)—then I feel or know rather that all I would need is that one trembling word to be whispered or spoken into my ear. AMERICA. And I could hold myself back no longer and blubber like a baby. (SHF, pp. 363–364)

And the last comes in the "Epilogue" in the short letter Peter receives from Cass after his return to the "whole smart-Alex

[20]

[*sic*], soft-headed, baby-faced, predigested, cellophane wrapped, doomed, beauty-hating, land":

> Charleston will never become the Florence of the New World Im afraid but the Sunday amateurs are keeping me busy & Im up to my ears in work. Also, another trauma. Overpopulation. Race-suicide. Poppy is having another baby next June & Ive been walking around Charleston like a wounded elephant, staggering with the usual pride and despair. Kinsey was distinctly wrong. A man doesnt even get started until he moves in toward il mezzo del camin. . . . Who was it in Lear who said ripeness is all. I forget, but he was right. (SHF, pp. 505–506)

Cass's allusions to the opening lines of *The Divine Comedy* and to Edgar's urgent moral to the blinded Gloucester (with, on Styron's part, we suspect, a muted symbolic echo of Cass's traumatic experience on the Cape) underscore his dissent from nightmare and surrender and his assent to growing lucidity and acceptance. It is, indeed, ascent after descent. As Dante's vision of Beatrice on the Ponte Vecchio inspired such a descent into the Inferno that led to Paradise, as Gloucester's false tumble from the Dover Cliffs brought about the eleventh hour rescue of lost, interior vision, so Cass's sinking into the dissipation, sensuality, and imprisonment of Sambuco prepares for the "new birth" in Charleston. An exile like Dante and Gloucester, Cass has learned that "Men must endure / Their going hence, even as their coming hither." But he returns to America as more than an exile; he returns as a human being.

Toward this condition, this value, *Set This House on Fire* tends from the opening. But it is clear from the opening, too, that we are still in the world of the white and the privileged. All barriers to becoming human are raised after plans laid down by the grotesque or unsteady architecture of the self. As charged as Styron's first three novels are with man's struggle to locate and define his humanity, possibly none does nor could measure the scope of the struggle so eloquently as *The Confessions*. Not one man nor two, not a half-dozen men come under scrunity; not the Old nor the New South; not the alienated nor expatriated; not the soul damned nor in revolt, but—through their history, myth, atavisms, and avatars—all men, all times.

[21]

For *The Confessions* is a novel about humanity: a large claim, we realize, to make for any novel, but in this instance scarcely an exaggerated one. Through Nat—the activating force in Styron's paradigmatic, spent, doomed world—we watch the desperate and impossible struggle of a man wanting to assert his humanity, the realization of how improbable the recognition of it is, and the glorious, insane attempt to generate chaos in thrusting beyond both impossibility and improbability. Like Styron, we are compelled to meditate on the historicized myth *and* the mythicized history, though finally we must abolish the distinctions that have brought as much articulate denunciation of the novel as applause for it. The compulsion is an imperative dictate because *The Confessions* is, before being either myth or history, art; it is an archetypal tragedy; and Nat is the archetypal tragic hero, here torn between dream and reality by the disparity between promise and fulfillment. Nat's struggle was, as with others it now is and chances are with others to come will be, the timeless, universal struggle to achieve, no matter how horrendous existence becomes, his essential humanity.

To drill into our consciousness, as well as to preserve in our conscience, this ultimate value is surely the finest achievement of any writer. But what makes the novel even grander in design is that Styron's agon of man against himself, against society, even against his God goes beyond being a confessions of aspiration to become a testament of affirmation. Horror, shame, and death brood over the novel only because they brood over much of American and human history concerned with struggles identical to Nat's. Yet apart from merely acknowledging their dark presence and grim persistence, *The Confessions* tries to show how man transcends them. This is why Nat's bitter negation and rebellion cannot finally be envisioned as blind alleys into solipsism, but as prime movers of self-definition; and why one cannot read the novel closely without finding it more hopeful than ambiguous. For *The Confessions* holds out the promise that joy may come out of anger, justice out of injustice, quietude out of fear, redemption out of damnation, good out of evil, charity out of brutality and vengeance. Despite the deprivation of physical and spiritual love, Nat in the end still comes to love, still vindicates his rights as a human being even after committing those senseless and terrible acts that not only seem, but are monstrous. In the end, too, something on the order of blood brotherhood arises out of the nightmare of blood baths to signify that inhuman theories and the dehumanizing collective can never destroy man's intrinsic, instinctive sense of his own worth and dignity.

Long after *The Confessions* ceases being criticized as muted racism or the muddled apologia of a chuckleheaded white southern liberal, or read as a parable on or parallel with the rise and fall of black power, these things Styron has shown will be his chief legacy to literature and the times. To date, *The Confessions* crowns his achievement as a novelist. It is fitting that it should. For it demonstrates how the insurrection of the human spirit leads to the resurrection of the artist's soul. This transformation is what any great writer undergoes in wedding his own private vision with enduring values; it is, we think, a transformation William Styron has undergone. Few achievements could be more desirable —or more lasting.

Notes

1. *Paris Review* 1 (1953): 13.
2. "William Styron: The Metaphysical Hurt" from *The Art of Southern Fiction: A Study of Some Modern Novelists* (Carbondale, Ill., 1967), pp. 145–146.
3. See the interview with William Styron in this collection, p. 34.
4. *Fearful Symmetry* (Princeton, 1947), p. 8.
5. *Young Man Luther: A Study in Psychoanalysis and History* (New York, 1958), pp. 260–261.
6. From the interview with William Styron, following this introduction, it would appear that the theme had been further amplified in his forthcoming novel, tentatively titled *The Way of the Warrior*, which is concerned with "the military mind in America." See p. 43.

ROBERT K. MORRIS

An Interview with
William Styron

The following interview with William Styron was conducted in part in the summer of 1972 at Mr. Styron's home on Martha's Vineyard, and in part in the subsequent summer at his home in Roxbury, Connecticut.

Q. In the last twenty years material about you and your work has appeared in some forty books, seven doctoral dissertations, about two hundred or more critical articles, and countless book reviews. Would you care to comment on how it feels to be, if you'll forgive the blatant phrase, "an American classic"?

A. That's a very good way to start the interview, especially inasmuch as I do not consider myself an American classic. I don't have any illusions, really, about what literature is. I think one generation's classic is another generation's corpse; and it's a chancy thing to talk about being a classic in your time. There's a book I haven't read written by the emeritus head of Duke University's English Department, Jay Hubbell, that has to do with just such matters: who are the acclaimed writers of their time. One of the interesting things I recall reading in a review of Hubbell's book is that in 1920 or 1921 there was a list drawn up of the sure-to-live immortals of that particular time. And heading the list, I *believe*, was Joseph Hergesheimer, followed closely by Booth Tarkington (or maybe it was the other way around); and Dreiser was something like number fourteen. This was a reputable poll, too, taken among serious critics. And so things like that make me a little itchy and nervous about answering what it is to be a classic.

Q. But by the same token there hasn't been that much written about Hergesheimer and Tarkington. Why do you think so many people are writing about you?

A. This is probably the time when people write things about writers to a degree they did not before. I think had the critical and academic apparatus been as lively and vigorous as it is now, Hergesheimer and the others would have had similar activities surrounding their work. Of course, it's nice to know you're alive and kicking, that you have a readership of some sort, that people are involved in your work, and that there is interest in it throughout various fields; but whether you are an American classic or not is still up to ol' posterity!

Q. Have you any feelings or reactions, one way or the other, about having your novels taught in the university?

A. I'm pleased when my work is taught there, very pleased. As I've said before, I really don't know how much validity can be given to the idea of the writer as a cult figure—and I'm thinking of the cult writers dating back to Salinger and Golding and moving on up through to Vonnegut. Yet at the same time to have the feeling one is being read by young people is a very inspiriting and happy state.

Q. You don't feel—even after *Nat Turner*—that you're a cult writer?

A. No, I don't; that is, I haven't any evidence pointing to it. But I do get enough responses to know that I am taught with some frequency and some currency at a large number of universities— and that pleases me.

Q. Is there any rough estimate you could make to the number of letters you receive from the people who read and like your books: letters not necessarily from those in the university?

A. It depends. When a book of mine comes out, all of a sudden I am inundated; and then it peters out to a sort of steady trickle of appreciative letters: sometimes several a day, but certainly several a week.

Q. Does receiving these letters gratify you?

A. Well, most of the time, yes. Most of them are "unsolicited testimonials" to the work, and that's pleasing; it makes you feel that what you've done has touched someone.

[25]

Q. Do you get any negative letters?

A. Yes, some. I got many, of course, after *Nat Turner*. But on the whole I get surprisingly few. Most people don't seem to want to sit down and write a negative letter.

Q. Do you think that the longer scholarly and critical pieces about your novels have been, in general, sound in evaluating your work? I mean, has what you considered the best of such criticism come closer to the mark than not on what you were planning to do?

A. I would say that, by and large, there has been a great deal of mediocre criticism which doesn't seem to get anywhere near the mark. On the other hand, you get really extraordinary insights by certain critics, who seem to smell absolutely, exactly what you're up to. They're in the distinct minority, however; but perhaps you can't expect any more than that!

Q. When you were interviewed for the *Paris Review* in 1952, immediately after the publication of *Lie Down in Darkness*, you remarked that bad notices always give you a "sense of humility, or perhaps humiliation . . . but they don't help [you] much." Do you still find that true?

A. Yes, substantially. Except I would now amend that to say that I don't know if they give me a sense of either at all.

Q. You've become hardened to criticism?

A. Yes. I think I've become as inured to criticism as it is possible for a writer to be.

Q. Has any salient criticism about an earlier book made you change or ponder direction in the writing of a later one?

A. No, unequivocally. I can't say there's been any connection between them.

Q. What kind of criticism, if any, do you find at least helpful, or is it all one?

A. I don't imagine a writer really finds any criticism helpful when his career is in full swing. I think possibly when he's young some criticism could be useful; but certainly by the time he is going full blast he should be aware of what his direction is, and there is very little profit I can see that he could derive from criticism. He's got his own voice, his own style, and I just don't see what the critic could tell or teach him.

Q. How do you feel about your books once they are published?

A. I feel a tremendous sense of fulfillment and gratification in terms of completion. Rightly or wrongly, you've done the best that you can do—or you *think* you've done the best that you can do—and all you can have is a sense of achievement.

Q. In that same *Paris Review* interview you also disclaimed being a southern writer, yet you've continued to write about the South. Is there any inconsistency there?

A. Well, I wouldn't stand irrevocably on what I said twenty years ago, because I was in no position to know what I really meant. I think, probably, I had an honest impulse in saying what I did then about *not* being a southern writer, and in disclaiming southern roots. But as I go along I do understand there is still a strong pull in my work toward trying to explain or express certain southern biases, certain southern sympathies, certain southern apprehensions. And therefore I would amend that to say I was wrong. I do not consider myself a southern writer in the sense that, let us say, Eudora Welty might consider herself one. She is, and Flannery O'Connor is another, an almost perfect example of a fine "regional" southern novelist. Basically, I guess, I am trying to make a distinction between southern regionalism (which can be a very strong, fine thrust in literature), and my own work, which is southern, but perhaps not regionally southern.

Q. Has your living in New England for the past twenty years changed your emotional or intellectual responses to the South?

A. I would say distinctly so. But even before that I resolved to remove myself from the South because I simply did not find it compatible with what my moods and aims and ambitions were.

Q. Did you feel you were too much dogging the footsteps of the well-known southern writers—regional or otherwise? I'm thinking in particular, of course, of Faulkner.

A. Yes, surely. I think I perhaps also anticipated—and I don't mean to sound smart-ass—the fact that southern regional writing was about to become a thing of the past. And, generally speaking, I think it has. I felt a far more cosmopolitan sense of direction, and I needed to get out of the South because it was no longer a deeply involved part of my psychic nature.

Q. Are there any young southern writers today whom you feel have suffered by aligning themselves with this regionalism?

A. I would say that you have to be an exceptionally *good* writer to still set up shop as a "southern writer." One very good writer who has done well in this mode is Reynolds Price, but I don't know of many others. It's not to denigrate his talent to say that I think those writers very rare who claim in a strong and aggressive way that they are, with a capital *S*, Southern. I do not. Though to answer your earlier question I find to my surprise that I am never quite able to divest myself of southern thought.

Q. Do you align yourself with *any* school of writing?

A. No.

Q. With the exception of *The Long March*, each of your three major novels runs close to several hundred thousand words. Is there any particular reason why you write long novels?

A. Certainly *Set This House on Fire* is a very long book, but *Nat Turner* and *Lie Down in Darkness* were of more graspable dimensions—in terms of pure length. I don't think they're extraordinarily long, either one of them.

Q. Is there any reason why *Set This House on Fire* was longer, then?

A. In retrospect I think it's overly long. I wish I'd cut it down by a lot. But that's one of those mistakes you make that you can't repair. But even it, by certain standards—compared to the length of *The Brothers Karamazov*, say—is not long. My own feeling is that if you sit down to write a novel you need space to move around in—and a lot of space, in order to give this sense of movement and life to people in the book. Therefore I have always thought of the novel as being a commodious vehicle, one that would take tens of thousands of words, hundreds of thousands if necessary, to tell a story in.

Q. Then why did you make *The Long March* as short as you did?

A. It seemed to have its own length. I don't think there was any quarrel in my mind or any problem as to how long it would be. It just seemed to tell itself. As a matter of fact it started out as a short story. I was going to try to do it in 4,000 words, but it became something in between a short story and a novel.

Q. Did any of your other novels originate as short stories?

A. *Lie Down in Darkness* and *Set This House on Fire* started as novels, *Nat Turner* as a novella. I thought it was going to be something I could clean up in about eight months. Of course I realized fairly early on in its writing that it could not possibly be a short novel; it had to involve the whole time-space concept.

Q. You're intensely occupied with the dimensions of time and space in your novels, aren't you?

A. It seems to me *the* problem a novelist has to conquer, and to do it in a way that pleases his own esthetic and his own demands upon himself as an artist.

Q. It's been mentioned on several occasions that you don't go on with a succeeding chapter until the previous one has been polished to your satisfaction. Does that mean you really do little revision once the novel is completed?

A. Yes. The only place where I did any lengthy revisions was in *Set This House on Fire*. For some reason there was a lot of pruning to be done there, but I'm glad it *was* done. I would say with everything else I've written, including essays and reviews and reportage, that, with minor exceptions, when it's done, it's done.

Q. Were these revisions your idea or your editor's?

A. My editor, Bob Loomis at Random House, has a very "light hand," I'm glad to say; but with *Set This House on Fire* we mutually saw there was a great deal that could be peeled away, and it was.

Q. Can you remember what the revisions were?

A. Not exactly, because I'm not that close to the book any longer. But I do recall that great stretches of dialogue were made more concise through editing: long stretches, which even now are a bit long, were much longer, and they were simply pulled out. Also in Peter Leverett's descriptions of himself there are a lot of things he overly described—self-conscious reflections about himself—and I remember distinctly (though not exactly where) Bob Loomis and I got them out of there.

Q. You told me earlier today that your play, *In the Clap Shack*, underwent "endless revisions." Why?

A. Well, I *think* I know, but I'm not sure. Quite frankly, a play is simply a strange thing for a novelist to write. Its structure is different entirely: more like a poem, in that there is a direct line of mood that should be maintained from beginning to end, and there is a subtlety of expression that has to be—though this is not quite the best way to describe it—"formalized." A novel, almost by definition, is a form in which you can pour four extra paragraphs that seem to work, and do work: literally, because the novel is a kind of broad, marvelous, expansive form which allows for such latitude. There are flights one can take which to some degree seem, and may even be, extraneous. But in a play this doesn't apply. That single mood must be sustained. And when I discovered—as I did in this play—that I had mixed my moods, I was forced to go back and tear away all the superfluous detail.

Q. Of the four novels you've written, have you a particular preference for any one of them?

A. Most writers seem to be partial to the novel they've last completed. Whether that's a good thing or not I don't know. I think I've put most of my mature thinking into *Nat Turner* and I believe it's the one that says the most. But over the past few years I've gone back to *Set This House on Fire;* and though it's a somewhat less perfectly formed work than the others, at the same time it has some of my most passionate and best stuff, and I'm proud to have written it.

Q. Would you call *Nat Turner* a work of maturity and *Lie Down in Darkness* a work of youth? Could that account for your strong feelings about *Nat Turner's* place as your favorite?

A. I think it is my favorite only because I am so close to it. It still has resonances in my mind because of its nearness.

Q. I take it these resonances go beyond the social implications and critical reception of the novel?

A. Yes. It has nothing to do with these: just personal feelings. At the same time, I don't think I'll ever get over the sense of commitment and involvement and passion I experienced in writing *Lie Down in Darkness*, which was almost my life's blood when it came out. I think it's impossible to ever relive that first lyrical outburst (so poignant really) which every writer has in his twenties: when whole arteries and veins are pumping away.

Q. Was the creative process involved in writing your other novels different, then, from that in writing *Lie Down in Darkness?*

A. All the novels I've written were very difficult for me to write. I would say that once I got into *Lie Down in Darkness*—after the initial problems of composition—that it was the easiest to write. It seemed to pour out of me in a curious way; *The Long March*, too, but to a somewhat lesser degree. *Set This House on Fire* and *Nat Turner* were terribly difficult to write, and for some diabolical reason it seems to get more and more this way than the other way around.

Q. Critics seem to feel there is a more "objective intensity" in the books after *Lie Down in Darkness*. Has the process of writing become more intense for you, would you say?

A. Really, the sense of intellectual responsibility has come down upon me. The novel I'm writing now—one I've tentatively called *The Way of the Warrior*—seems to be almost insuperably difficult to write because I want to say things which are intellectually and morally important to me, and I think important to say. And the telling of these things in an artful way has become a wretchedly difficult thing for me to do.

Q. Do you look upon novel writing as Dylan Thomas did upon poetry as a "sullen craft and art": tremendously alone, private, agonizing?

A. Yes, absolutely; in spades. And sometimes almost hopeless!

Q. You mentioned somewhere that the actual technique of *Lie Down in Darkness* stumped you for a whole year. Did you have equal difficulty with the technique of your other novels?

A. Not so much in *The Long March*. That seemed to come with some ease, as I recollect. It took, for me, almost a negligible length of time to write: about six weeks, in Paris, in the summer of 1952, hot as it is now, in a little hotel room on the Left Bank. But with *Set This House on Fire* and *Nat Turner* the technique was very, very difficult.

Q. Why?

A. I think it was a matter of finding the true voice and rhythm of the narrative: programming the narrative so the voice merged with it in time and space, and so that there was a credibility at work. At one point in *Nat Turner* I stopped dead in my tracks for a long time. Months. Where it was was at the beginning of "Part Two," the flashback into Nat's past. I didn't have the momentum after "Part One" to just plunge ahead into this very, very tricky area in which I was trying to do a lot of things at once: among other things, to try and define what it must have been to be a slave growing up as a child, in that day and in that place. I finally, suddenly seized upon the idea that I must (as I did) meticulously outline the boy's life so that his subsequent actions would be credible.

Q. Was that flashback originally *conceived* as a flashback?

A. No, not originally. It just came; and had to become a flashback: a long flashback of 45,000 words.

Q. Do you generally find imagination dictating technique as you go along?

A. I think you could say that. The two really intermingle.

Q. Concerning the matter of technique, your novels tend to develop elaborate symbols and motifs. Have you any set idea of how these symbols are to work in your novels? Do you at all formulate them before you begin, or do they evolve in the creative process?

A. It depends on what you mean by symbols. I know "they" are there; but my own feeling is that they tend to spring up out of the soil of the work, to arise naturally from the narrative. Most of the time they simply seem to work. I just don't really know. I think it's an unanswerable question.

Q. Along those lines, your three major novels all seem preoccupied with dreams. Is there any particular reason for this?

A. Yes, I think so. I think if there's any reason at all, it is because dreams are a very impressive part of my subconscious. They linger with me (as I'm sure they do with many people) and *seem* to be teaching me something. I don't know if they do or not, but they are a momentous part of life for me, and therefore they must have their own significance somewhere: where and how, exactly, I'm not prepared to say.

Q. Have you ever incorporated your own dreams in your novels?

A. Yes, I think I have; in fact, I know I have.

Q. You have in your novels a penchant for long descriptions, many of them pertaining to nature. Do such descriptions always serve an integral function, or are they sometimes a flexing of technique?

A. I think they serve a very important function: at least in my work. I know that other writers tend to ignore nature completely; it doesn't seem to have any effect on them at all. But it's an important thing for me because I see it as an important component of the way people drift through existence. At this moment, for example, we're sitting on a porch on Martha's Vineyard. I'm enormously conscious not only of sitting here talking to you, but of being hot, of the water being out there, of hearing birds. These are components that I think we're never free of; and therefore I've always felt them a very important aspect of my work. For the same reason, I'd like to add that there is no extraneous nature writing in my novels. One critic came down rather heavily on its being extraneous in *Nat Turner*. But every bit of that writing about nature is crucial. Many critics—urban critics in particular —are probably not aware that a little black boy and a slave growing up in Virginia in 1831 had nothing *but* the presence of nature; and that nature, in fact, is where most of the black southern legends and myths derive from.

Q. All of your three longer novels are framed by epigraphs of a religious nature; yet in the novels themselves religion, per se, or at least Christian ritual, comes in for hard knocks. Is this intended simply as a controlling irony, or something more?

A. I think I've always been partially intent on contrasting the spiritual impulse as it is defined by Christianity with the hypocritical ritual and hypocritical shallowness and thought that surround much of its manifestations in life. So I consider the use of epigraphs an important device of irony.

Q. Why did you choose epigraphs from seventeenth-century

[33]

writings: Thomas Browne for *Lie Down in Darkness*, John Donne for *Set This House on Fire*, the King James Bible for *Nat Turner?*

A. With *Nat Turner*, of course, it had to be. With the others I was, at the time I wrote them, still very much steeped in seventeenth-century poetry and prose; and I seemed to want to strike chords that were common both to that time and ours.

Q. Can you explain why your protagonists tend to be visionaries, often of an apocalyptic sort?

A. That's an interesting question. I never quite thought of it that way. Perhaps I'm grounded in some manner of unconscious transcendentalism that makes me believe people really are striving for some impossible state. Perhaps they're all hopelessly romantic. (I don't know if that's the word, but perhaps it's as likely that as something else.) Anyway, this is an impulse I see in myself, and therefore it may take over these characters.

Q. In your novels any display of heroism is attended by a tragic outcome. Do you believe that "our age [to quote Lawrence] is essentially tragic"?

A. I think all ages are tragic, that heroism is always succeeded by tragic outcome, and that this is the human condition.

Q. Do you mean that all ages are tragic for the people involved in the age, or for the writer who transmits its vision?

A. I would say the two go hand in hand, and that they're inseparable in a way. If they are tragic for one, they're tragic for the other.

Q. In *Set This House on Fire* Cass Kinsolving is torn by, among other things, feelings of ambivalence about America: now loathing it, now longing for it. Were those your own feelings at the time, and have they changed any in the thirteen years since the novel was written?

A. I would say that if my feelings were validly expressed in the character of Cass, they're about the same now as they were then; perhaps even more so in both directions. You can't separate love-hate relationships; in fact, maybe this is what gives rise to viable and interesting literature.

Q. You realize, of course, that many contemporary American

writers avoid writing about "America" as a concept. But you don't; you seem to engage it wholly.

A. Yes. I continue to and I don't know why. It's not particularly a value situation; it's certainly not a necessary component of good writing to have this awareness. I just simply happen to have it to the point of preoccupation, and I imagine I always will in whatever I happen to write.

Q. Another concept, "sex," seems a cosmically destructive rather than a personally renewing force in your work: motivating in many instances the tragic outcome of your characters. Why?

A. I suppose you're being fairly accurate about that as a function in my work. I've often felt that what Freud called "this mighty urge" was, in the scheme of things, and in the contexts of things I've been writing about—the time, the place, the ethos—more destructive than constructive because of the prevalent morality. *Lie Down in Darkness* is a good example of what I believe you mean: the time and place being the thirties and forties in America, which was still very restrictive, especially in the South. Sex was the thing which one kept buried, I think unhealthily. I rejoice, really, in the new freedom of today, but in that time I believe it was a destructive force.

Q. Do you feel that if Nat Turner had "found his woman" the slave revolt would not have come about?

A. I don't think you can pose the question that way, but I'll try answering it by citing an example I've used before. Other revolutionaries—I'm thinking specifically of Martin Luther—consciously eschewed this matter because they believed that women, sex, etc., got in the way. And I think this has been demonstrated over and over again. Nat wasn't sophisticated enough to look at it in that fashion; but probably the reason he did *not* have a woman —and I still stick to my guns in saying that the historical record is, at the very least, obscure about the matter—was because he unconsciously felt this would obstruct his own revolutionary impulse and idealism: that the cause had to be served by steadfast asceticism.

Q. Several critics have noted in your novels recurrent motifs of master-slave relationships: e.g., Dolly and Milton in *Lie Down in Darkness;* Mason Flagg and Cass Kinsolving in *Set This House on Fire;* Nat and his owner, Hark and Nat. Is there any special reason for this, or is it purely fortuitous?

A. I've noted it myself. I suppose life is probably that way to a degree. Maybe I tend to focus on it more than other writers; but perhaps for me life is a demonstration of oppression and submission, and variations upon them.

Q. Has this anything to do with your southern origins?

A. I think it does, to some degree, yes.

Q. Since I'm asking about recurring patterns, can you explain why your heroes all happen to be thirty? Fitzgerald said that after thirty a man can't lie to himself anymore. Is thirty the age for "the moment of truth"?

A. I wish I knew. I would say that maybe it's fifty or fifty-five. But really, you can't ever lie to yourself. Actually, I hadn't thought of thirty as recurring as often as you say, but I guess it is a kind of crucial age in that you're no longer a youth; you're an adult. I think you could say it's an arbitrary age. There was a time when I was under thirty that I thought things would float along; and when I hit thirty, all of a sudden I had to get hold of myself. I don't know if that was the exact age or not, but when I turned thirty I was kind of glum. I see in retrospect how stupid the whole thing was.

Q. Your first full-length play, *In the Clap Shack*, was presented on December 15, 1972, at the Yale Repertory Theatre in New Haven, Connecticut. What decided you on play writing?

A. This particular theme, this episode seemed (like nothing else I've ever written) to outline itself as a play. The two acts, the setting, everything literally seemed to form itself in my mind as a play. And it did come very easily. Whatever the merits or demerits of the work, I certainly think it's a very theatrical piece.

Q. Did you find it easier to write than fiction?

A. Much, much easier. Let me qualify that. Harder in a curious way, but not harder in a more important way: harder in a kind of nit-picking way.

Q. Did you approach the writing of the play in the same way as you approached the writing of your novels?

A. More or less, yes. I sat down and did those four or five pages a day. I found they went very rapidly, and that it took me only two and a half months to write the play. Of course the revisions took a lot longer: and that's the big difference, for me, between play writing and novel writing. There's a lot of work to be done after the first draft is laid out.

Q. *In the Clap Shack* is a comedy. Isn't the writing of comedy something of a departure from your normal mode of writing?

A. Put it this way. I would like to think that all my work has some humor in it, and I think it does. But you're basically right. The comic mode has not been my . . . dodge! But I do think the irony that's necessary to both tragedy and comedy is in me. And it was easy to switch to comedy as long as I understood that the play was going to be a satire—which it is: a satire on a lot of things.

Q. What were the critics' reactions to the play?

A. *The* critic, namely Clive Barnes, saw no value in it at all. Too bad that he's *the* critic, because that destroyed, at least immediately, any chance of its going on to better things. However a lot of the other critics liked it. In places like the Hartford papers and *Variety* it got rather good reviews. Brendan Gill, a man of taste I think, saw it and liked it very much, though he saw it too late for a *New Yorker* review. In fact he wrote me a letter and put down Barnes rather severely for having failed to see anything in the play.

Q. Even more importantly, I was wondering what your reactions were to the initial production in New Haven.

A. I thought there were good and bad things. I thought there was bad casting in several instances, namely in the Magruder part. But also I thought the play had some very strong casting in the parts of Schwartz (Eugene Troobnick) and Clark (Hannibal Penney, Jr.). I thought they superbly fleshed out the characters. As I look back on it, I think the production probably lacked imagination. I think it was done too conventionally. It needed an ele-

[37]

ment of extravaganza about it. The whole thing needed to be done more surrealistically to have given it bite, and to have removed it from the rather conventional sort of setting.

Q. Do you think (since you *are* a playwright now) that a playwright can or deserves to be satisfied with a production of his play?

A. I think so. I'm not knocking the production I got. I was very glad to have a production. I was pleased, above all, that though the audiences in New Haven are variable, they almost universally enjoyed the play.

Q. Do you feel, now that the play has been published, as close to it as to your novels?

A. No, absolutely not. At the same time I don't mean to sound as though I'm trivializing my relationship to it. I put much work and effort into it, and I respect what I achieved in it; but I don't have the same commitment to it emotionally, in any sense, as I do to my novels, nor even to some of the essays I've done.

Q. Robert Brustein, dean of the Yale Drama School, helped you in the revision of the play. Could you tell me what his most valuable contributions were to the final script?

A. He saw the unity I was trying to achieve but not achieving. The play was diffuse in its tone. It was a tragicomedy, whereas the comic tone should have been ascendent. So he made me, in effect, and I gladly did, cut out the extraneous things which tended to be grim and morbid in favor of the humorous elements.

Q. I would scarcely have called these other elements "grim and morbid." I remember them from the first drafts as memories or reveries, mostly Magruder's. Would you say those elements, whatever we might call them, were the novelist intruding on the playwright?

A. Yes, I would definitely say they were a hangover from novel writing.

Q. As a novelist, then, would you like to see the earlier drafts published with the "cuts" restored: to see the play, I mean, published not necessarily as a drama in the acting version but solely as a piece of writing?

A. I don't think it would serve any purpose. I'm happy with it the way it evolved. It's my belief, among other things, that of all art forms, of all literary art forms, play writing is the only one that's really collaborative. And that it allows for collaboration without compromising the integrity of the original creator. If an editor had taken the manuscript of a novel of mine and done as much changing as Bob Brustein suggested I do in this play, I would have felt compromised. But in terms of the play I don't feel that at all. I feel that's one of the aspects of play writing which is constant: that it lends itself so readily to a collaborative point of view.

Q. How did you "see" the play while you were writing it, and how did your vision of it change (if it did) when it went into the final production?

A. Very little. I think the two coincided very well. But from *this* vantage point, that is now, retrospectively, I still think it could have been transformed into something more exciting by the use of some experimental stagecraft, lighting, stage effects, and so on. I don't have all the theatrical jargon down, but what I'm trying to say is I think it could have been more exciting.

Q. I'd like to ask you a question about the acting itself. Would you respond to how you felt the actors supported, distorted, or changed your meaning as *you* wrote the play?

A. Let me be specific. I think that the actor who played the doctor, Glanz (Jeremy Geidt), is an excellent actor, and I wouldn't fault him for a moment, but I thought he was miscast in this particular role. He's an Englishman and he has an English gloss. In fact, we had to add things in the script to give his accent credibility. When he announces his pedigree to Magruder he says things like medical training at the University of Budapest, and Guy's Hospital, London. This was done in order to establish a foreign background. But even that wasn't enough to keep from distorting the role. I visualize, and I think he's central to the play, a very important figure in the play, a kind of mid-Western efficiency expert. I always saw someone very deadpan, getting his laughs out of the lines. Jeremy got a lot of laughs out of the way he played it, which is O.K., it's legitimate. But ideally I saw someone like Hume Cronyn: a combination of malevolence and illness, on the order of Queeg from *Caine Mutiny*, though much funnier. For me the role fell far short of what it should have been.

The role of Magruder, too, I thought was miscast. The part needs a young stud instead of the round, pink-cheeked, little innocent it got.

On the other hand, the ensemble playing was excellent; and, as I said before, so were the actors who played Clark and Schwartz. Also there were some very imaginative minor roles.

For instance the Catholic chaplain, in his one little scene, did a marvelous job. As a matter of fact I remember Bob Brustein or Alvin Epstein (the director) thinking about taking that whole scene out because it seemed to interrupt the tempo of the play. But in the acting it "worked"; he got a hand every night. In fact, to give an example of the collaborative aspect of play writing I mentioned before, the actor (Bill Gearhart) changed some of the lines during one rehearsal, and changed them beautifully. At one point, you remember, he's arguing about whether it's a Protestant or Catholic who's dying, and he pulls out a very official paper. Now I had the line reading, "I have a message from Battalion Headquarters saying that a Catholic *is* dying on D Ward." And he changed the tense to say "a Catholic *will be* dying." I think that's a nice piece of imaginative ad-libbing on the part of an actor. And of course we left it in because it turned out to be a funny, funny line.

Q. There is a difference, of course, in seeing a play on paper before it goes into production, and even in realizing what the actors are doing by way of bringing the written play to life. But an equally important dimension in the theater is the audience. Do you think the audiences' reactions influenced your original conceptions of the themes and characters? I mean, you created them one way; the audiences responded to them in another way. Or did they?

A. Well, that's curious, because I never realized before I'd written a play the way that audiences vary. For example, I was supposed to go—but I missed a plane somewhere and couldn't—on the night Phillip Roth went, and apparently I missed a fantastic evening. Apparently there was continuous laughter, according to Phil, who's tried play writing himself and is a very tough guy to please. He couldn't contain his enthusiasm for the way the play went *that* evening. And then Howard Stein, who knows theater as well as anyone, I guess, said it had been a marvelous audience; he said there had been a chemistry. After the show there were "Bravos" and a standing ovation—just one of those incredible theatrical exchanges between actors and audience. Then I went on several occasions after this. One evening there was a rather small audience; the house was about two-thirds full and there was a kind of intimacy in the theater. The audience responded (I thought) happily to the way *I* saw the play. And then I went to another production with a much larger audience—it was a performance toward the end of the run—and this audience was taking it as a straight play. Lines which had universally "cracked people up" (including the "famous" night Phil Roth went) fell dead! Now this is an indication for me of a very important thing about the theater. Audiences vary of course. Everyone "in theater" knows it. But *I* didn't know it until I became a playwright.

Q. Were the production to be done again, say on Broadway, what changes if any would you make?

A. I think that would be up to the director. I think it needs a different, more imaginative setting. That's one criticism Clive Barnes made that I would agree with, where he said that it was adequate and what else can you do with a hospital ward. Well, I think a set designer can do a lot of things with a hospital ward. It needs a new concept.

Q. I'd like to ask you something slightly more "literary." Dialogue in novels may have as many connotations as there are readers to interpret it. In a play, though, the audience is chained to the director's and actors' interpretations. Do you find this adds a significant limitation to the dramatic form?

A. I think it can work both ways. Obviously if the actor is inadequate to the dialogue he's going to convey that inadequacy. On the other hand, if an actor sees depth in a role he can often bring to the dialogue a new dimension. And I think within the framework of this play I had good examples of both possibilities.

Many of the lines delivered by Glanz lacked the irony and bite they should have had because of the failure of the actor to fulfill that role. It just wasn't his part. The lines did not have the resonance and abrasiveness that I saw. Conversely, I thought the two best actors, who played Clark and Schwartz, brought, surprisingly to me, dimensions to the lines I had given them. Penney's marvelous laugh, for example, that seemed to encompass the audience at many points in the play was just superb. I had not visualized, in the writing of the play, that kind of range and effectiveness.

Q. Even were scenes like these to be found in a novel, you couldn't really imagine them being enriched in any way by the sensitive interpretations of readers themselves? What you're saying, it seems to me, is that in many cases it was *the* way you wanted a scene, though you didn't conceive all its possibilities in the writing!

A. Yes. And that's a salient difference between novels and plays. If I had wanted to write about this black man's evil laugh I would have had to describe it in that way, glossing the whole thing. But what happened here is that Hannibal Penney (who I think is a promising actor and someday will be a fine one) brought it all off automatically. It was part of *his* concept. And that's the great difference between these two literary forms.

Q. Do you have in mind any real limitations of the novel form over the dramatic form?

A. Basically I'm still a novelist and partisan to the novel. To put it the other way round, one of the things that makes writing plays so pleasant is their length: the fact that you can dispense with those endless descriptions, those sunsets, those entrances and exits, all that furniture and nuance which is part of the tedium to me of novel writing. This gives play writing a basic attraction.

Q. Then you do plan to write more plays.

A. I think so. Not immediately, but I do intend to.

Q. You're presently at work on a novel, *The Way of the Warrior*, about the marines. One chapter of it, as a matter of fact, appeared in *Esquire* for September 1971 and was called "Mariott the Marine." Will this be a long novel, too, and have you been working on it for long?

A. It's going to be "longish": shorter than the other three long novels, but of reasonable length. I've had stops, many hung-up moments, but I've been working fairly steadily off and on.

Q. Do you feel that after *From Here to Eternity*, *The Naked and the Dead*, *Catch 22*, and *Slaughterhouse Five* there still might be interest in a war novel?

A. I think it depends entirely on the approach. What I'm writing about is very unusual. It's not in the "war novel" tradition. It's becoming, I think, a rather thickly textured examination of the professional military mind in America.

Q. That last is a very intriguing phrase. Can you elaborate on it, or would that be giving away a good portion of the novel?

A. The phrase, really, has become in *my* mind a symbolic representation of what America has been up to for many years. The hero is an idealistic military man. He is a man who joins this primitive, militaristic organization called the Marine Corps as it was forty years ago, at the end of the twenties and thirties when it was simply an arm of American imperialism, a kind of police or enforcing arm for the First National City Bank. The man comes of age through World War II and becomes someone who sees the necessity for civilizing military life in order for us to proceed as a civilized nation. An idealistic point of view, but nonetheless one based on a very real and tragic apprehension of existence: namely, that war is an absolute component of life, one that will never vanish so far as we can tell from the human condition. In other words, he's a kind of Fifth Columnist for the "good": a man who has almost some quixotic notion that if he can change the way that military people live, he will change the face of life.

Q. Isn't it paradoxical to bring the idea of "civilization" into the military?

A. Of course it is. That's one of the points of the book. This is what makes the man, I think, a rather splendidly unique sort of character.

Q. Does the military mind, per se, frighten you personally?

Are you obsessed by it in any particular way, or only as a vehicle for the novel?

A. It doesn't frighten me as an abstraction, no. I think the military mind has been badly misunderstood in this country, mainly because we have a unique military establishment. It doesn't follow the patterns of the professional military establishments in other nations. It's a product of democracy after all; whereas, generally speaking, the military establishments of other Western nations have been the product of an aristocracy. It takes a different form. It's a reflection really of what we are as a nation. But it's a far more complex thing than many people envision it. The cliché of the "dumb military man" is simply not true.

Q. Is the novel in any way a roman à clef?

A. In no way, no way at all.

Q. What decided your turning to military subjects for your last two works? *In the Clap Shack* has a military setting; so does *The Way of the Warrior*. Was there any direct inspiration for writing it?

A. I'm like Edmund Wilson in this respect. I'm fascinated by the Marine Corps: its traditional glamor, the fact that it's an elite and dedicated establishment within an Establishment, and that it very distinctly has in our time involved men of courage and action. I'm fascinated by a sort of amalgam of personality about it. Perhaps like so much of what one writes it's a working out of one's fantasies. And who knows but whether this character I'm writing about is not a kind of projection of my own fantasies: the idea of a man who is at once a man of incredible physical courage, yet a man of learning and culture, a man who is, in addition, an idealist who wants to put an end to war: at least to bring civilization to the art and science of warfare.

Q. But the inspiration for this character wasn't pulled out of thin air. There were, are people who may have served as models.

A. Like everybody one writes about there is a figment here. There is a man who crossed my life at one point or another who resembled the character I'm writing about; but basically he is an imaginative projection.

Q. *The Long March* and *In the Clap Shack* are based on actual marine experiences. Is this true of *The Way of the Warrior?*

A. No. Well, I'm only being partly accurate. There is a lot in the book that's semiautobiographical.

Q. *Set This House on Fire* is written in the first person. *Nat Turner* is written in the first person. Long and substantial sections of *Lie Down in Darkness* are monologues, which can almost be considered first person narrative. And even *The Long March* might qualify for a first person narrative considering its "central intelligence" as James called him. Why do you prefer this voice, or something akin to it?

A. I tend to gravitate toward it because of its immediacy. It lends a kind of authenticity to a narrative that is sometimes quite lacking when you're describing a third person situation.

Q. It doesn't make the writing of the novel any easier, does it?

A. It certainly doesn't. It often makes it quite harder because it tends to start limiting your point of view, and you've got to find a way to get into the other peoples' heads. You trust to luck or skill that that happens.

Q. Is it still luck, at this point in your career? Don't you know what you're doing at every moment in the writing of a novel?

A. Obviously if it works it works. I've been criticized for many things but rarely for not being convincing.

Q. In *Nat Turner* you ingeniously devise a separation and synthesis of biography, history, and fiction. From what one gathers from the excerpt from *The Way of the Warrior* in *Esquire* it seems that your point of departure for that novel is autobiography: which means you are working this separation and synthesis between *autobiography*, history, and fiction. Are there any new techniques (new to you, that is) you had to adopt or invent in achieving this fusion?

A. No. Again it's a matter of tone, I think. Clearly, I have to gain the reader's confidence and credulity; and in order to do this I've had to say at certain points: "Look, I don't know what this man is thinking, but I'm trusting you, the reader, to go along with me in an imaginative exploration of this man's mind."

[45]

Q. Is it significant in any way that the narrator is a novelist who is almost or quasi-William Styron?

A. That's another thing. I wanted definitely to leave the impression that it was I, William Styron, telling this story, though I never refer to myself by name nor is my name ever mentioned. But this is the impression I want to establish. Again, I don't claim by any means to have invented this technique, because it's been done before. But I don't believe it's been done terribly successfully or very much: this writing in the form of a fictional memoir. In other words, a fusion of two forms, in which you start off distinctly giving the reader that it is you, William Styron, writing, and yet merge this into fiction. It gives the impression of autobiography but in reality it's not. It's something much different.

Q. The autobiography is there to establish the credulity only?

A. As in a court, yes, so you'll have an unimpeachable witness to things.

Q. Of course we're talking about a work in progress. I mention this because I wonder if current events, relating not only to the military, but to the government to which it is subordinate, changed the direction of the novel since you began writing it?

A. Yes. Well, I would think that events in Vietnam have illuminated things a lot. I think that through the evolution of recent history I have been able to see insights into this man that I am writing about which I did not have before. This has been a slow evolution for me because I did not realize what the philosophic center of this book was until pretty recently. And it is just what I've described to you a few minutes ago: a kind of symbolic rendition of what is very much part of the American spirit and embedded in it, this kind of blind, almost puerile groping for a national identity, part of it taking the form of wanton imperialism. It is a chapter about twentieth-century American history which has never really been fully written yet.

The fact is that we have, for example, been criminally involved in Latin America. Of course everyone who is sophisticated knows this, but hardly the extent of it. And that ever since the turn of the century, ever since the Spanish-American War, we have been involved in these criminal activities which have been mini-Vietnams.

We had no business there, torturing civilians, fighting guerillas, and so on. It prefigured this war we are still ostensibly, despite what passes for a truce, fighting.

And what I want to do is show how a man is able to come to a moral consciousness, even as he has been engaged in these things. He starts out, you see, as a young, cultured, hothead Virginian of the old-fashioned type, VMI graduate, but brought up partially in France, with a great flair for languages and a great appetite for life. He's a young lieutenant of twenty-three or twenty-four, commissioned into the regular Marine Corps, in Nicaragua on patrol, and he hates these Communists. He comes from an anti-Communist background (what could be more anti-Communist than Virginia?). Well, three Nicaraguan guerillas are captured, and he cheerfully presides over cutting their throats with a bayonet. He does it himself. So I'm trying to show how this man evolves through a career in the Marine Corps up through the Second World War and the Korean War into by this time a colonel who sees his mission in life as a man who is going to pacify the military: a man who *knows* through his sense of destiny that he's going to become commandant of the Marine Corps. The book begins with a fantasy where, now a general and in his fifties, in the year 1963, he persuades John F. Kennedy to get out of Vietnam. I think you'll have to wait for publication to see how it ends.

Q. The novel does seem to depend a lot on history. Would you call it, like *Nat Turner*, another "meditation on history"?

A. No. I wish it were; it would be easier to write; I'm having to invent it all.

Q. In any case you are consciously avoiding writing a war novel after the accepted style.

A. Yes. And when I reflect on this book it has many of the themes you brought up today—master-slave relationships, destruction by sex, America, and other of those various motifs.

Q. I read sometime back that *Nat Turner* was going to be made into a movie. Have they begun filming it yet?

A. It's been bought and paid for—thank God—but that's all. It hasn't been produced, though the production came close to being started. I went to Hollywood for a week and stayed at very posh quarters and wrote a "treatment" which was never used because the producers began to get very upset over the black reaction. And that became a stumbling block. Finally for that reason, and probably for financial reasons, they postponed it or put it on the shelf, or whatever they call it out there.

Q. Had you ever written for the films before you did this treatment?

A. I collaborated on a screenplay just recently which was bought—or rather an option was taken on it. It's a screenplay based on a 1927 murder in New York (quite famous in its day) called the Snyder-Gray murder case, which was an especially gory triangle murder having to do with a woman, her paramour, and her husband. It was a big cause célèbre and ended up in the double execution of the woman and her husband. It's called *Dead! A Love Story* and was sold to Paul Newman and his production company who've recently renewed the option.

Q. Would you like to see your work filmed?

A. Well, this I would. It's something that grabbed me and also my collaborator who is John Phillips (the son of John Marquand). We had great fun doing it; but I doubt very seriously that I'd care to make script writing a career.

Q. I think what I meant was did you ever want to see your novels turned into films?

A. Every one of them has been optioned at one time or another; scripts have been made for all of them, with the exception of *The Long March*, which had a disastrous run on television in the fifties: the last live broadcast on *Playhouse 90*. With the exception of that, everything has fallen through for one reason or another. The only novel that *I* think would possibly make a good movie is *Nat Turner* because it has an exterior scope. The others are too interior. Not that *Nat* isn't interior to some degree, but I can visualize it as a panorama more readily than the others.

Q. Along rather different lines again. I recall that you taught a seminar in creative writing at Yale.

A. Yes. Just for a semester. Several years ago.

Q. Did you like teaching?

A. I enjoyed it, yes.

Q. Did you have any luck teaching people to write?

A. I *think* I did; in a funny way. Unless I'm terribly mistaken I think the students improved. I had thirteen students. Most of their things looked awfully poor at first, and then at the end they looked better. And I attribute *some* of that to my guidance.

Q. Do you have any particular tack you take in teaching people to write, besides just criticizing their writing? Do you emphasize certain things?

A. I think I pointed out to them certain important things about language that they were vague about: the specific choice of words. I tried to point out that language, after all, is behind all this, and that many of them had great visions but not much linguistic capability, and that was because they were not being very careful about how they wrote. I pointed out rather primitive things at first. For example, if you sprinkle too many sentences with adverbs they're clumsy sentences, mostly if not always.

Q. What did you deal with after language, which I think we would all agree is the primary thing in teaching writing?

A. A combination of things. The students were college sophomores and juniors, so they were not very old, and so far as writing went not very experienced. I tried to point them toward a fusion of vision and language, emphasizing that subject matter was important, that they should avoid cliché situations, that there were certain mechanical hurdles to get over. Another thing I tried to get them to do was a lot of reading, because many of them had not. I had a suggested reading list and most of them went along with that. And I think profited from it, because at an early age writers profitably imitate.

Q. Was this a short story writing course?

A. More or less.

Q. You yourself don't write many short stories. Do you feel in any way that the short story is a dead form?

A. No, I don't think it's a dead form. I'm not attracted to it very much because I think it's a limiting form, and that I work better in a larger medium. I remember the ones I've tried always restricted me; I felt the need to expand. As the case with *Nat* which, as I mentioned, started out as a novella.

[49]

Q. Would you care to express your feelings about the younger writers, thirty-five and under, of today? Have you any particular favorites?

A. There *are* two writers whose careers I've followed. One is a writer named Donald Harrington, who's very clever, and who's written several novels: none of which has gotten the attention it deserves. The other is Michael Mewshaw who went to the University of Virginia, and who, I think, is an awfully talented writer.

Q. How about the writers of your own generation: Capote, Salinger, Mailer, Bellow? Have they in your opinion come through or fallen off?

A. I don't like to comment on other writers too much. I used to, but I don't like to any longer because I don't feel competent in doing so. The writers you've mentioned are all good writers, worthy of our attention. I think it's a very various and lively gathering of writers we have in America and have always had. Today is a very vital, good, fruitful time; and I think it's clear that this is where the major voices are and where the action is.

Q. What are your feelings about critical collections such as the present one?

A. I don't think they do any harm; they might do some good. I think as an introduction to a writer's work it can be useful; and it can also be useful as a guidepost for the time when, if your work is fortunate enough to last, it will be a thing for people to consult.

Q. You've never, to my knowledge, expressed positive disdain for critics, as some of your contemporaries have.

A. Actually I think I have, but *when* I have I haven't really been sincere. I think I value the critical function very highly; it's ridiculous not to. I think it only becomes unfortunate when the critical faculty is esteemed over the creative faculty, which it was for some time—ten, fifteen, twenty years ago. There was a time when it was thought that to be a critic was to be superior to a writer of prose fiction. It was, fortunately, a passing phase, and criticism today when good is very valuable.

LOUIS D. RUBIN, JR.

Notes on a Southern Writer
in Our Time

In 1951 a young Virginian, William Styron, published his first novel. Entitled *Lie Down in Darkness*, it was the story of a young woman whose existence grew increasingly desperate until finally she took her own life. The novel was received with considerable acclaim, and reviewers prophesied a distinguished future for its author.

In an interview with David Dempsey, Styron readily admitted that he had first begun *Lie Down in Darkness* immediately following an intense reading of the novels of William Faulkner. And indeed, there were more than a few obvious similarities to Faulkner's fiction, notably with *The Sound and the Fury*. Both novels were set in the South. In both there were a family with an alcoholic father, a selfish mother, and several children, one of them mentally retarded. Both had protagonists who wandered about a city far away from home, clutching a timepiece, before jumping to their deaths. Both had faithful Negro servants who went to church to mourn the disintegration of their white folks. Another Faulkner novel, *As I Lay Dying*, was built about a family's journey to inter a coffin. In *Lie Down in Darkness* a family's trip to the cemetery to inter a coffin provides the frame for the novel. And so on.

All the same, Styron's novel was not simply warmed-over Faulkner. For one thing, it had a contemporaneity to it, a sense of dealing with moderns in the modern world, that is not present in Faulkner. For Faulkner's attempts to use the contemporary urban milieu to create fiction, notably in the last two volumes of the Snopes trilogy, have been melodramatic and unsatisfactory. By contrast, Styron's novel was set convincingly in a contemporary setting, and was fully of the present moment in its concerns and attitudes. Where so much fiction by younger southern writers seemed like inferior Faulkner, Styron's talent was recognizably his own; and as with the better Faulkner novels, it had the sense of *mattering*, of dealing with characters who definitely stood for something as human beings. Nor was it composed with the terse understatement typical of so much present-day American fiction. It had the high rhetoric, the sounding language, of the best fiction of Faulkner, Wolfe, and Warren.

Here, then, was a novelist who seemed to write squarely within the southern tradition, and yet was definitely his own man. He was, furthermore, quite young—only twenty-five when his first novel appeared—and he obviously possessed the kind of stylistic mastery emblematic of the truly gifted writer. There was no apprehension of his first novel's having been a fluke, depending for its impact on a lucky combination of topical subject matter and the author's momentary psychological attitude, as was true of a novel such as James Jones's *From Here to Eternity*. The novelist who could write *Lie Down in Darkness*, one felt, could and probably would follow it with other novels of similar or higher caliber. This opinion was confirmed a year later when Styron published a novella, *The Long March*, a vigorous tale of Marine reservists called back to duty. It too bore the mark of the writer thoroughly in control of his craft.

What happened then was very strange. For almost a full decade, William Styron did not publish another novel. Though rumors of a new work in progress recurred, year after year went by with no new fiction by Styron. Yet paradoxically, instead of gradually dropping from sight in public reputation as novels by other good writers were published and achieved recognition, as one might expect to happen to the author of a good first novel who did not produce additional work, William Styron's stock kept right on rising. On the strength of that one novel and the novella, he came to enjoy the kind of literary prestige that few other writers commanded. Critics habitually referred to him as one of the handful of really distinguished novelists of his generation. He was interviewed, quoted, repeatedly cited, and discussed. For the better part of ten years he possessed a reputation that the author of a half-dozen good novels might well envy.

Lie Down in Darkness was a good book, and everything that was said about it in the way of the augury it held was justified. But good as it was, one is hard put to explain the extraordinary growth of Styron's reputation in terms of it. It was no *Look Homeward, Angel* or *The Sound and the Fury*. It was surely not, for its time and place, the kind of novel that *Sister Carrie* had been during the 1900s. To an extent it was derivative. It had flaws aplenty. Though it thoroughly warranted its author's being marked as a man to watch, a potentially important novelist, it was after all only a single, well-written, medium-length novel, and not a sustained body of literary work. So that one might ask why its author, during the 1950s, gained the astonishing reputation he enjoyed. Was it something else besides the book itself? One of Styron's contemporaries, Norman Mailer, jealously hinted as much in *Advertisements for Myself*, suggesting that it was Styron's own doing. "Styron has spent years oiling every literary lever and power which could help him on his way, and there are medals waiting for him in the mass-media," Mailer wrote. Exactly how Styron managed this feat Mailer did not bother to explain.

In any event, the reputation was there, and it outran the novel, with the result that when in 1960 Styron did bring out a second novel, what happened might have been expected. *Set This House on Fire* was treated to a torrent of critical abuse the like of which has seldom been seen in our time. On all sides it was roundly condemned. If one believed most of the review media, it was almost inconceivable that any novelist could have produced as bad a work as William Styron had done in his second try. The Most Promising Young Novelist Of His Generation was thoroughly denounced. The popular critics and the academic reviewers seemed to compete in the rage and intensity of their abuse, and not content with demolishing *Set This House on Fire*, some went back and decided that *Lie Down in Darkness* was not really so good, either.

Was *Set This House on Fire* really so bad as everybody said it was? Not at all, I think. In fact, it was quite a good book. Like its predecessor it had flaws, perhaps more vulnerable ones, but in

almost every way it was a more ambitious, more deeply perceptive work. It was a novel such as no other writer of Styron's generation could have produced; it contained some of the best writing
of its day. But if this is so, then what explains its devastatingly
hostile reception? Why was it singled out for such a barrage?

The answer, I think, is to be found in the *kind* of book that *Lie
Down in Darkness* was, and the reasons why that novel, in contrast to the second book, enjoyed such a stunning success. It has
to do with the difference between the kind of book that *Lie Down
in Darkness seemed* to be, and the kind of book it really was. For
when it first appeared it seemed to be something very different,
and much more familiar, than what it actually was; and the reasons
for this have to do in large part with southern literature from
Faulkner onward. The history of Styron's two novels is closely
tied in with what southern writing has been during the past several
decades, and what it can and might be in the future. I want now
to discuss Styron's work in this light. For what is involved, I believe, is not only the history of one young novelist's career and
reputation, but the whole question of the continuation of a literary
mode into a new generation. I am not talking about "influences,"
nor am I concerned importantly with cultural history as such.
Rather I shall seek to deal, by inference at least, with the deepest
and most elementary relationships between a book and its times,
between art and culture, between one writer who comes from a
particular region and the writers of that region who preceded
him. And without claiming for a moment that the concerns I shall
be examining are the *conscious* concerns either of writer, or region,
or reader, I shall seek to show what, in William Styron's own time,
which is ours as well, it means to be a "southern" writer.

The central character in *Lie Down in Darkness* is a young
woman, Peyton Loftis. Born of a well-to-do Tidewater Virginia
family, she grows up in the seaport city of Port Warwick. Her
father, Milton Loftis, is a lawyer. Once he had political ambitions, but over the years he has become much more interested in
his golf game and in social drinking. Helen Loftis, Peyton's
mother, is the child of a sadistic, puritanical army officer, who has

left her a substantial fortune. Peyton is the older of two daughters; the second child, Maudie, is mentally defective. Milton Loftis is inordinately fond of Peyton, and far too indulgent. He cannot bear to jeopardize her affection for him, even momentarily, by denying her anything she demands. By contrast, Helen Loftis is highly resentful of her daughter's hold over Milton, and at crucial moments her jealousy is revealed in words and acts of great cruelty. The older Helen grows, the harder her personality becomes. Milton, meanwhile, becomes infatuated with another woman, Dollie Bonner, who gives him the idolatry and the softness that his wife will not provide.

After a violent scene with her mother, Peyton goes off to school at a fashionable Virginia women's college, and never really returns home to live, though several times she tries and fails. Her life becomes increasingly unhappy. At crucial junctures Milton fails to provide her with the guidance and firmness she needs in a parent, while Helen denies her the motherly affection she craves. When Maudie sickens and dies, Helen accuses Peyton of causing her death. Several times a reconciliation between mother and daughter is attempted, but Helen's insane jealousy always wrecks it, despite the advice and encouragement that an Episcopal minister, Carey Carr, attempts to give to Helen.

Finally Peyton goes to live in New York, where she falls in love with a Jewish painter, Harry Miller. In a final effort to gain her mother's love, she comes home to Port Warwick for the wedding ceremony, but just when all seems to be going well, the mother's obsession and hatred are viciously reasserted, and the day ends in bitterness and misery. Peyton and her husband return to New York, and Peyton thereupon steadily destroys her own marriage by continually "testing" Harry's love through acts of selfishness and cruelty. At length she begins to sleep with other men, whereupon the tormented Harry forces himself to leave her; and, when a final, pathetic attempt at reconciling him fails, Peyton commits suicide by leaping from a building. Her body is brought home to Port Warwick and buried. Thus the plot of *Lie Down in Darkness*.

First let it be reiterated that is is a *good* novel; there is no doubt of that. Styron's sense of psychological complication is such that the descent of Peyton Loftis into darkness is convincingly motivated. Just as in Faulkner's *The Sound and the Fury*, the novel is an account of the failure of love. Had Milton Loftis's love for his daughter been less selfish, so that the father had been willing to incur his daughter's momentary displeasure by insisting that she do what was right rather than what she wished to do; had Helen Loftis's firmness been the product of genuine love and understanding for Peyton and not a hypocritical mask for jealousy and hostility; then Peyton might have grown up into someone who is able to love in her turn. But Milton sought in Peyton the affection that Helen did not provide him, and Helen struck out at Peyton in order to punish Milton. Thus Peyton has known for love only indulgence on the one hand and poorly masked jealousy on the other; and when she marries, she seeks a relationship on just those terms. She demands and must have continual forgiveness, and the acts she commits in her quest for proof of such forgiveness are too reprehensible for her husband to condone. Along with this goes an insane jealousy, in which she magnifies small failures on her husband's part into evidence of monstrous unfaithfulness; no sooner does she feel that Harry has forgiven her for her own misdeeds than she begins at once to berate him unreasonably and psychotically for imaginary infidelities. Thus Harry must play the part of forgiving father on the one hand, and erring husband on the other, neither of which roles he merits. In psychiatric terms, Peyton must first reenact her relationship with her father, and then her mother's relationship with her father. It is too much, finally, for Harry to accept, if he is to retain his own sanity. Whereupon, denied the only kind of love that she can recognize, Peyton takes her own life. A father's weakness, a mother's cruelty have brought about a daughter's destruction.

Set against a background of upper–middle-class, urban, southern society, the story is one of real dramatic tension. Peyton's struggle to save herself (more rending because of her own recognition of her plight) deeply engages the reader's sympathies. Intelligent, compassionate, with a great capacity for loving and being loved, she is doomed to frustration and pain, and when finally she succumbs to the forces that are dragging her downward, there is a genuine tragedy in her fall. Similarly, the characterization of Milton Loftis is a moving picture of weakness and ineffectual love. Milton too is aware of his plight, and his efforts to save himself and his family are pathetically moving. Helen Loftis, I think, is somewhat less effectively drawn; the psychological motivations for her conduct are never fully apparent, and must only be conjectured. The role of the family's Negro servants is too obviously contrived. Unlike Dilsey and her family in Faulkner's *The Sound and the Fury*, Ella and La Ruth in *Lie Down in Darkness* do not fill the dramatic position in the fortunes of the Loftis family that would justify Styron's use of them as tragic chorus.

Despite such flaws, however, *Lie Down in Darkness* is a successful, well-written work of art. As a first novel it surely justified those who saw in its author a writer of much promise, who might be expected to produce other works of distinguished fiction. To begin with, it was decidedly moving, and had genuinely tragic overtones; and it was the first novel to appear in the postwar period by a young writer of whom that could be said. Not one of the other postwar writers had been able to produce such a book. The best of their novels were ponderous, naturalistic works such as Mailer's *The Naked and the Dead*, and Jones's *From Here to Eternity*, both the products of writers of obvious passion, but written, I think, somewhat crudely. Both were war novels. Of the two Mailer's was the better written, but much of its power came out of its author's, and its readers', detestation of war and military life. In Jones's case that was about *all* that could be said for his book. In each instance a sense of civilized outrage, on the part of novelist and reader, contributed much to the success of the work.

By contrast, Styron's book was not a war novel. Its intensity was attained by the author's fictional craftsmanship, his talent at characterization, his insight into the tension and desperation of a modern, godforsaken urban existence. Such a novel had not appeared in some time, and the public was hungry for a writer who could produce more. It was thus quick to hail *Lie Down in Darkness*, and to hope and expect that Styron would be able to follow with other and even better books. Furthermore, in the decade that followed its publication, no other competitor appeared in sight. Good as Saul Bellow's *The Adventures of Augie March*, J. D. Salinger's *The Catcher in the Rye*, and other novels by writers such as Nelson Algren, Bernard Malamud, and Herbert Gold were, their works seemed infinitely more private, less public in their dimensions than Styron's one novel did. There was not the sense of any of these authors speaking so directly to the experience of his time as Styron did in *Lie Down in Darkness*. Peyton Loftis's downfall seemed to say something about the day and age that the more limited predicaments of the heroes of other novels did not. Styron alone seemed capable some day of producing really important literary work, novels that could stand up to the best books of the prewar novelists.

More specifically, *Lie Down in Darkness* seemed very much in the Faulknerian mode. Not that it was derivative; quite the contrary. There had been and would continue to be numerous Southern novels that *were* derivative, that seemed to be imitation Faulkner. William Humphrey's *Home from the Hill*, for example, was almost a parody of the Yoknapatawpha novels, until halfway through when it left the primitive milieu of such stories as "The Bear" and descended into modern melodrama. The thing about Styron's novel was that, while it seemed to come out of the same literary and cultural tradition that had made Faulkner's fiction so profoundly moving, it created its own kind of tragedy, and did not rely on the secondhand insights of Faulkner and his contemporaries. Styron, in other words, seemed to be doing what good writers have always done: he used his tradition, rather than let himself be used by it.

That literary mode, it must be emphasized, had produced much of the finest American fiction of the twentieth century. It had avoided the sodden determinism of the naturalistic school of Dreiser, Dos Passos, Steinbeck, and Farrell, and had been able to achieve fiction in which human beings could be made to behave as free agents, able to pit their wills against their society and the limitations of their mortality in meaningful dispute. It had been able, too, to depict men in a necessary and inescapable relationship to society, so that the conflict between the private conscience and public circumstance could seem real. The characters of Faulkner, Wolfe, Warren, Lytle, and the others were not in arbitrary, casual contact with the world around them; they were inescapably a part of society, and any lasting isolation from society constituted a tragic condition. If society was hostile, it was never indifferent. Furthermore, these men's characters were not creatures of the moment; they existed in time, and the past affected them in crucial ways. Finally, the basis of their morality and the sources of their behavior were not only social and biological but religious as well; their transgressions were not ultimately against men, but through men against God.

When *Lie Down in Darkness* appeared, the southern literary mode had been the productive force of distinguished fiction for almost three decades. It had set up certain expectations on the part of the reading public. The reader had become, as it were, habituated to conceiving of tragedy along certain lines. When Styron's novel came along, therefore, it fell heir to a by-then familiar literary tradition, and was read in terms of that tradition. Here was another fine southern novel, with the implied promise that the author would be able to sustain and develop his talent within the accepted mode. The southern literary tradition was thus manifestly continuing into the postwar generation.

This seemed all the more important since, up until then, and in the years immediately following the publication of *Lie Down in Darkness* as well, no other southern novel by a younger writer seemed to hold out such promise. Truman Capote's *Other Voices, Other Rooms* had been too exotic, too private to allow one to feel that its author would be able to produce major work. Carson McCullers's fiction, interesting though it was, seemed limited in its scope; it stopped short of the tragic, contenting itself with a poignant exploration of surfaces. Flannery O'Connor's decidedly promising talent was limited in range and breadth; it seemed to fulfill itself adequately only in the short story form. Certainly James Agee's *A Death in the Family* was an excellent and quite original work, containing passages of great beauty and force; but its mode was not that of high tragedy, and besides, Agee had been dead for two years when his novel appeared. To be sure, Robert Penn Warren was obviously of major stature, even though he never seemed to repeat the achievement of *All the King's Men;* while Andrew Lytle's *The Velvet Horn* was both its author's best work to date and as good a novel as almost any written by a southern writer. But these two, like Faulkner, were members of the previous generation of southern writers, the generation of the high renascence. So for that matter were Eudora Welty and Caroline Gordon; both had been publishing fiction since before the Second World War.

In the post–World War II generation of southern writers, then, Styron stood alone in his achievement, and in the nature of that achievement. If the southern literary mode was to retain its importance in contemporary American literature, William Styron seemed to be the writer who would lead the way.

Assuredly, I do not mean that the average reader was aware of all this when he encountered *Lie Down in Darkness*, though I suspect that many reviewers were, and to a greater extent than they perhaps realized. But I do think that when Styron's novel was published, it appeared to fit into a literary mode that a generation of excellent novelists had educated the reading public to understand, so that the reader was able to bring to *Lie Down in Darkness* an expectation and a frame of reference that the novel seemed to fill. This made possible a kind of cumulative public response that, at the time of publication and during the decade that followed, helped to give the novel its vogue, and contributed greatly to the nature and extent of Styron's reputation. Here, one felt, was another first-rate writer in the familiar southern style, one seemingly able to create genuine literary tragedy. And that it *was* tragedy he had managed, there could be no doubt; had not Faulkner, Warren, and the others already done just that, and in the same way?

Let me quote from one of Styron's more perceptive critics, John W. Aldridge. Writing in 1956, Aldridge spoke of the "Southern elements of the novel—particularly the elements of fundamentalist religion, regional guilt, and the contrast of races," as being "so powerful that if anything they seem excessive to the motives of the characters and perpetually to overcome them." He noted Helen Loftis's "Southern gentlewoman madness" and "the whole Southern blood-guilt." He remarked that "it is significant that it is after she marries and goes North that Peyton becomes overtly psychotic." Or lest I appear to single out Mr. Aldridge, who I believe has somewhat different thoughts on the matter now, let me quote from a review that I wrote of *Lie Down in Darkness* shortly after it appeared in 1951. I find, rather to my astonishment, that I did not have much to say about Styron's southernness as such, but even so the criteria I used for the evaluation were clearly taken out of the familiar experience of the southern novel. I remarked that "the Loftises want something, and none of them knows what it is. What they want is a purpose, a reason for being. In the final chapter Mr. Styron contrasts their aimlessness with the happy faith of their Negro servant, who is untroubled by acedia. The servant believes, and on the foundations of that belief is able to conduct a satisfying life." Note that this is an accurate description of the role of Dilsey in *The Sound and the Fury*—but not at all, as I shall try to show, of the servants in Styron's novel.

The question I should like to propose now, a decade after *Lie Down in Darkness* was first published, and with the hindsight that comes of having observed the progress of Styron's literary fortunes over ten years, is whether such inferences as Mr. Aldridge and I made, and those of many another critic as well, were accurate. Was *Lie Down in Darkness* a novel of originality, but one written essentially within the accustomed southern mode, achieving its tragic force in approximately the same manner as the novels of Faulkner, Warren, and others in the southern tradition? Or did the "southernness" only *appear* to be important, and was *Lie Down in Darkness* in important and vital respects quite another *kind* of novel than those of Faulkner and the others, significantly different in its version of human experience, its conception of society and of people, so that the familiar southern motifs were considerably less important than had seemed true at first reading? In other words, had Mr. Aldridge and I and various other critics reviewed William Styron's novel, or had we in effect reviewed a new novel by William Faulkner?

[61]

Earlier I noted some obvious resemblances between *Lie Down in Darkness* and Faulkner's *The Sound and the Fury*. Since the latter novel is one of its author's two or three greatest works, and since the dimensions of the tragedy of the Compson family are so central to the southern mode—were instrumental, indeed, in fashioning that very mode—I want to compare the manner in which that novel realizes its tragic potentialities with the way in which Styron's novel does.

The Sound and the Fury is concerned with the collapse of the Compson dynasty in the modern world. Once great, the family has fallen upon evil days, and the novel describes its death throes and final spiritual extinction. The failures of the fathers have been visited upon the children. Jason Compson III drowns his days in alcoholic futility; his wife is a self-pitying hypochondriac who prattles about her past while failing to give her children the love they need. Quentin Compson holds forlornly to an outmoded concept of Compson honor, and when its inadequacy becomes apparent, commits suicide by drowning. Candace Compson seeks to find in promiscuity the affection denied her by her mother. Jason IV survives by abandoning all pretense of Compson honor and becoming a Snopes in everything but name, a vicious, embittered, small-time speculator and defrauder. The degradation of the family is symbolized by Benjy, whose helpless imbecility represents the dead end of a century of family tradition.

At first glance *Lie Down in Darkness* would seem to involve a greatly similar situation. Milton Loftis is a father who numbs his futility in alcoholism; indeed, his own father had a way of talking that was much like Jason Compson III's manner of addressing Quentin. Like Mrs. Compson, Helen Loftis is self-pitying and selfish, and takes out her frustration on her daughter. Peyton Loftis, like Candace Compson, turns to promiscuity in her need for affection, and like Quentin Compson she walks about a northern city carrying a timepiece before seeking the oblivion of suicide. And the mentally defective Maudie is surely the Loftis counterpart of Benjy Compson. In both families, too, there are faithful Negro retainers who mourn the downfall of their white families.

Yet are the situations really similar? Like the Compsons, the

Loftises are the modern descendants of a once-distinguished southern family. But the implications of this in *Lie Down in Darkness* are very different. The Loftises exist entirely *in the present*. Milton Loftis's alcoholic stupor is not importantly the result of changed times. There is no outdated concept of Loftis honor, no heritage of former leadership to be lived down. Milton is not the sot he is because of the impossible burden of the past; his failure is entirely the result of personal weakness. His spinelessness must be blamed on his own character, not on the decadence of a fallen dynasty. Likewise, Helen Loftis is no Mrs. Compson; she is no morose worshiper of her family's past, but a twisted psychotic, whose sin is not hypochondria but insane jealousy. And her daughter Peyton's tragedy is not the result of a massively decadent family past, but of the personal failure of her parents. Though both Peyton Loftis and the young Compsons seek hopelessly for love and strength, the causes of the absence of those commodities are very different; with Peyton they lie in her parents' personal shortcomings, while with Quentin and Candace they are the result of the degradation of a dynasty in their time. They are *dynastic*, not personal. They are caused by *history*.

The difference is all important. For where the downfall of the Compson family symbolizes the crash of formerly great dynasties in time, and the central tragedy consists of the downfall of a once-great family, the death of Peyton Loftis in *Lie Down in Darkness* involves no such sense of the collapse of generations, no important implication that the sins of the dynastic past have caused the debacle of the present. In other words, in Styron's novel the historical dimension is almost entirely absent. Peyton is not the product of a family's and a region's history; she is a young woman whose own parents' failures rob her of the hope of happiness. What she is and is not can be blamed on Milton and Helen, and, in any important respect, no further back than that. Where Faulkner created a Greek-like tragedy, reminiscent of the fall of the House of Atreus, Styron produced a domestic tragedy that had no element of fated dynastic downfall about it.

We can see this clearly if we compare Maudie Loftis and Benjy Compson. The idiot Compson child is the proof of a family's down-

fall and disgrace, the barren fruit of exhausted loins; Maudie
Loftis is only an unfortunately marred child. We do not see in her
plight the judgment of fate on a dynastic collapse; she is not symbolic of the guilt of generations. She is a poor, pathetic little girl,
bereft of her faculties, and nothing more. Missing entirely is any
kind of implied commentary on family ambition and ancestral
failures; Maudie's idiocy is the chance result of a biological freak.
Not history, but biology, is to blame.

If we think upon the meaning of all this, we will recognize, I
think, something essential about *Lie Down in Darkness*. And that
is, that it is not a community tragedy but a private one. The relationship of the Loftises to the city in which they reside is vastly
different from that of the Compsons to the county of Yoknapatawpha. Upper-class Port Warwick society, as seen in the occasions
upon which it gathers in *Lie Down in Darkness*, is pleasure-
seeking, decadent, even dissolute. But it is not anachronistic. It is
not a holdover from a better day. There is little sense that what has
happened to Milton, Helen, and Peyton Loftis is symbolic of the
historic decline and fall of the Tidewater Virginia gentry. Port
Warwick society is urban, cosmopolitan; it clings to no historical
image of itself and its role. We can, if we wish, *infer* the death of
the aristocratic tradition from its present condition, but any such
inference will be based on our extraliterary historical knowledge,
not on the manner in which Styron actually builds his tragedy.
There is no concept of Loftis role within the community, no pre-
sumption of leadership that is no longer respected. Milton Loftis
had political ambitions at one time, but not because he felt a sense
of an expected family role, of habitual function of command. It is
entirely a matter of personal ambition with him. And when he fails
to act on those ambitions, there is no feeling of his having betrayed
a public trust, but only of his personal inability to make something
of himself.

In short, the Loftises live in Port Warwick, but they are not and
were not Port Warwick, in the way that the Compsons once *were*
Yoknapatawpha County. If their decadence mirrors that of the
community's upper social stratum, it is not the decadence of an
historical tradition gone to seed, but that of a very modern, hedo-

nistic segment of urban rich society living without faith and purpose. In *The Sound and the Fury* the emphasis is on an aristocratic family's abandonment of historical role; in *Lie Down in Darkness* it is on the general immorality of modern society. How the society got that way is, whether explicitly or by implication, not part of the story.

Contrast, for example, the description of Quentin Compson's last day at Harvard with Peyton Loftis's last day in New York City. Both are far from the country of their origins. Both are doomed souls. But how different are the implications! Quentin's estrangement from his home *constitutes* his tragedy. His alienation from Yoknapatawpha County is emblematic of his failure to cope with the modern world; he is the ineffective oldest son and heir of the once mighty Compson dynasty, and his isolation is not only one of place, but of time. What Quentin is estranged from is the role of the Compsons as leaders of the community, a role that is vanished in time. Cut off from his tradition, he wanders aimlessly about Cambridge, meditating on his plight, until finally he weights his clothes with lead window sashes and dives from a bridge into nothingness.

With Peyton Loftis, by contrast, we have no sense that her tragedy consists in her isolation from Port Warwick, no feeling that she belongs not in New York but in the community into which she was born, and that she is walking forlornly about the city because of her family's failure to fill its accustomed historical role back home. John W. Aldridge, as we have seen, noted that "it is significant that it is after she marries and goes North that Peyton becomes overtly psychotic." But is this really significant, in any important dramatic sense? It is not because Peyton is unable to go home to Port Warwick that we are distressed; on the contrary, we were rather relieved when we learned that she had departed, and our distress is at her isolation *in* the metropolis, from the husband she loves and who loves her. Is it a matter of New York's having *caused* the appearance of the psychosis in overt form, or was the psychosis already all but present, and was the move to New York only a futile attempt to postpone its imminent onset? Peyton's flight is her one last chance to retrieve her life; and her destruction is fated because of what her parents have been and have failed to be to her, not because of her estrangement from the society into which she was born.

In both novels the cause of the isolation is ultimately spiritual. Both tragedies symbolize the plight of human beings in the modern world. But where Faulkner saw it in historical terms, involving the blood-guilt of generations, Styron saw it in social terms, an indictment of modern society as symbolized by the selfishness and weakness of the Loftis family. In *The Sound and the Fury* a dynasty collapses; in *Lie Down in Darkness* a family breaks up.

Much has been made of the religious implications of Styron's novel. In my review of the novel, as already mentioned, I contrasted the aimlessness of the Loftises with the sturdy faith of their Negro servants, and remarked, rather clumsily, that "the servant believes, and on the foundations of that belief is able to conduct a satisfying life." To be sure, the religious implications are there, but is it as simple a matter as I proposed, that of a mere "contrast of races," to use Mr. Aldridge's phrase? I think not. For Styron does *not* neatly juxtapose the futility of the Episcopal minister Carey Carr's attempt to lead Helen Loftis to true repentance on the one hand, with the magnetic efficacy of Daddy Faith's healing spiritual balm for the Negroes at the riverside in the final chapter. Instead the contrast is much more complicated, and considerably more ironic. For while it is true that Carey Carr's gentle, benevolent brand of modern theology is so lacking in moral force, so watered down in precept, that it cannot persuade Helen Loftis to overcome her jealousy, is Styron actually proposing in its stead the kind of primitive fundamentalism displayed by Daddy Faith and his constituency? Hardly. For Daddy Faith, effectiveness is clearly attributable entirely to the ignorance, the lack of sophistication, the love of flashy showmanship and weakness for dubious hocus-pocus of his audience; Daddy Faith is a faker, a false prophet. "Who loves you, my people?" he asks. "You, Daddy! Daddy Faith! You loves us! You, Daddy!" they shout back. "You, Daddy! Yes, Jesus, you loves us!"

But Daddy Faith certainly is not Jesus Christ; he is in no sense divine; indeed, his establishment is a gaudy parody of all known

religions. He is effective in his charlatanry because of the gulli-
bility of his audience. The idea, then, that Styron was criticizing
the diluted intellectualism of Carey Carr's religion and its inability to provide ethical guidance for Carey's white parishioners
by tellingly contrasting it with the primitive soundness of Daddy
Faith's fundamentalism, is a misrepresentation of Styron's attitude. If anything, he seems to be making a much bleaker pessimis-
tic observation, which is that the moral usefulness of religious truth
decreases in direct proportion to the increase in the intelligence
and sophistication of the believer. The implication is that religion
can function effectively as a morality *only* when its communicants
are ignorant and superstitious.

Here again the difference between *Lie Down in Darkness* and
the comparable occurrence in *The Sound and the Fury* is revealing.
The scene in Faulkner's novel in which Dilsey momentarily leaves
the Compson household in the throes of its disintegration and takes
Benjy to the Negro church to hear the preacher from St. Louis
is one of the most dramatic in the novel. But contrast the two
preachers. Daddy Faith is a flashy, gaudy showman. The preacher
in *The Sound and the Fury*, though no mean performer in the
pulpit, has nothing of the humbug about him. Though primitive
and untutored, his sermon rings with sincerity, and his congrega-
tion is deeply moved. The minister's words speak directly to Dilsey, and she is moved to utter her simple but rending summation
of all that has happened to the Compsons:

> "I've seed de first en de last," Dilsey said. "Never you mind
> me."
> "First en last whut?" Frony said.
> "Never you mind," Dilsey said. "I seed de beginnin, en now I
> sees de endin."

The point is that Faulkner's presentation of the Negroes at
church, though written in dialect and presented in a kind of pas-
toral simplification, is deadly serious. There is no sense of ironic
qualification, no element of condescension involved. The variety
of religion is simple, but not ignorant. Unlike Styron, it seems to
me, Faulkner *is* contrasting, directly and dramatically, the form-
less chaos of the white folks with the unlettered but deeply felt

faith of Dilsey, and this quality of belief in Dilsey enables her to give to the Compsons some of the love and strength that they themselves cannot attain. In her loyalty, her compassion and faith, Dilsey is clearly superior to her white employers. Dilsey believes, and can act on her belief; believing, she endures, while the Compsons, who have no such firm theological conviction, are doomed to perish.

To recapitulate, then, the apparent resemblance of Styron to Faulkner in respect to certain important aspects of experience is only a surface similarity. Upon closer examination Styron turns out to have a significantly different attitude toward many things. Where Faulkner envisions the disintegration of a leading southern family as something dynastic, the result of the spiritual and moral exhaustion of generations of aristocratic southern life, Styron portrays it as being psychological, the result of the personal weaknesses and sins of a father and mother. Faulkner's tragedy is historical; Styron's has no important basis in the past. The failure of the Compsons is the failure of the southern aristocracy; that of the Loftises is the failure of the effete rich. Faulkner's tragedy is deeply rooted in a region and its history; Styron's takes place in a recognizable place, but its dramatic causes lie almost entirely in the present. For Faulkner the fatal consequence of the breakdown of traditional southern leadership is to isolate its heirs from their heritage; in Quentin's and Candace Compson's separation from Yoknapatawpha lies the tragedy. In Styron the isolation is not from an accustomed heritage and role, but from society in general, whether in Port Warwick or New York. Thus, while both writers see isolation from human society as tragic, the older writer's conception of society is of something involving a particular locale and region, with a known history, while the younger writer conceives of society in much more general terms. Quentin as a character could properly exist only in Yoknapatawpha County; Peyton might have done as well, if not better, in the metropolis.

In other words, each writer's attitude toward society is the same —each sees a man's isolation from it as a violation of his human position; but with Styron this is only an attitude, while for Faulk-

[68]

ner the attitude is inextricably connected with a particular society and a particular history, and the very nature of the man is inseparable from the man's historical role within his society. And while, as with Faulkner, Styron's attitude likely is the product of a particular kind of society and a particular history, the specific circumstances and the specific occasion that brought about the attitude are largely missing in Styron's work, while in Faulkner the attitude goes hand in hand with the circumstances that produced it.

That this is an important difference is clear: for the difference, it seems to me, is precisely that between the South in which William Faulkner grew up and that in which William Styron grew up. It is the difference between two separate generations of southern writers and of southern life. For the South of the 1900s and 1910s was painfully caught up in the process of breaking away from the old concept of community, the old, fixed patterns of life in a society in which inherited beliefs and accustomed roles played a central part in the conduct of life, in which the individual's identity was supposedly still defined within the community. Faulkner's novels, and in differing ways those of the other writers of his generation, record the breakdown of this older South before the onset of modern urban life. The attitudes toward society, toward history, toward theological and ethical values had been clearly embodied in specific institutions: a particular society with established roles and customs, a specific history, an accepted theology with a revealed ethic. In the growing failure of these specific and concrete institutions to provide order and authority for the human beings who sought to live within and through them, there lay either tragedy or comedy, depending upon the literary imagination concerned with them.

In Styron's South, however, that of the 1920s and 1930s, the process of social dissolution had proceeded much further, and the institutions had ceased importantly to embody the attitudes any more: no longer were there accepted and established roles. The history was no longer a living and concrete reality. And the particular theology could no longer be accepted as gospel truth. To an important degree the attitudes that grew out of these institutions still remained valid, and still do so: a belief that the individual belongs in society, that he is not a creature of the moment, that he needs the authority of religious conviction to guide his conduct. These are indeed present in Styron's novel. They are, however, no more than attitudes; they are not embodied in tangible institutions. And if Styron, as I think, is the leading southern writer of his generation, and if he is in any important sense representative of his generation, then there would seem to be a significant change in the southern literary imagination in the present generation, those writers who were born during or shortly after the First World War, growing up in the changing South during the 1920s and 1930s and writing their novels in the years after the Second World War. They would appear to constitute a generation that is much further removed than its predecessors from the concepts of a particular kind of community, of man as a creature of a particular history, and as a creature whose life is ordered by a particular scheme of theological belief.

For Styron's generation of southern writers, who grew up in a greatly changed South, only the general attitudes, the general ways of looking at human experience, remain real. And what we might expect from these writers, then, is a literature that involves the examination of these attitudes as they survive, or fail to survive, in a very different kind of experience. That, I believe, is what we have in *Lie Down in Darkness:* not a Faulknerian tragedy at all, but a literary exploration of the potentialities of certain surviving attitudes for imparting meaning and order to modern human experience, an experience that by no means is identical with traditional southern life as described and assumed in the work of the earlier writers.

If all this seems far removed from the accustomed concerns of fiction, think of it in specific terms. What, once again, is the difference between Dilsey at church on the one hand, and the contrast between Carey Carr and Daddy Faith on the other? Is the difference not that Faulkner assumes the reality of the theology, and measures the decadent Compsons against it, while Styron does not assume the theological reality, but instead explores its validity, showing both its failure to possess any meaning for the Loftises, and in the case of their servants, the charlatanry that must accompany the religion for it to succeed? Faulkner is not examining the validity of the theology; Styron is doing precisely that, and his implication that theological conviction would be desirable for the Loftises is the product of an attitude toward religion and society, not because of the theological validity of the particular religion itself.

What Faulkner *is* questioning is the validity of the historical tradition of aristocratic Compson leadership in the twentieth-century South. But here, by contrast, Styron conducts no such examination. He cannot even take such a tradition seriously; what little he presents of it is mouthed by Milton Loftis's aged father, long before the events that constitute the central tragedy of the novel. And Milton's memories of his father bear little dramatic relevance to the condition in which Milton finds himself as an adult. The theme of decline and fall, so far as it relates to a particular historical tradition, does not importantly exist in Styron's novel. By implication he may be said to show the results of the failure of such a tradition, but if we reach such a conclusion it is because of what we know about southern literature and southern history, and because of Styron's attitude, but not because Styron gave any dramatic embodiment to the theme of historical decline and fall in his novel, and thus attested to its concrete reality.

And, finally, consider again the inescapability of Quentin's relationship to Yoknapatawpha County in *The Sound and the Fury*, as compared with Peyton's to Port Warwick in *Lie Down in Darkness*. Faulkner, it seems to me, *assumes* that Quentin should have a role in the community of his birth, and in Quentin's inability to discover such a role Faulkner sees a commentary on Quentin and in the times. But Styron does not make that assumption at all. He examines Port Warwick, finds it wanting; whereupon he sends Peyton northward. There is no sense of a killing estrangement, no sense that Peyton's failure to find a meaning for her life in the metropolis is due to the fact that she does not belong there, but in Port Warwick. Either kind of community would do for her, New York perhaps better than Port Warwick—and neither kind will do. The trouble is in Peyton, and in her parents' failure, and in crass modern times in general. We do not feel that because

[71]

Peyton cannot live in Port Warwick there has been a historical betrayal of what the community should have been and what Peyton should have been. What we do feel is that Peyton belongs somewhere, a part of some society. And once again, this is because of the author's attitude toward the individual in society, not because of any inference that there ought to be a community such as Port Warwick presumbly used to be and that Peyton ought to have been able to find a role and a meaning for her life within that particular kind of community. Styron's imagination is not wedded to that kind of community, and that kind of person. He does not see the disappearance of either as fated, and therefore tragic.

So far as southern writing in our time is concerned, then, the question that William Styron's fiction occasions is the whole problem of continuity. If there has been developed over the course of several decades a kind of southern literary mode, a tradition as it were, then, on the evidence of Styron's books, how is it surviving today? Just what is the relationship between southern literature as we have hitherto known it, and a southern writer of a new generation who does not assume the inevitability of a relationship between his characters and the kind of historical community that we think of as southern, who cannot take seriously the importance of the continuation of a tradition of leadership in the modern South, and who does not measure his characters' ethical and spiritual conviction by their obedience to the authority of a particular kind of Protestant theology?

We should have to conclude, I think, that such a writer's relationship to that tradition is significantly different from that of any of the older writers within that mode. We should have to conclude that he is joined to them, insofar as those things are important, principally by his attitude—an assumption on his part that a community role is desirable, that a traditional basis for experience is a good thing, that men without theological conviction live fragmented, chaotic lives—but an assumption not embodied in concrete institutions and shared experiences.

And, if, then, it is only a matter of the survival of an attitude, not of the embodiment of the attitude in particular institutions, is not the next order of business the examination of the *assumptions themselves?* Not the institutions, but the assumptions. And insofar as a specific southern literary tradition is concerned, where does that leave us?

It leaves us, I think, with William Styron's second novel, *Set This House on Fire*. For almost a decade preceding its publication, and on the strength of one good, medium-length novel, Styron was widely held to be America's Most Promising Younger Novelist. I have conjectured as to why this came about—the particular state of the American novel at the time of the appearance of *Lie Down in Darkness;* the emergence of a novelist who could *write*, and not merely relate; the inherited prestige of a particular literary mode into which it seemed to fit so well, a mode that had been notably proficient in producing distinguished fiction, so that the reading public had been educated to respond to the dimensions of that mode. And I suggested that because *Lie Down in Darkness* seemed to fit into that mode, and yet to possess an originality of its own, reviewers and readers were quick to recognize Styron as potentially a very important writer.

In short, it was as if the appearance of *Lie Down in Darkness* constituted an assurance that the kind of contribution Faulkner, Wolfe, Warren, Welty, and the others had been making to American fiction for two decades and more was not going to dwindle and die, but could flourish for another entire literary generation.

Nine years elapsed, during which time a new novel by Styron was often rumored and once even announced, but without its appearing. Then, in the late spring of 1960, finally came *Set This House on Fire*. Unlike its predecessor, there was nothing tidy and portable about it; it was a big, hulking affair, two hundred thousand words long, the size of *Look Homeward, Angel* almost. It did not take place in Port Warwick, though the narrator came from there. In fact, though it was remembered and related by two men while fishing and reminiscing in Charleston, South Carolina, it did not importantly take place in the South at all, but in New York, Paris, and a small Italian coastal town. None of the customary trappings of the southern novel was present: there were no Negroes, no First Families, no church services, no blood-guilt of generations, no oversexed southern matrons. It was thoroughly,

[73]

completely modern, even cosmopolitan. There were expatriate artists, Italian peasants, Greenwich Village cocktail parties, pornographic orgies, American tourists in European cities and towns, movie making, Army PX's, philosophical Fascist policemen, and so forth. People quoted Ortega y Gasset and Wilhelm Reich, listened to Buxtehude and *Don Giovanni*, preferred Frankie Lane to Johnny Ray, worried about the decline of American capitalism. And—quite unlike most southern novels—the protagonists engaged in long, probing psychological analyses of their inner souls, after the manner of Proust and Dostoevski. The story told was not at all Faulknerian; it was about a young artist who after a frightening stay in the lower depths won his way back to sanity. It was as if Eugene Gant had gone through the kind of furnace experience that Jack Burden underwent in *All the King's Men*, perhaps— but in Europe, not in Louisiana, and politics and the South were not involved. But to say that is to say very little, for Jack Burden never really ceased to take seriously all manner of verities that Styron's Cass Kinsolving not only flouted but even ignored. Styron's new novel was simply not a "southern" novel at all, in the way that southern novels had been written by his predecessors.

The new novel, as I have noted, was straightaway treated to a hostile critical barrage such as few other important works of fiction in our time have received. It was called romantic, melodramatic, pompous, sentimental, inflated, chaotic; it was self-pitying; it was even un-American. To repeat, the Most Promising Younger Novelist of his generation had fallen flat on his face.

The question I asked before was why, if *Set This House on Fire* was as I think a quite respectable novel, it came in for so hostile a reception. And the answer I proposed had to do with the nature of Styron's first novel, *Lie Down in Darkness*. That book had earned its author an impressive reputation, partly on the strength of the kind of novel it had seemed to be. To repeat, it seemed to be "southern," Faulknerian; it seemed an extension, into our own day, of the southern tragic mode, to fit into the mode even while giving it an original twist. But in reality Styron's first novel was significantly different; the specific experience that it related was not handled in the traditional way; only the attitudes remained close to the tradition, without their accompanying embodiment in concrete experience.

Set This House on Fire confirmed that break. And this time, there could be no mistaking the difference. By all rights, Styron should have produced in his second book another "typical" southern tragedy. But he did not. He did not write the kind of book he was supposed to write at all. The novel that he brought forth after nine years of silence was far removed from the familiar mode of southern fiction. And this, I think, caused a tremendous disappointment.

The nature of that disappointment was all too obvious: this young, talented novelist, so heralded, so praised, had failed to do what was expected of him. He had not continued the literary mode of Faulkner, Wolfe, and the others into the new generation. Seemingly he had veered off in another direction. And the new direction did not permit the familiar kind of tidy, smoothly formed tragedy that *Lie Down in Darkness* had seemed to be. By its very nature it demanded the groping, restless, searching type of novel that Styron produced.

What I am suggesting is that, just as readers and reviewers read *Lie Down in Darkness* as if it were automatically a novel in the Faulknerian mode, and praised it highly for that, they read *Set This House on Fire* with precisely the same expectation, and since this time the novel did not remotely fit the mode at all, they denounced it. Styron, the apparent heir to the best of the southern literary tradition, had seemingly betrayed that tradition.

Yet had he? I am not so sure of it. It seems to me, rather, that Styron's second novel *was* an extension of the southern literary imagination into a new generation, was in fact perhaps *the only possible way that the mode could be made to stay alive*. And I believe that, when we look back in retrospect at the first novel, we can see that *Set This House on Fire* was exactly the kind of novel we might have expected Styron to write, if what we took to be his major stature was true; it grows squarely out of the implications of the first novel, and represents a coming-to-grips with the true concerns of the author's experience—an experience, I believe, that is still very much southern, but in significant respects not that of

[75]

the previous generation of southern writers. To illustrate what I mean, I must first review the plot of *Set This House on Fire.*

There are three main characters in the novel: Mason Flagg, a would-be playwright, Cass Kinsolving, a painter, and Peter Leverett, a lawyer. Flagg is a wealthy, clever, bedeviled young man, who is always "going to write" a play but never does. Handsome, conversant in the arts, a brilliant talker, he spends his days and nights in quest of some ultimate sensation, usually sexual. Sex, he keeps insisting, is the only frontier left to modern man. Essentially Flagg is a fraud, a poseur, in some ways reminiscent of the character Starwick in Thomas Wolfe's *Of Time and the River.*

Cass Kinsolving is a painter who cannot paint. A southern boy, he is wedded to a sweet and not very intelligent woman named Poppy, and they have several children. A considerable portion of his time is spent in getting and remaining drunk.

Peter Leverett, through whom much of the story is related, is a boyhood friend of Mason Flagg's, who goes to visit Flagg in the Italian coastal town of Sambuco, where the major events of the novel take place. Peter is from Port Warwick, Virginia, the scene of *Lie Down in Darkness.* The new novel begins when Peter travels to Charleston, South Carolina, where a now-regenerate Cass Kinsolving is living and painting, and together they piece out the details of what happened in Sambuco, where a young peasant girl had been raped and Mason Flagg killed.

We see Mason Flagg, in other words, through the eyes of two persons—Peter Leverett, who knew him as a youth and as a young man, and Cass Kinsolving, who knew him in Sambuco just before his death. It is here that the chief structural flaw of the novel lies. For if this novel were primarily a study of Mason Flagg, what made him into the harried and driven creature he was, what drove him to his death, then the structural scheme that Styron chose to give his story might have sufficed.

But important though the character of Mason Flagg is in this novel, it is not in him that the chief meaning of the story is to be found. Rather, the central figure is the painter Cass Kinsolving.

For most of the novel, Cass is a man in bondage. In Paris, before he goes to Sambuco, he lives in an alcoholic daze, tortured by his inability to paint, spending his time drinking, wandering about, pitying himself, doing everything but confronting his talent. At length he moves his family down to Italy, where he comes under the sway of Mason Flagg. At one point Flagg even forces him, in exchange for his largesse, to paint a pornographic picture for his collection. Cass also becomes enamored of an Italian peasant girl and steals medicines in a hopeless attempt to save the life of her father, an old man in the last stages of tuberculosis .

Peter Leverett, about to leave Rome for the United States, drives over to Sambuco to visit Mason Flagg, arriving in time to witness the cataclysmic events that end the novel. The peasant girl is raped by Mason Flagg, then brutally murdered. Flagg is found dead at the foot of a cliff. The solution to these crimes is discovered by a philosophical young Italian policeman, who allows the culprits to go unpunished by the law.

The meaning of these events exists, as I have said, not in Mason Flagg's life but in Cass Kinsolving's. When Peter Leverett and Cass meet several years later to analyze what happened at Sambuco, Cass is well again, doing the painting he could not do in Europe, earning a living, caring for his wife and family. And though this novel is a murder mystery, the principal question it proposes is why Cass was for so long in bondage, unable to paint the pictures he wanted to paint and unable to receive and return the love of his wife and children.

In the events that come to a climax at Sambuco, I think, we do find out why. Cass was unwilling to accept the responsibility of his own talent, unwilling to face up to the fact that it alone could accomplish its own perfection. He wanted to find a form for his art outside of himself, when he alone it was who could give his art, and therefore his life, reason for being. He could not put up with his creative limitations and work his way out of them. He looked outside of himself, to the society, the people, the institutions surrounding him, for what could be found only within himself.

This was the hold that Mason Flagg had on him. For Mason could provide wealth, afford the glamor and excitement of "life," "experience"—or so Cass tried to pretend. Throughout the novel Cass attempted to deny the personal responsibility of his talent, attempted to substitute external experience for the dedication to artistic creativity that for him could be the only true account. He sought escape into "life," in alcohol, in false visions of Wordsworthian "ecstasy" that gave him the illusion of beauty, in Mason Flagg's largesse and phony dilettantism, in an insubstantial, idyllic romance with the peasant girl, in a quixotic and forlorn attempt to doctor an old man back to health. All these activities were ways of avoiding his own true mission and refuge—the remorseless requirements of discovering how to paint the pictures he wanted to paint. And because he was an artist, all these false externalizations of his need failed.

The attainment of this realization, through grief and pain, constitutes the development of the novel, and though it requires five hundred pages and two hundred thousand words, as a story it is dramatically and artistically convincing. When at last we put down this novel, we have witnessed the resolution of a rending conflict within a man.

Why, however, is Cass so constituted that it takes him so long to find out what at last he learns? We accept the reality of his bondage to "life"—but how, we may ask, did it come to be? The answer is there, but—and this, I think, is the major structural defect of *Set This House on Fire*—it does not lie in the experience of Cass Kinsolving. Instead, it is found in the characterization of Peter Leverett.

For it was Peter, not Cass, who grew up with Mason Flagg, who through him was exposed to the delusion of self-fulfillment through external "experience," instead of through personal creativity, who was progressively tempted by Mason Flagg's advocacy of false gods. The spiritual duel between Mason Flagg and Cass Kinsolving that constitutes the dramatic struggle of *Set This House on Fire* was begun long before Cass went to Sambuco and encountered Mason Flagg. It commenced in Virginia, when Mason and Peter were students in preparatory school together. As Peter wrote of his attitude toward Mason then, "his wealth, his glamorous connections, his premature ease with the things of the flesh—they worked on me a profound fascination." It is this attitude that is transferred, as it were, by the author to Cass Kinsolving, a Cass who has been miserably wasting his time in Paris trying to be an artist without painting, and who wanders down to Sambuco when even the opportunities for self-delusion possible to him in a city such as Paris begin to fail.

Mason's last, despairing attempt to "own" Cass Kinsolving by raping Cass's girl friend was the culmination of a long battle. Why did Mason try to dominate first Peter Leverett and then Cass Kinsolving? Because he knew that they alone, of all those who comprised his acquaintanceship, could judge him as an artist. Tempted though they both were, they alone did not confuse what Mason did with the true artistic responsibility. At one point, early in the novel, one of Mason's admirers praised him to Cass in these words: "That Mason. Now there's a boy for you. A genius. Figure everything he's got. The eyes. The nose. The *expression*. Everything. It's uncanny, I tell you. Just like his dad." "You've read his play?" Peter asks him. No, the man replies, "but he's told me about it. It can't miss, I tell you. It's a natural. The boy has genius." But genius is a matter of plays written, not plays talked about, and Peter and Cass know it. Mason could bribe others, but he could not bribe them. They would not be owned.

But what is Cass Kinsolving's relationship to Peter Leverett? In the novel ostensibly both are friends of Mason Flagg, and that is all. Dramatically, psychologically, however, they are more than that. *They are one and the same person.* We meet Cass Kinsolving in mid-passage, a painter who cannot paint, a created, believable character. It is Peter Leverett's past history, not Cass's, that explains why Cass cannot paint. Peter Leverett, in other words, *becomes Cass Kinsolving.*

Now from a strictly logical point of view, that ought certainly to compromise Styron's novel. How can the experience of one character serve to create the characterization of another and entirely different man? But I want to emphasize that nevertheless we *do* believe in Cass Kinsolving. As a character he is convincing, and the events that give the novel its conflict and its resolution happen to him, not to Peter Leverett. So perceptive and imaginative is the characterization of Cass that the explanation of how he got that way, though interesting, is not finally of primary importance. Though logically we know that the early experience happened not to Cass but to Peter Leverett, dramatically and psychologically the development of the characterization is so secure that as readers we do what in terms of plot logic we should not be able to do: we give Peter Leverett's experience to Cass. We accept him, when he turns up in Paris, for what he is on the basis of what we know about Peter Leverett.

Building upon it, Styron succeeds in making Cass emerge as a formidable characterization, a figure that almost anyone who has ever attempted to paint or write or otherwise create artistic work can recognize. Cass Kinsolving is a familiar and crucial figure of our time, the artist seeking reality, confusing it with "life," struggling to locate it in his work. And coming as Cass Kinsolving does to us, the heir, so to speak, to a generation of fictional protagonists by southern novelists, it seems to me that his plight thoroughly mirrors the situation that confronts the southern writer of Styron's generation—a generation for whom the traditional institutions and embodiments of values have been so seriously modified that a new relationship between attitudes and values on the one hand, and "real life" on the other, must be created. To do that, the values and attitudes themselves must be examined. And what Styron makes his fictional artist learn is what Allen Tate once said about the poet Hart Crane. Crane, he declared, "is betrayed, not by a defect in his own nature, but by the external world; he asks of nature, perfection—requiring only of himself, intensity." The poet, says Tate, did not face up to the obligation "to define the limits of his personality and to objectify its moral implications in an appropriate symbolism." The Cass Kinsolving whom Peter Leverett visits in Charleston several years after the events of Sambuco has accepted that obligation, though he never speaks of such things at all. Wrongly constructed or not, the characterization is there.

Why, one asks, did Styron separate his characterization in this way? My own notion is that Styron himself did not fully recognize the essential connection between Peter Leverett's experience and Cass Kinsolving's. The actual origins he gives for Cass are not important to the novel. Cass was a boy from a small coastal town in North Carolina, the son of an Episcopal minister, who was left an orphan at the age of ten and brought up by a Methodist uncle and aunt. During the Second World War he landed in an army psychiatric ward, took up painting as therapy, was later married, and went to Europe to live and paint. It is interesting, though, that when Cass wins his way to sanity and takes his family back home to America to live, he goes not to North Carolina, but to Charleston, South Carolina, a seaport city—precisely what Port Warwick, Peter Leverett's home, was.

As for Peter Leverett, he too goes home in the novel, but early in the story, before he visits Cass in Charleston and they recall the events of Sambuco. When Peter stops by at Port Warwick there is a moving scene in which his father takes him driving about the city, and he is greatly struck by the changes that have taken place. Port Warwick now

> had grown vaster and more streamlined and clownish-looking than I thought a decent southern town could ever become. To be sure, it had always been a ship-building city and a seaport (visualize Tampa, Pensacola, or the rusty waterfront of Galveston; if you've never seen these, Perth Amboy will do), and in official propaganda it had never been listed as one of the ornaments of the commonwealth, but as a boy I had known its gentle seaside charm, and had smelled the ocean wind, and had lolled underneath giant magnolias and had watched streaked and dingy freighters putting out to sea and, in short, had shaken loose for myself the town's own peculiar romance. Now the magnolias had been hacked down to make room for a highway along the shore; there were noisy shopping plazas everywhere, blue with exhaust and rimmed with supermarkets; television roosted upon acre after acre of split-level rooftops and, almost worst of all, the ferry-boats to Norfolk, those low-slung smoke-belching tubs which had always possessed their own incomparable dumpy glamour, were gone, replaced by a Yankee-built vehicular tunnel which poked its foul white snout two miles beneath the mud of Hampton Roads.

Port Warwick, that is, is the *New South*—the South of modern times, in which the comfortable, sleepy old landscape is hardly recognizable. Peter and his father stop at a service station, and while there, Peter suddenly divines that almost on the very spot of reclaimed land where the gasoline pump now stands, there had once been a marsh creek where he had almost drowned and had been rescued by a Negro crab fisherman. Awed at the thought of the change that had taken place, in himself above all, he thinks that

> perhaps one of the reasons that we Americans are so exceptionally nervous and driven is that our past is effaced almost before it is made present; in our search for old avatars to contemplate we find only ghosts, whispers, shadows; almost nothing remains for us to feel or see, or to absorb our longing. That evening I was touched to the heart; by my father's old sweetness and decency and rage, but also by whatever it was within me—within life itself, it seemed so intense—that I knew to be irretrievably lost. Estranged from myself and from my time, dwelling neither in the destroyed past nor in the fantastic and incomprehensible present, I knew that I must find the answer to at least several things before taking hold of myself and getting on with the job.

But what does Peter find out, in the ensuing story? He finds out what happened to Cass, not to himself. So if, as I have suggested, the young Peter Leverett is the young Cass Kinsolving, then several things are obvious. Peter's (and therefore Cass's) past is, figuratively and literally, buried in time. The creek where he almost died is covered by acres of fill dirt, upon which the properties of the new industrial South have been constructed. He cannot, as he says, dwell in the "destroyed past." When Cass Kinsolving, in effect the adult Peter Leverett, goes home, it is to a city which in many ways is like Port Warwick, but which is not Port Warwick. Charleston resembles Port Warwick in that both are seaports, both are on tidewater, both are surrounded by salt marsh; but except for the fact that both are seaports, their particular histories are quite different. There is thus, so far as Cass is concerned, no continuity of community, of history, of family role. But in Charleston, to a much greater extent than in Port Warwick (which is Newport News, Virginia), the evidence of the past does survive into the present. It is very much more a historical town, much more leisurely and quaint, in its waterfront areas at least, than Port Warwick. In other words, the general climate of everyday life in the older, less-industrialized South remains for Cass, but *without any personal, institutional ties to it on his part.* He lives there, but he is not of it.

Before Cass comes to Charleston, he is adrift, homeless, cut off from his past. He wants to paint; he cannot. He is married, with children; he wants to love them and care for them, but he cannot. He cannot discern any order and meaning to his experience. What he finally learns, in the frenzied chaos that produces the catastrophe at Sambuco, is that only through respect for his own personal integrity, as a human being and as an artist, can he give his life the order he seeks. He cannot look for his order and purpose in "life," in the institutions of the exterior world, in his environment, but only within himself. He must face his responsibilities, paint his own pictures. Then, and not until then, can he go home, to America, to the South.

What Cass had to know, before he could go home, was what Peter Leverett knew, about his childhood, about the place where he grew up—that it was, in Peter's words, "irretrievably lost." But also, as Cass finds out, that for a man to live and create, it must be replaced by order and purpose within oneself. For a world without order and purpose, without the values of love, self-respect, compassion, and responsibility for one's fellow human beings, is a world of chaos and fragmentation, ending in the blind destructiveness of Cass at Sambuco. The results of what Peter Leverett has known produce the condition in which Cass finds himself in Paris and Sambuco. From this condition Cass manages finally to extricate himself.

In effect, Cass Kinsolving completes the symbolic journey begun by Peyton Loftis in *Lie Down in Darkness.* In the first novel Styron's protagonist left Port Warwick. In the second novel Cass Kinsolving comes home to Charleston. Earlier I sought to demonstrate how Peyton's background, society, and tradition had failed, not in terms of directly producing her own dramatic plight, but through their absence, their failure to be importantly present at all. Peyton dies in New York, estranged not only from Port Warwick but from human society as well. Now Cass Kinsolving comes back to the South, but not until he can furnish within himself the order, stability, and continuity he needs to exist, to live with other human beings.

What I am getting at is that *Set This House on Fire* is, among other things, an examination of the validity of certain precepts by which people live: an examination conducted on *southern* terms. Cass Kinsolving's particular past is dead, forgotten, inoperative— but Cass as Styron describes him is nevertheless a man who requires the stability of belonging to a place that is anchored in time and that possesses order and stability. As Cass tells Peter Leverett in Charleston,

> "Funny thing, you know, in Europe there sometimes, when everything got as low as it can get for me, and I was hating America so much that I couldn't even contain my hatred—why even then I'd get to thinking about Charleston. About how I'd like to go back there and live. It almost never was in North Carolina, or the pinewoods up there in Columbus County where I was brought up. I didn't want to go back there and I sure as hell didn't want to go back to New York. It was Charleston I remembered, straight out of these memories I had when I was a boy. And here I am." He pointed across the wide harbor, radiant and gray-green and still as glass, then in an arc around the lower edge of the town where the old homes, deep in shade, in hollyhock and trumpet vine and bumblebees, had been defiled by no modish alteration, no capricious change. "You'll search a long way for that kind of purity," he said. "Look at that brickwork. Why, one of those houses is worth every cantilevered, picture-windowed doghouse in the state of New Jersey."

What Styron has done has been to describe the terms on which a man such as Cass Kinsolving can find such order and tranquillity for his life. It is emphatically made clear that Cass is unable to do without these commodities, but equally there is no intimation that he can find them in the life and institutions lying outside of himself. He must do it on his own. Cass can finally live in Charleston, when Peyton was unable to live in Port Warwick or New York and he himself in Paris and Sambuco, because he is creating— which is to say he is drawing his spiritual sustenance from within himself. Until he can do this, the environment makes no difference and the past is of no help. Cass himself is an orphan; Peter Leverett's Port Warwick is buried beneath the fill dirt; the traditional southern circumstance, with its historical notion of role, its institutions, its community order, means nothing anymore.

We remember Faulkner's Quentin Compson in Cambridge; for him too the southern past no longer enabled him to define himself as a man. The difference is that Quentin's failure to discover his role was inextricably connected with his failure to embody the values of a Yoknapatawpha County that no longer existed; while, contrariwise, Cass's eventual success in finding his place comes *before* he joins the community. Quentin left the stability behind him, geographically and in time; Cass brings to the community his own stability. Cass is in effect a new man, prepared to sink down roots in the community—but a different kind of a community for him, one in which there are no historical and social links with his past. Quentin's hope for stability and sanity rested in institutions, traditions, concepts of role, theological authority that no longer existed. Cass Kinsolving knows nothing about such things; he creates his own salvation.

The stability and order he finds cannot be dissociated from religious values—the ability to love, to care for one's loved ones, to act justly and responsibly, to be kind and generous. And these things Cass has learned to do, through realizing his own private integrity as a human being. "A man cannot live without a focus," Cass remarks at one point. "Without some kind of faith, if you want to call it that. I didn't have any more faith than a tomcat. Nothing. Nothing! . . . I was blind from booze two thirds of the time. Stone-blind in this condition I created for myself, in this sweaty hot and hopeless attempt to get out of life, be shut of it, find some kind of woolly and comforting darkness I could lie in without thought for myself or my children or anyone else." But let it be noted that if Cass has acquired such faith, it is personal, and apart from any revealed theology. We recall that his father was an Episcopal minister, and that he was brought up by Methodists. At one point, too, Cass describes his first sexual experience, with a female member of the Jehovah's Witnesses sect, who comically remarks to him that "that's one thing you'll find out about us Witnesses. We're right liberal as concerns social contacts." If we wish finally to describe Cass's attitude as being essentially religious, there is certainly no hint that its basis lies in any of the theological systems of his childhood. In describing Cass at Sambuco, Styron examined what Cass needed to do in order to achieve order, integrity, and tranquillity and showed Cass living in hell on earth when he tried to do without spiritual conviction and moral responsibility. The redemption was from within.

I have spoken of Styron's fiction as embodying the traditional southern attitudes toward man's place in society, his need for order and stability, his desire for the love and responsibility that come from the authority of religious conviction, but without the institutions, the experience of life that embody those attitudes. I have said that *Lie Down in Darkness* possessed those attitudes, but without their fictional grounding in the traditional southern institutions. In *Set This House on Fire* Styron may be said to have proceeded with an examination, inherent in the fictional process, of the terms by which such attitudes can survive and flourish in modern life—how Cass Kinsolving, a southerner of our time and place, can live and cherish and create. It is as if, where the hell of *Lie Down in Darkness* lamented their absence, the purgatory of *Set This House on Fire* described their reacquisition. But the conditions whereby they could be regained necessarily involved a complete alienation from the time and place in which they had once existed, and from which they had disappeared. Cass Kinsolving's entire separation from the South was, in effect, a severance from all lingering institutions and traditions that once might have, however inadequately, embodied those attitudes. He was indeed a man without a country. So that for Styron, *Set This House on Fire* represented a clearing away of the debris, as it were, of the southern fictional texture—all the accustomed embodiments of setting, history, community that for so long have provided the experience from which southern literature has been created, now swept away, like Peter Leverett's memories of the past, in the fill dirt upon which a new and modern experience was erected. Not in Port Warwick, but in Paris and Sambuco, was Cass Kinsolving's full initiation in the cauldron of modern experience conducted. All his surviving attitudes, his ideals, his emotions were there examined and tested and finally made to depend for their reality on his own inward and personal acceptance of them.

Whereupon he returned home. What, though, of Cass's alter ego, Peter Leverett? It may be noted that Peter Leverett no longer lives in the South. At the end of the novel, Cass writes to him that he "wanted to tell you how glad I am that N.Y. goes O.K. for you now." And there is no reason to suppose that Peter Leverett will be any more or any less happy living in New York than Cass seems to be in the South. To each one, "home" means something different. It is involved more importantly with what is going on inside them than with the place in which they have settled down to live and to work. For both these fictional characters live in a faraway country now, and that country, bound though it is to the "real world" by the pinions of time and memory, is finally a country of the mind.

Even so, it still bears a notable resemblance to a particular American region. Thus Cass Kinsolving, seated with Peter Leverett in a boat, fishing:

> He rebaited his hook and cast out the line again, squinting against the light. The river shores were immensities of shade—water oak and cypress and cedar; the heat and the stillness were like a narcotic. "September's a good month for this kind of fishing," he said after a long spell of silence. "Look over there, over those trees there. Look at that sky. Did you ever see anything so *clean* and beautiful?"

For Cass, who has come back, there is still the marshland, the water, the fishing, the sun. Changed and altered almost beyond recognition in many respects, it is even so the South.

JOHN O. LYONS

On *Lie Down in Darkness*

It is sad that Peyton Loftis cannot love another as herself. It is sad
that her father Milton loves her to excess in compensation for the
love that his wife Helen lavishes on their crippled and moronic
daughter Maudie. And it is sad that Helen cocoons herself in the
memory of her father's sterile world. But it is not tragic. Much
of the commentary of the novel insists on its tragic mold, but I
think that Styron depicts a world which is beneath tragedy. This
is not just a matter of our age's being unsuited to tragedy, although many have insisted that man is now too diminished for
Aristotelian prescriptions. It is more a matter of the emotional level
on which the characters in *Lie Down in Darkness* experience their
lives. Styron, through allusion and symbol, attempts to impose a
weighty significance on these events, but the characters tend only
to blubber under the burden of their lives. Even the admiring
critics allow the work tragic dimension with one hand, and then
take it away with the other. Jonathan Baumbach, for example,
speaks of the novel as echoing the fall of the house of Atreus and
sees Peyton as Electra, "(also Orestes)," but finally says that the
work "may fail ultimately."[1] This is the hedging tone often taken
with impressive first novels, but in the past two decades *Lie Down
in Darkness* has received more plaudits than pummelings. It may
seem uncavalier to raise a dissenting voice now, but Styron's reputation is secure and will survive my animadversions. I also believe
that my comments may be instructive in the matters of the risks
of ambitious first novels, Styron's style, and perhaps the novel of
generational crisis in general.

The derivativeness of the novel is invariably commented upon.
Even the casual reader notes traces of Wolfe, Joyce, and of course
Faulkner. Baumbach calls this indebtedness "unassimilated,"[2] but
David Galloway writes:

That Styron is able to succeed so well and so personally with techniques that are associated with Faulkner and Joyce is in part, of
course, a tribute to his enormous skill as a writer, but in part, too,
the result of historical accident; for Styron is not essentially an
experimenter, and therefore does not run the dangers which Joyce
and Faulkner often ran of becoming overwhelmed by technique
itself. Character and story are of immense importance to Styron,
and his intense fully drawn characters give the novel concentra-
tion and unity, just as such characters give substance to Faulkner's
best work.[3]

Perhaps in this Galloway is also saying that Styron's indebtedness
is unassimilated, for he could be saying that the techniques of
Faulkner and Joyce are used as ornaments to the narrative. No
matter how certain passages of the work are read, it seems to me
that we not only read the passage for what it says, but we read it
with an ear open to the way that the young Styron manipulates
his literary enthusiasms. This is not the case when we read Joyce
in which the spore of Ibsen, say, is virtually indetectable, or when
we consider in turn Faulkner's use of Joycean fictional time in
Light in August or the interior monologue in *As I Lay Dying*.
When a writer has assimilated his sources he creates an artifact
that stands—even in literature—almost independently of the refer-
ent. I think this is a case with Joyce and Faulkner, and even Wolfe,
but in *Lie Down in Darkness* the fine writing proposes to make
the reader see and feel the action as clearly as possible—but through
its gauze.

There are many novels (I think of those of Hardy or Lawrence, for example) that have their roots deep in the journalistic
tradition. In them the narrative is the end, and so the often plod-
ding prose does not stand in the reader's way for it does not pretend to do other than narrate, and its infelicities make little
difference. Styron has chosen to be a different kind of writer, and
his way is a demanding one for he wishes to make us both see a
scene and the process of seeing it. There are some extraordinary
passages in the work that are brilliant in their subject and technique. When, for example, Milton Loftis is called to Charlottesville where Maudie has been hospitalized he finds Helen in the
solarium trying to control her anguish.

Below, Halloween horns blew amid a garland of cowbells, a
football sound, and the old invalid suddenly strangled behind
them, horribly and obscenely, with a noise like the last gurgle
of water sliding down a drain. They both turned; the man looked
up, perfectly composed. He had a huge scimitar of a nose from
which the skin had begun to peel away in flakes, eyes pressed so
deep in his head that they seemed, to Loftis, like billiard balls
sunk in their pockets. With a shock Loftis realized that the man
had no hair on his body at all. And with the disregard for convention which is the privilege of lonely old people, he made no
introduction but stared at the two of them from the caves of his
skull and stretched a skinny, hairless arm toward the hills.
"Might as well be frank," he said. "I came up here to die. I
came up to die near Mr. Jefferson. There he is—" he pointed
toward Monticello—"there he is, up on the hill. On clear days you
can see it from here. Yes sir, I sit here in the afternoon and look
up at the hills and it takes a lot of the pain away to know you're
near Mr. Jefferson when it comes time to shuffle off this mortal
coil." His voice rose, thin, tremulous and old; Loftis saw a tiny
flake of skin fall from his nose, but now there was a touch of color,
too, on his cheeks, somehow rather dangerous. "I came all the way
from the Eastern Shore to spend my last days here and Mr. Jefferson, if he was alive he'd appreciate it, I think. He was a gentle-
man. He was—." (LDD, pp. 191–192)

The passage does much with unusual economy, for the flaking
man suggests not only the way Milton feels his life to be flaking
away in what appears to be wholesome sunshine, but the lost
human dignity of a Thomas Jefferson is soon to be echoed in Milton's memory of his own father's meeting with the angelic Lincoln.
Yet even here the simile of the "billiard balls sunk in their pockets" is a little strained and self-conscious. Much too often the
reader is invited to admire the process of narration, and this turns
into a contemplation of Styron's sources. Early in the work we
have a coal car making a "wild descending lisp of steel on steel,"
and a few pages later a locust making a sound, "shrill, ascending
then, like something sliding up a wire." The metaphors are descriptive of the sounds, but one might wonder if language was
carried fresh to the experience or if Styron had heard them through
Whitman's "the carpenter dresses his plank, the tongue of his
foreplane whistles its wild ascending lisp" from section 15 of
"Song of Myself." The result of such as this is a kind of pastiche

in which images are dragged in by the heels. When we get to Peyton's own narrative just before her suicide (which must be thought of as read over the omniscient author's shoulder) her style is astonishingly like that used by Styron in the rest of the work, except that it is liberally sprinkled with allusions to writers and painters she was exposed to at Sweet Briar and thick with images of clocks, drowning, and wingless birds.

It is the Faulknerian ghosts that are most often remarked in *Lie Down in Darkness*. Louise Gossett points out the likenesses between Peyton and Caddy Compson and Maudie and Benjy in *The Sound and the Fury*.[4] One could add the likeness between the use of the small dark juggler who amazes Maudie and Faulkner's mysterious dark vessels of magic and ritual, such as Sam Fathers or the unnamed father of Joe Christmas. But more important, I think, is Styron's use of Faulkner's rhetoric. He loves the Faulknerian negative prefix which gives the world he describes a dying Gothic beauty, beautiful because it is sepulchered and motionless. This can be seen in "by the dahlias light fell upon the figurine dresser lamps, upon those beribboned eighteenth-century lords and ladies frozen timeless and unaltered in some grave and mannered dance, the light and the heat and the silence in the house suddenly all becoming one, with form, it seemed, and with substance, inert and unyielding," or "yes, perhaps now it will be upturned, the chalice he has borne of whatever immeasurable self-love, not mean, yet not quite so strong as sin." In this passage the chalice and the circumstances under which it is borne suggest the chalice borne through a throng of foes by the romantic little boy in Joyce's "Araby." In the first passage there is also Faulkner's use of the suspended adjective, which can be seen again and again—"Milton who, fascinated, tries vainly." Styron also employs Faulkner's characters' sense of a doomed prescience, as in "committing himself, he somehow knew, with foreknowledge and awareness, as if to an exciting and perilous journey." "Was this part of the plan, the nightmare?" Milton thinks later. And as the old Packard hearse of the undertaker, Llewellan Casper, repeatedly breaks down under its burden (shades of *As I Lay Dying*— but updated) so that the characters can mull upon their past, the

Faulknerian formulae are used to introduce their meditations. Carey Carr reflects, "She had come to him six years ago, he remembered, on a rainy Sunday night in October," which requires our being reminded ten pages later of the narrative situation: "Here Helen paused, Carey remembered, and had turned away." This process of remembering is refined: "But later he was able to reconstruct the scene in his mind." This all makes Carey Carr sound like a younger sibling of Gail Hightower, whom he also resembles in his narrative function as confessor. At the end of the work he is like that Tennessee furniture dealer (but without the humor) at the end of *Light in August:* "Then Carey saw something take place which he could never have predicted—much less, he later said to Adrienne, thought ever could happen at all, among civilized people of a certain maturity." Faulkner had read his Joyce and Conrad with care, but in his works the stylistic turns become part of a machine of his own design, and the reader properly takes delight in his delight at the invention. But here Styron seems to be riding another's bicycle, and although it is impressive how well he makes it work, it is still another's.

John Aldridge takes issue with Styron when he contends that the world of Port Warwick is a world that could be anywhere, that its events are universal.[5] Aldridge (perhaps because he is writing on southern literature) insists that this world is peculiarly southern with its militarism, its bourbon drinking, its strange combination of frigidity and sexuality, and its racial fears. Aldridge may be right, but Styron's world is certainly not Faulkner's —it is more suburban and upper middle class. This may be what makes the characters often sound distressingly like the soap operas they listen to on the radio or the Warner Brothers movies of domestic mayhem they see. Carey Carr even states his awareness of this likeness: "And after coffee and a talk full of stupid (he knew) reservations about a woman's right to happiness, all of which sounded vaguely like a soap opera." Milton has a similar thought: "And when Helen talked like this, just as they do in the movies, with such conviction." This may be a way in which Styron pillories—or at least characterizes—Helen. But most of the characters have this tendency. And, once more, this is possibly Styron's point—that the essential lovelessness of these people is a result of the watered gruel of their popular culture. The result, however, is to make the novel a series of case studies—of narcissism, self-indulgence, frigidity—so that the screeching is sad, but not tragic.[6]

When Styron's prose is on its own it tends to attribute thoughts in cadences that we have little reason to suspect the characters of possessing, and without the Faulknerian "he thought, or would have thought . . . ." Through the haze of champagne toward the end of the wedding reception, Milton reflects on his loss of Peyton:

> He drinks. The bells toll on through his memory. Seawardborne, they strike reefs of recollection, shatter and recover, come back to smother his soul like something heavy and outrageous. *Time! Time!* he thinks. *My God has it finally come to this, do I finally know?* And lost in memory, thinking not of Peyton but of this final knowledge—this irrevocable loss of her—he recalls the incessant tolling bells. With a steady, brazen certainty they had struck off the passing hours, marched through the house night and day forever. It seems that he had heard them for the first time, though they are silent now, motionless in their yokes. The guests reel giddily before his eyes, on his arm the dentist's clutch is raw and painful. *Those bells,* he thinks, *those bells.* Why now did they return to afflict him with such despair? *Count off twenty years.* The light in the room deepens toward gold, sending sandy threads through Peyton's hair. (LDD, p. 289)

If he is as bleary at this point as we are led to believe, it is hard to imagine him assembling these echoes from *King Lear*, Poe, Meredith, and of course Faulkner, ending with the maudlin "sandy threads through Peyton's hair." But then the prose often gets out of hand and metaphors sometimes turn upon their heels and march the other way ("a knot of sailors on the deck—she could see them, far out, as tiny as pins—scattered away like a broken cluster of pearls"), or the blacks—who appear to carry some of the burden of hope in their belief—sound like something from "Amos 'n' Andy" :

> "He gonna make de 'Pearance now."
> "He sho' is. I kin always tell."
> "How come *you* know?"

"I kin always tell. When de elder goes in, it's almos' time."
"De band gotta come yet."
"Dat's right. Wonder where dey is?"

(LDD, p. 393)

Even stranger is this comment on La Ruth, after she has given an astute reply to the Marse. Milton reflects, "If you were to peel back her skull, he thought, you'd find no convolutions at all on the brain, only a round, thoughtless, shiny sphere." From the passage it would seem that Styron is not trying to characterize Milton or that there is any sort of irony intended. Or could it possibly be that La Ruth is a black Maudie?

In his *Paris Review* interview Styron says that the greatest problem he had with *Lie Down in Darkness* was in handling "the progression of time."[7] He also says, of his indebtedness to Faulkner, that "I'm all for the complexity of Faulkner, but not for the confusion."[8] This novel tries very sincerely to combine the sense of the few hours that it takes to convey the body of Peyton from the train station to the cemetery with the memories of Milton, Helen, Dolly, and Carey which review the past that led to this day. Behind this scheme are the models of *As I Lay Dying* and *Ulysses*—and perhaps especially the "Hades" section of *Ulysses*. The chronology is very important to the novel if Styron is to keep the events and the motives clear to the reader, but he also wishes to present that chronology through the tormented jumble of the present moment. Styron establishes his "real" world through his allusions to historical events and people, and this creates a base on which the experiences and emotions of his characters play a kind of obbligato. This use of public events would seem to be mainly indebted to Joyce; the use of family history to Faulkner.

Yet Styron offers the reader a few quandaries where the dates are concerned. In one passage Helen has a memory of a visit to her brother Edward in Pennsylvania. She is twenty-four, which would place the scene in 1922 as Helen was born about 1898.[9] In this scene Maudie is talking—precociously for someone with her defects—as she appears to have been born just about this time, and Peyton is going for a walk with her uncle even though she wasn't born until 31 August 1923. This we know because she is nine

[94]

the spring of 1933, and her sixteenth birthday is 31 August 1939, "the day before the war began." But here the trouble with dates deepens. Milton has a letter from Peyton which he carries at the funeral and which begins, "Dearest Bunny, today I was 22." But Peyton's twenty-second birthday would be on 31 August 1945, and her suicide was on 7 August, the day after the atomic bombing of Hiroshima, and so she would have been dead for three weeks. On this day when we have Peyton's account of her life in New York she hears someone speak of Nagasaki—someone who must know what only the inner circle of the Pentagon knows, for Nagasaki was not bombed until 9 August. There is also a problem about what happened between these two significant dates. Peyton plunges naked from the washroom of a Harlem loft on 7 August. Since her body is unclaimed, she is buried in Potter's Field on Hart Island until she is claimed by Harry Miller, her estranged husband. The body is then shipped by train to Port Warwick for burial, but there is still enough time for it to show up there for the bombing of Nagasaki two days later on 9 August. Such matters, I think, rarely move so swiftly, but it appears that Styron wishes to sacrifice chronology for dramatic impact and larger significance.

His major purpose would appear to be to document the spiritual and emotional malaise of the Loftis family in these generations. He often suggests that theirs is a universal situation, but the characters themselves see their predicament as unique to the time and place and so they look to some past time as a time of happiness. For Helen it is a memory of her girlhood at Fort Myer where her stern and patriotic father, mounted on horse back, reviewed his troops. For Milton it is also his youth, thirty years ago, which he remembers as "a finer, more tranquil age." For him, however, it is a mixed memory, for he hates his father who dominated that age, who spoiled him and favored him with orotund homilies on prudence. One condemnation of this age comes from Milton's father as a result of meeting, when a little boy, Lincoln in Richmond shortly before the assassination.[10] It was as "if he had looked into the eyes of Christ, like he said: the last angel, the last great man who ever walked on earth." He adds that "we are a race of toads,"

[95]

and when Dolly accuses him of bitterness he says that he is not bitter, but that "we have lost our lovewords." Such passages appear to be taken seriously by the author as well as the characters, without that tinge of irony when, for example, Faulkner writes of the antebellum South or Joyce has Bloom ask himself if he were happier in former days. And I gather that we are to take seriously the sodden Weltschmertz of an old grad at Charlottesville who asks Milton, "I guess this generation's just lost the goddam Cavalier spirit don't you?"

It is in Peyton's relationship to her father and mother that the issues of what I have called the novel of generational crisis must rest. In the nineteenth century (I have in mind the way in which this subject is treated by Balzac or Turgenev) the youth are often hotheaded, mistaken, and invariably selfish, but there is an impressive vigor about their ideals even when these are nihilistic. This is not the case with Peyton. She seems so completely wrapped up in herself that she is more a case study than an adequate vessel of the larger issues. In New York she is asked flippantly if her psychiatrist said she was "dangerously abstracted or . . . psychogenically incapable of sexual fidelity." Either way the prospects are dim for her being a clear mirror of her age. If she is dangerously abstracted she might serve as an aloof commentator on the events of the novel and make the author's intent clearer, but this she does not do. If her problem is a Messalina complex which might reflect the gnawing hungers of the time this might serve, but Styron more often presents us with images of her flawless beauty than her unsatisfied lasciviousness. Her husband tells her that she is "absolutely incapable of love," that she "just can't love," and all the evidence indicates he is right. In these scenes on her last day she sounds dangerously like her mother, although Helen's syntax is more believable: "Then, Harry, I would say, why are you like this to me? Not for your defection so small, really, did I do my petty vengeance, but just because always you've failed to understand. Me." This is petty narcissism given the circumstances so that when she leaps to her death it is not our ills she is curing— the ravages of Time, the Bomb, and so forth—it is her own ills.

We are still offered some light in this gloom. First there is the character of Harry Miller. It appears to be in his favor that he is polite, his parents are dead, he is Jewish, he fought in Spain, and he is a painter who feels he has something to express. But (and here most of the critics agree) we are shown too little of him and, one could add, he turns the final deaf ear to Peyton in her distress.[11] Another reason for optimism might be found in the placid wisdom of Maudie who loves everyone in her dependence and refuses to be cast down although a cripple and prisoned in her child's mind. Helen insists that Maudie knows more than all of them, and this knowledge seems to be how to love selflessly. Helen reflects that "strange things make her happy," and this is true, but Helen herself is as mad as a hatter and an odd person to be allowed this testimony since Maudie cannot testify for herself.[12] The third glimmer of hope often remarked is the recurring figure of Daddy Faith (probably modeled on Daddy Grace), the black Baltimore revivalist who comes to Port Warwick every August to save lost souls. His gathering followers force the hearse to detour at one point, and in the epilogue there is a full account of a sunlit baptismal service which contrasts with the Gothic squalls that have gone before. There is certainly an impressive contrast here between the hysteria of the crypt and that by the water's edge, but the intellectual leap from an account of a sick white society to a wholesome black one is difficult. Perhaps the faith of these simple souls has to be more fully documented throughout the novel. But even if it were it still might not successfully imply resurrection for Peyton, for the contrasts between her life and that of the white gowned at the water's edge is remarkable. Cooper Mackin's comments on the novel end with the significance of the title from Sir Thomas Browne and the lines from Henry Vaughan's "they are all gone into the world of light" which Peyton trades with Dr. Holcomb at the wedding reception.[13] His point is that both passages emphasize that there is resurrection "one short sleep past," and he suggests that this is what we are to expect for Peyton. This could well have been Styron's intent, but the passages (especially that from Vaughan) are oddly imported. And if this is the intent

[97]

I am still troubled by the wingless birds ("dodos and penguins and cassowaries, ostriches," "the emus and dodos and ostriches and moas") in Peyton's final meditations. All of this makes it difficult to see the epilogue implying resurrection for Peyton.

But the main difficulty with *Lie Down in Darkness* is in the style. This has been much lauded and it is certainly a remarkable performance for a writer of twenty-six, but I think that it tends to obscure where it proposes to make clear. This is probably the most awesome trap that first novelists encounter, for their style is almost of necessity gleaned from their literary enthusiasms, and when their matter runs counter to the style, very difficult choices must be made. When the work is ambitious—in style and subject—those choices are virtually impossible.

Notes

1. Jonathan Baumbach, *The Landscape of Nightmare* (New York, 1965), pp. 130, 133. Ihab H. Hassan calls the novel "a vision of tragic ambiguities and ironic necessities, of human experience spanning the abyss," but ends his essay saying that "the reader's mind is purified without recourse to a genuinely tragic catharsis." "Encounter with Necessity," in *On Contemporary Literature*, ed. Richard Kostelanetz (New York, 1964), pp. 603, 606.

2. Baumbach, p. 123.

3. David D. Galloway, *The Absurd Hero in American Fiction* (Austin, Tex., 1966), p. 54.

4. Louise Y. Gossett, *Violence in Recent Southern Fiction* (Durham, N.C., 1965), p. 126.

5. John Aldridge, *In Search of Heresy* (New York, 1956), p. 146.

6. Hassan writes, "For Peyton's darkness, however 'clinical' it may seem—and there is no doubt that it is more dramatic than clinical—must still illumine the universal urge of human beings to clutch some impossible idea of eternal childhood or innocence, must illumine and expiate that urge" (p. 599). Here I do not agree and feel that Hassan himself uses *must* in a very delicate way.

7. Peter Matthiessen and George Plimpton, eds., "William Styron," in *Writers at Work: The Paris Review Interviews* (New York, 1958), p. 280.

8. Matthiessen and Plimpton, p. 275.

9. Helen might have been born about 1900, which would place the scene in 1924, but this still creates problems.

10. Lincoln visited the ravaged Richmond 4–5 April 1865.

11. Galloway, p. 61, for example.

12. On Maudie see Cooper R. Mackin, *William Styron*, Southern Writers Series (Austin, Tex., 1969), pp. 6–9.

13. Mackin, p. 11.

JAN B. GORDON

Permutations of Death: A Reading of *Lie Down in Darkness*

Riding down to Port Warwick from Richmond, the train begins to pick up speed on the outskirts of the city, past the tobacco factories with their ever-present haze of acrid, sweetish dust and past the rows of uniformly brown clapboard houses which stretch down the hilly streets for miles. (LDD, p. 9)

The train came on with a clatter, shading the trestle, and its whistle went off full-blast in a spreading plume of steam. "Yeah! Yeah!" Another blast from the whistle, a roar, a gigantic sound; and it seemed to soar into the dusk beyond and above them for-ever, with a noise, perhaps, like the clatter of the opening of ever-lasting gates and doors—passed swiftly on—toward Richmond, the North, the oncoming night. (LDD, p. 400)

Like the Tidewater which serves as its setting, the predominant movement of William Styron's *Lie Down in Darkness* is the slow rhythm of sedimentation and withdrawal. If the novel's first para-graph places the reader aboard a train homeward bound from "Columbus or Detroit or wherever," its final page places the po-tential passenger back aboard an outbound train highballing it for the night of the eternal snow, the North. The excursion period which separates the two segments of this unique round trip is in effect the novel itself. The reader is a stranger, trapped between inbound and outbound trips in a novel that moves almost im-perceptibly when it moves at all. That is to say that the narrative serves to fill in those interstices of character and motive rather than to develop a plot. It is not that Styron's novel is written backward, as is say, *Wuthering Heights* or Faulkner's *Absalom! Absalom!* where we know the events of the novel and read in order to dis-cover causes and motives, but rather that the action seems to eddy. *Lie Down in Darkness* circles about Peyton's funeral, accumulating details of fragmented lives rather than giving us a fragmented picture of lives which we must piece together through narrative disjunction.

All of this is to say that the action of the novel is structurally analogous to those estuaries that dot the coastline north of Cape Hatteras; neither all sea, nor all river, nor all land, but a curious hybrid geography. Its stillness is perhaps the closest one might come to that other cycle of growth and decay—the great Dismal Swamp which flanks the Tidewater on the lee side of the coast. That bit of primeval America is, of course, the place where life and death meet insofar as it is an arena where the processes of decay yield to new energy. The swampland south of Port War-wick, like the worship of the black revivalist, Daddy Faith, is an intersection of growth and decay where denizens on the verge of extinction are making a last stand of sorts, and whose space remains almost impenetrable. The epigraph to the novel is drawn from Sir Thomas Browne's *Urn Burial:*

> And since death must be the Lucina of life, and even Pagans could doubt, whether thus to live were to die; since our longest sun sets at right descensions, and makes but winter arches, and therefore it cannot be long before we lie down in darkness and have our light in ashes; since the brother of death daily haunts us with dying mementos, and time that grows old in itself, bids us hope no long duration;—diuturnity is a dream and folly of expectation.[1]

Like Keats's urn later, Browne's is a repository where the relationship between a civilization's ruins and its ceremonies are the occasion for a discourse upon the nature of immortality. Among the questions posed by Browne's inquiry upon the discovery and dis-interment of the ancient graves (which parallels the exhuming of Peyton's body from Potter's Field in *Lie Down in Darkness*), is the nature of death and immortality. And Styron's novel really explores the same themes, notably the relationship between death-in-life and life-in-death in a civilization which is itself trapped between the two, the cavalier coast of a Virginia where all that remains of the life of southern aristocracy are the empty forms of a way of life, perhaps best symbolized in the label from the Jack Daniels bottle that slips off into Milton Loftis's perspiring palms.

One of the primary objections raised over the years by critics of Styron's achievement is the derivative nature of his style and thematic interests. Inevitably, comparisons with Faulkner or Eudora Welty or Robert Penn Warren are used to the detriment of Styron's reputation. Yet, in the largest sense, Styron is a "second generation" southern writer whose stylistic interests and thematic concerns set him apart from the mainstream of southern fiction. In the first place, Styron does not imagine himself as a member of some larger agrarian brotherhood, but rather as part of a different world:

> Much of the power of a writer like Faulkner, for instance, or Flannery O'Connor, derived from their ability to see the bizarre connotations of this *difference* of the South, to perceive the ironies and contradictions involved when people inheriting so directly the manners and mores of a nineteenth-century feudal, agrarian society collided head-on with the necessities of an industrial civilization. . . . Yet now as this difference is erased and the contradictions smoothed out, now that the South to everyone's amazement proves to accommodate itself to racial integration far more gracefully than the North . . . now that the difference has gone, and no one save a few antiquarians and scholars and readers of Faulkner can know what the Old South really was; now, in short, as the South is truly absorbed into the substance of the rest of the nation, I think that Southern writing, if it doesn't fade away altogether, will certainly no longer correspond to anything we recall from its illustrious past. Possibly the works of Walker Percy give a clue.[2]

Interestingly, Styron seems to believe that the South is in the process of being "absorbed"—that is losing its separate sense of identity. Somewhat later, in the same interview, he speaks of southern writing having entered a "grey" area, almost as if, like the "emerging majority," the nation would take its strength from those border kingdoms, geographic and psychic. William Styron does not create a separate fictional region, like Faulkner's Yoknapatawpha or Conrad's Costaguana, but rather makes use of the local geography as it is. There is no effort to recapture as fictional space something that has been lost, and the corollary to such an attempt at reclamation, the pervasive myth of the fall of the Old South, is seldom a part of his imagination. In short, Styron's South deserves special attention precisely because it is so radically different from what we might expect: the lawyer has replaced the farmer; shopping in Washington, D.C., is a habit among the respectable middle class and the stern Calvinism that was part of the land's curse in earlier southern writing has been relaxed into the mannered and more socially acceptable Episcopalian mutterings of Carey. It is a world different in both kind and degree from that of all, save perhaps the late Faulkner. It is the Faulkner of *The Reivers* with its wild ride to a Memphis racetrack that is closest to the emotions of *Lie Down in Darkness*, emotions that are part of a newer urban South where some ancient curse upon the land is replaced by some similarly ill-defined neurosis which afflicts the collective psyche.

A large part of the final one-third of *Lie Down in Darkness* is set in New York where Peyton lives with her husband, Harry Miller, a Jewish painter with somewhat radical politics. Although Miller is not a well-drawn character, the reason for his sketchiness is clearly related to the very functional role that he plays in the novel. He is always on the periphery of a group of metropolitan intellectuals and pseudointellectuals who engage each other with all the fads: orgone boxes, oriental mysticism, and such neohumanistic bombast as the generalization, "the evil in man is both beautiful and preordained." This realm is one of almost incredible pretense, where a psychiatrist named Dr. Irving Strassman can tell Peyton she is "hopelessly abstracted" without recognizing that in the mere use of such phrases he is more abstracted than she. Her final soliloquy, as a matter of fact, is filled not with abstractions, but with the most concrete memories of her childhood in Virginia: the sea gulls, picking flowers, and the sound of guns— all of which we have read about earlier in the novel. But the conversations at Albert Berger's house *are* hopelessly abstracted and the names that swallow up Peyton provide some insight into the nature of the allegory that Styron has constructed: Gould, Fischer, Liebowitz, Freeman. In a sense, her journey north and into the darkness, like that of the train at the conclusion of *Lie Down in Darkness*, is the saga of the South being absorbed into the life of the growing urban areas of the country, complete with the conversations of spoiled Jewish intellectuals. All that is missing from Berger's gathering, alas, is poor Portnoy, and he lurks, fictionally at least, just around the corner. Several years ago, Norman Mailer severely criticized Styron as one of those "uncircumcised dogs" whose values were antithetical to the "arrival" of Jewish fiction in the early sixties. And more than once, Styron has been accused of antisemitism in his fiction and in his public pronouncements. Yet, Miller is drawn with considerable sympathy, and Peyton is surely as spoiled by her father as the various Jews at Berger's apartment have been spoiled by their mothers. The tragic last pages of *Lie Down in Darkness* are much more complicated than such easy interpretations will allow. Surely, these last pages are an allegory of southern fiction in the process of being supplanted by other values, of the shift of a fictional generation. If the last chapter ends with the baptismal party of the black revivalist, Daddy Faith, the penultimate section concludes with a glimpse of Harry Miller's painting, showing a rabbi with upraised arms and eyes walking through a desolated city. The IRT local runs beside one and the Port Warwick–Richmond express runs beside the other, but both represent some attempt at life triumphing over death. Thus each image is undoubtedly symbolic of various fictions common to their respective regions: the dying faith of the Old South and the dying martyrdom of the urban rabbi who must cross a desolated landscape. Perhaps *Lie Down in Darkness* will someday be read not as the last gasp of southern fiction, but rather as a self-reflexive commentary upon the history of the nation as well as the history of her fiction.

Perhaps the one feature, however, above all, that sets William Styron apart from the mainstream of twentieth-century southern writing is his emphasis upon *nostalgia* as opposed to *memory*. Were one to attempt to locate a common denominator in the development of an American literature, the pervasive influence of memory manifested as some ancestral curse would loom large. Almost inevitably some sin, usually sexual in nature, exerts an influence upon later generations as they struggle to do penance for acts which now exist only as a part of history. Hawthorne's *The House of the Seven Gables*, Ahab's wound in *Moby Dick*, the visit of those ghosts upon a governess in James's *The Turn of the Screw*, the mixture of incest and miscegenation in Faulkner's *The Sound and the Fury*—all share in the American penchant for a literature of atonement. It is perhaps what we might expect from a nation of vagabonds who successfully mounted a rebellion against their colonial master long before the rest of the children fled the imperial household in the nineteenth century. Perhaps a civilization which sees itself as the naughty child invents a sin for which it might legitimately feel guilty. But if the typical orphan of nineteenth-century British fiction felt himself duty bound at some point to reclaim the ancestral family estate (whose names—*Mansfield Park*, *Wuthering Heights*, *Bleak House*, and *Howard's End*—provide the titles for major Victorian novels), his American counterpart seems to revel in his outcast state. Rather than the pattern of departure and return which J. Hillis Miller sees as a central structural motif of the nineteenth-century British novel,[3] the American rogue seems intent upon authenticating his illegitimacy a la Huck Finn. Instead of affirming legitimacy by acknowledging his inheritance (and thereby being cut into all those disputed wills that pervade deathbed scenes in Victorian fiction), the outlaw of American fiction typically becomes a combination explorer, confidence man, and purveyor of folk wisdom. He creates his own space rather than returning to that of his father. But memory always haunts him, as if somehow civilization were indistinguishable from history. It is when history itself is called into question that memory is replaced by nostalgia. Although the precise relationship between the two is often difficult to establish, memory is generally a function of our ability to recapture either traumatic or highly pleasurable moments. By contrast nostalgia tends to screen those traumatic aspects of memory in favor of an aestheticization which takes a segment of time and spatializes it, so that say, the late fifties return on our "rock" radio stations as "greaser days." As its root would suggest, nostalgia is a collective experience —an attempt, often sentimental, by a civilization to write its own history.

Unlike most southern fiction where memory is often represented as the product of some elder white or black sage/prophet, there are few such old people with clairvoyance in *Lie Down in Darkness*. And the absence of such a figure tells us something. Rather than being trapped in its own unique history, the country surrounding Port Warwick is forever unable to recapture any part of its collective past, except as nostalgia. Lyrics from songs popular at the time recur throughout the novel: "Try Me One More Time," "Saturday Night (Is the Loneliest Night in the Week)," and "Deep Purple." These are all tunes that were popular during and immediately after the Second World War, but, more importantly, they are all songs whose lyrics speak to a certain decadence of romance, of a desire to recapture the golden age of love: " 'Member, Helen? 'Member how we used to drive up to Connellsville in the summer? Marion and Eddie's? 'Member the time when Peyton almost got stung by the bees?" We have entered a realm once removed from memory through the vehicle of self-consciousness. As part of the attempt to recapture an idyll (perhaps something like the fateful summer of '42?), these words participate in the nostalgia that they attempt to describe. Although *Lie Down in Darkness* was first published in 1951, the events of the novel are set back six years to August 1945, since the newspaper headlines during Peyton's last days read of Hiroshima and of the hopes for a quick truce. Then six years before 1945, in August 1939, Milton Loftis and his mistress, Dolly Bonner, had first made love during the celebration surrounding Peyton's sixteenth birthday. That, we also know to have been "to call back ancient history . . . the day before the war began." On that day, there was, we are told, "talk about a Corridor." This chronological scheme which seems always to involve intervals of six years accomplishes something else, notably a synchrony between the human events and international circumstance. What is happening among the nations of the world parallels the events that afflict the Loftis family. It would seem that Styron, like George Eliot in *Middlemarch*, has set his novel back as a way of talking about disjunction in time. The people who walk through the pages of *Lie Down in Darkness* are literally dispossessed; like the orphans of Victorian fiction, they have no knowledge of their origins. There is a certain organic rhythm that links Peyton's death with the deaths of thousands of Japanese and Milton's attempts at a truce with his estranged wife to the global effort to seek peace between the Allies and the Axis powers. Yet,

somehow, it all seems too late for that. In this novel, history is
never determined a priori by blood lines, nor is it a part of some
rigid Calvinistic eschatology, but rather history is made by hu-
mans and human interaction. There is little suggestion of regional
uniqueness in *Lie Down in Darkness*, but rather the complaint of
Mrs. La Farge that "the international Jewish bankers are con-
spiring to send my Charlie into war" floats above a Virginia cocktail party much as it floated around the earth on the eve of World
War II. The mysterious "corridor" could as easily apply to the
strip of Tidewater as to the devastated finger of Poland. The
struggle between colonial-suburban Hellenism and urban Hebra-
ism is seen as part of the systoles and diastoles of the civilization.
It impacts the largest kingdom as well as the smallest person, this
collective guilt which prompts Peyton to marry Harry Miller. And
for that reason, *Lie Down in Darkness* is a great panoramic novel
of the order of, though finally a lesser achievement than, say *Middlemarch* or *War and Peace*.

Yet, because they make their own history, none of the figures
of Styron's novel can ever rise above these events. The "world" of
Styron's novel is a world where no resolution is possible, and it
must be read with that proviso in mind. The question that the
novel poses on 9 August 1945, the day of Peyton's funeral, is no
less than, "How did we get here?" It is a question to be applied to
the Loftises, Dolly Bonner, the blacks of the household, and to a
nation—all of which find themselves looking death in the face
after a long struggle. It may also represent, at least allegorically,
the history of the American novel looking at its own death.
Throughout the sixties, critics like Leslie Fiedler and Richard
Poirier were speaking of the demise of the "traditional" American
novel with its various existential outlaws: Dimmesdale, Ahab,
Huckleberry Finn, and the Snopeses. Although the argument var-
ied in its details, there was a sort of Turner Thesis applied to the
development of our fiction: as the frontier filled, there was simply
no more new territory to which one might "light out," and the
image of the populist rogue, that combination "Confidence-Man"
and "Rifleman," that has permeated our literature and our politics
was transformed. With the advent of "beat" fiction in the late

fifties and sixties, the "road" of Jack Kerouac and the circuitous path of Richard Fariña have led neither into the future nor the past, but only into a world that lives in an eternal present. Lacking both history and prophecy, the hero of this new fiction quickly became the perpetrator of "instant history," the persona of a new naturalism who marched with the *Armies of the Night*. If the "old" American novel was dominated by the individual of strong will, the new fictional antihero tended to be among the "beautiful losers" tossed about by events whose causality was indeterminate. Although not the outcast from society, these urban dwellers felt aliented from themselves, and any terror stemmed not from the unknown and the unsettled, but rather from some mirror image: the encounter with an alternative self. History, when it appears at all as an influence, is invariably a psychologized history, so that vague guilt tends to be a substitute for a definable evil that has been watered by relativism. Peyton's plight in *Lie Down in Darkness* is not unlike the plight of the American novel in the fifties and sixties: having depleted her existential spaces, she becomes unable to complete any act save that of a morbid fascination upon her own genesis.

Not so of Helen Loftis. Whatever else we might say of her, a fixation upon the past is her most noticeable trait. Combined with a sense of languor and infirmity, she is the modern day descendant of Dickens's Miss Havisham whose every effort is part of some colossal attempt to return to a prior state of which the reader is only dimly aware:

> Now she did something that she had done many times before. She pulled the skin of her face taut over the cheekbones so that the web of lines and wrinkles vanished as if it had been touched by a miraculous and restorative wand; squinting convergently into the glass, she watched the foolish and lovely change: transfigured, she saw smooth skin as glassy white as the petal of gardenia, lips which seemed but sixteen or twenty, and as unblemished by any trouble as those she had held up to another mirror thirty years before, whispering "Dearest" to an invisible and quite imaginary lover. (LDD, p. 24)

Her entire life has had the same psychic dimension as that exhibited in the revelatory scene during which we first meet her. Between glances at the morning paper announcing the possibility of a truce with the Japanese, she looks in the mirror at a face artificially, albeit magically, transformed. Her husband, Milton, has already telephoned the paper requesting that the announcement of Peyton's suicide be deleted. In both of her glances then, Helen faces a profound absence. It is almost as if one could successfully transform that which has happened into that which has not simply by living a lie. The look into the mirror involves the refusal to accept the scandal of time, and the reading of the newspaper involves a similar doctoring of events to avoid a more social scandal. Both involve the need for repair by excision, and more than once in the novel, Helen Loftis expresses the desire to actually live the death that has been her existence for a quarter century:

> "Don't try," she said sighing. "Oh, it's so hot!" And thought, *Indeed if I consider Charlottesville that will be all. Which is worse, past or future? Neither. I will fold up my mind like a leaf and drift on this stream over the brink.* (LDD, p. 149)

This desire to fold oneself up is, stated another way, a wish for a life that is all boundary, that walls oneself up behind identifiable barriers. And that condition is perilously close to the nothingness of death. As R. D. Laing has suggested in his astute examination of the defensive personality, *The Divided Self*, such individuals come to imagine themselves as being disconnected, quite literally out of touch. From another perspective, they are all outer wall or surface which implies that the interior or "inner" self is all emptiness, a word which occurs with increasing frequency as we read through *Lie Down in Darkness*. We inevitably see Helen alone within some confined existential space. Neither the look in the mirror nor the cursory reading of carefully edited news is a look outside the self. For most of the novel, Helen Loftis's life alternates between the bedroom where she weeps herself to sleep under the influence of tranquilizers and another interior chamber, that of the boozy country club where everyday is an Old Forester kind of day. The bright glare of a funereal sun on the day of Peyton's last return home to Port Warwick blinds her. Helen's light, when it does exist at all, is always reflected or refracted—the light of the mirror, the muted Japanese lanterns at the country club, the twilight cocktail parties, or the wild summer moon out of whose dim glare she arrives at the home of the Reverend Carr to seek marital advice.

In every way Helen Loftis leads a derivative existence; having little sense of her own selfhood, she attempts to contain it by erecting barriers that compartmentalize both her physical being and her soul while creating a similar distinction between self and other: " 'Just a minute, Milton. I'm not finished. Let me tell you, too. Let me tell you. I know what sin is,' she repeated, and the word *sin* was like the cold edge of a blade sunk deep somewhere in his body. 'I do. I do. In knowing that I'll always be superior to you.' " For Helen Loftis, knowledge is the equivalent of mental property insofar as it is to be hoarded. As her Virginia ancestors imagined a relationship between the ownership of land and personal salvation, so she believes that her knowledge of sin places her just outside the domain of the devil. For her, all knowledge of sin in the world represents a bit of the soul's space reclaimed from the Kingdom of Death. But Helen's speech reveals as much about her as her Protestant fundamentalism, for hers is the language of an incredible emptiness for which the personal pronouns *I* and *me* provide the fiction of a center. Actually, in the ensuing discussions with her pastor, the reader discovers that Helen Loftis really has very little knowledge of sin. It is truly one of those "hopeless abstractions" of which Peyton is later diagnosed by Dr. Strassman. Helen's is virtually a satellite existence; forever on the periphery, always attempting to claim some space of her own, she manipulates and is in turn manipulated by others. Their daughter, Peyton, can use her body to manipulate her father into granting whatever she wants. Helen Loftis's temptation, then, is a representation of Milton's rejection of her body, internalized as the self-hatred of her own body, and then reprojected (mirrored) as envy upon her daughter's relationship with her husband. The love triangle involving Dolly Bonner is no different from the triangle which exists in her own family; two women vie for the love of a single man.

If Helen Loftis's words in *Lie Down in Darkness* are only barely memorable, Milton Loftis speaks far too much. His excessive verbosity is a complement to her weary silence. If her lie is the assumption of knowledge where none exists in order that the self might thereby be more effectively buttressed ("her only hope . . . was to supply her soul each day with new attitudes, new bulwarks"), Milton blurs the boundaries between self and other by the alcoholic's diffusion of being. In his physical appearance, spreading middle age means that all of those limits to being are exceeded, and the proper metaphor for such a condition is the hangover:

> At the age of fifty he was beginning to discover, with a sense of panic, that his whole life had been in the nature of a hangover, with faintly unpleasant pleasures being atoned for by the dull alleviated pain of guilt. Had he the solace of knowing that he was an alcoholic, things would have been brighter, because he had read somewhere that alcoholism was a disease, but he was not, he assured himself, alcoholic, only self-indulgent, and his disease, whatever it was, resided in shadier corners of his soul where decisions were reached not through reason but by rationalization and where a thin membranous growth of selfishness always seemed to prevent his decent motives from becoming happy actions. (LDD, p. 153)

Milton Loftis had been told by his cavalier father that love and passion have an inverse relationship, one with the other. As the flames of passion are extinguished by the sands of time, love ripens and endures. It is the everlasting light that matters rather than the witches' bonfire: "*My son, never let passion be a guide. Nurture hope like a flower in the most barren ground of trouble. If love has fed the flame of your brightest imaginings, then passion will perish in that flame and only love endure.*" Of course, such a vision is merely another way of saying that love is the reward for having conquered passion, legitimizing a frightening double standard. Milton Loftis, having lost one, seeks the other in Dolly Bonner. His relationship to his mistress is symbolically represented by the peculiar syntax that is vehicle for the expression of that "love." The use of the spider web and of the word *entanglement* is a perfect representation of Milton Loftis's speech:

> The eccentric manner of twisting words into grotesque parodies of themselves, his supplications—"Oh, God" or "Oh, Jesus" when something went wrong—uttered with such profound and comical

intensity to the heavens; and his own particular wit, the subtleties of which she often did not get: to listen to that steady flow of words, the fine enthusiasms and the wry, damning accusation of things in general. (LDD, p. 71)

Milton Loftis is the ringmaster of a linguistic circus, and most of his utterances are the verbal equivalent of the "shambling procession of lies and excuses" which stroll through his mind. Milton's problem, like that of most wandering men, is that he must be in too many places at the same time. Covering his tracks while meeting Dolly in Washington or Richmond, he must always account for time spent, and there are the inevitable overlaps that short-circuit one-on-one relationships with a kind of verbal overkill, the oratorical equivalent of rationalization. After a few drinks, he is always tongue-tied, the internal correlative to the "knots" that comprise his pseudoaffections. Although his excess is the other side of Helen's empty silences, both live a perpetual lie. Milton is no more in touch with Dolly Bonner than he is with his wife. Although he and Dolly occasionally share a bed, the net result is not much different from that love which stems from the separate bedrooms inhabited by him and his wife:

> In the darkness, taking his hand, with nothing troubling her secret glow of triumph, she lay down next to him on Helen's bed. Soon, "Have you?" she said.
> "Not yet."
> "Have you?"
> "No. I can't," he groaned.
> "Now?"
> "Yes, yes," he said.
> It was a lie but she couldn't tell. (LDD, p. 187)

Clearly, his parody of lovemaking parallels the parody of the language, that other form of communication. Although Milton continually alleges that Dolly's hips drive him wild, it is quite clear that he is driven wild only from a distance. That the hand redeems—one of the aphorisms of Carey Carr—is never fully recognized. Milton Loftis, unable to get both sides together, must forever live with distance providing the basis for desire. In other words, Milton Loftis is a voyeur *manqué:*

[112]

"I wish I had been a poet."

"Oh, you could do it, Milton," she burst out, forgetful of his slight.

"You keep saying that. Why don't you do it? What would you start writing now?"

"Pornography. As befits a dirty old man. The way we make love, that's what I'd write about. The way I love it. The way—."

(LDD, p. 179)

May the good Lord protect his readers! The blank in this dialogue is the visible emblem of the absence at the heart of his life. Whenever that which he desires enters the range of possibility, Milton Loftis must use a flood of oral or written verbiage in order to defeat the possibility. His desire to write pornography is but another excuse, yet another apologia for failed connections.

The two children share the attributes of each parent. The crippled Maudie, a study in arrested development, inhabits the spaces of silence. Unable to move or to comprehend anything beyond the most immediate family relationships, she passes her life folded up in a heap. Peyton is her opposite; flirtatious, gregarious, highly verbal, she, like her father, is all excess—too much liquor, too many false expectations, too many lovers, and too many midnight travels away from home. And, like Milton, she does not approve of nor enjoy sex. She is called "the body" at the Kappa Alpha dance after a University of Virginia football game, but it is a body she does not really possess. Whenever the young Cartwright wishes to embrace her gratuitously, she pulls away. Her desire is closely related to want (as in the episode where she kisses her father in return for the promise of a new red auto for graduation), and, of course, that is precisely the point. Since the other side of "want" is "lack," it must be expected that, serially, desire-as-want is easily transformed into *wanton* behavior. Unable to gain satisfaction, Peyton must move from lover to lover until her suicide. Just as Helen and Milton Loftis lead lives that border on death, so the two children who share in those lives both die—one by shrinking up into nothingness in a Charlottesville hospital, and the other by falling between New York skyscrapers, thereby filling up the abyss between structures.

In *Lie Down in Darkness* love is seldom freely given, since there is simply too much demand for reciprocity. Several times in the novel, *love* is equated with *need*, and the two abstractions are used interchangeably. Helen greets Milton's return following Maudie's death with a perfect instance of such a confusion: " 'Darling,' she said that afternoon, 'darling, darling, you have learned, haven't you? You have learned what I need, haven't you? You have learned. I believe you. Oh, yes, together we can never die!' " Peyton gets caught in the same bind, for at the onset of her honeymoon, she bases the connection on a mutual dependency, using almost the same language as her mother, while she and Harry cross on the night ferry:

> "I'm sorry for what I said, darling. I married you because I need you."
> He looked into her eyes. "Need?"
> "I mean—" She struggled to say something.
> "Need?" he repeated.
> "I mean—"
> "Need? Love?" (LDD, p. 320)

This identification of love and need have a number of consequences, not the least of which is addiction. We need those people whom we cannot do without, so that relationships based upon some love-need dynamic is usually strongly determined. In addiction need is the middle term in a dialectic which links love to hate. One fears absence so much that he cannot do with and he cannot do without. Even as love binds the two, the possibility of the "want-lack" permutation enters the relationship. We wish not for the presence of the other, but instead come to define the relationship negatively —as *not* wishing for the absence of the other owing to that which accrues to self. We feign affection for the other only as a way of avoiding any self-confrontation. This deceit is doubtlessly part of the lie by which love comes to be regarded as a need. The second manifestation of the equation of love and need is the growth of something akin to rescue-fantasy. Unable to love the other unconditionally, we imagine ourselves as rescuers of those in trouble so that we might disguise desire within the garb of salvation, thereby achieving the sharing of distance and desire once again. It is clear that Peyton does not love Harry Miller, and just as clear that what she does love is *not* to be abandoned. She loves a nothingness that is perilously close to suicide, even from the beginning of her saga. She desires not Harry at all, but rather she desires his desire of her and only then is she authenticated. She lives a double lie, once removed from the inauthenticity of her parents. In order to command his desire, she must always reenforce his role as a redeemer by threatening to live her own absence. She must make Harry chase her just as she made Milton chase her through the fraternity parties at Charlottesville: "You could have done something. But you weren't there. You left me just like you always do. When I needed you. Why didn't you come and rescue me? Didn't you see—." The elder Virginia gentlemen had enacted the ritual of courtship by the moonlight elopement on a horse. But Peyton Loftis is the decadence of such a romanticism; in her contrived parodies of rescue, she gives the lie to history. Only when she is in the extreme defensive posture can she love. Of course, as inevitably happens, one of the rescues fails or the signal is refused by the knight, and she is left only with the nothingness of her own death.[4] The relationship of *love, need, want* (as lack or absence), and the necessity of *salvation* in *Lie Down in Darkness* reads as practically a concordance to southern puritanism.

The final, and perhaps the worst aspect of the equation of love and need, is in effect a symptomatology. By the end of the novel, practically every white person is suffering the effects of some illness whose symptoms suggest the desire to reject some deep-seated evil. As Helen and Maudie fold themselves up in a defense against exterior pain, so Milton Loftis vomits bile and his daughter Peyton feels her selfhood draining away in menstruation. Vague trips to doctors are mentioned with increasing frequency, and the revelry of the football game is paired with a visit to the deteriorating Maudie in the hospital. Everyone seems to be afflicted with illness, either spiritual or physical, so that the entire novel comes to resemble a hospital room. The last stage in the evolution of this metaphor is the group therapy scene in Berger's house, where the only hope for community stems from the recognition that all the guests are sick. When love is made a companion to need, then every act of communion must be masked as therapy. Calvinistic notions of salvation are transformed into a dependency upon the psychiatrist or some other facilitator-mediator. And Peyton's last letter to daddy, which is a sort of suicide note that says "please save me," resembles in its broken syntax, the halting speech of Helen Loftis when she seeks out the Reverend Carr for her own midnight confession:

> Oh, Daddy, I don't know what's wrong. I've tried to grow up— to be a good little girl, as you would say, but everywhere I turn I seem to walk deeper and deeper into some terrible despair. What's wrong, Daddy? What's wrong? Why is happiness such a precious thing? What have we done with our lives so that every- where we turn—no matter how hard we try not to—we cause other people sorrow? (LDD, p. 38)

The novel itself might be considered as a survey of the various types of families and, long before social scientists were detailing its deterioration, William Styron was exploring the theme. Most family rituals in the novel conclude with some act of violence: Peyton's birthday celebration at the country club; the Christmas dinner when Peyton returns from Sweet Briar; or the ill-fated wedding ceremony. Love, whenever it does exist, is always the ac- companiment to threatened absence, whether it be Peyton's flight from home or Milton's flight back to his wife from Dolly's arms. Physical embrace and caress occur upon arrivals and departures, but never in the ordinary course of events. Even the embrace which briefly unifies Milton and Helen after the death of the crippled Maudie occurs only in response to a new absence in their lives. There is, of course, one family which is not deteriorating into a sick bay, and that is the family over which La Ruth and Ella Swan rule. Although this family is a stereotyped black family whose father has long since departed, love and the physical touch that is always an integral part of the deepest love, flourish. Even rebuke, such as that which occurs at Peyton's wedding when one of the children spills the tiny hot dogs being used as hors d'oeuvres, is always directed physically. Children are kissed as well as struck. Peyton's neurosis fits the standard Freudian definition as some "abnormal attachment to the past," and in her last days, she carries about the alarm clock that will enable her to know of time in the present. But La Ruth has a kind of internal clock that always tells her when someone will be late for dinner or at precisely what moment to bring on the next course. Her "family" is the entourage of Daddy Faith, whose witchcraft is of the same order as that of the shrink who is the spiritual father to the group of Jewish intellectuals with whom Peyton keeps company. Both find the necessity for constructing a fictional "origin" as the substitute for an absent father.

In order to find life in this Kingdom of Death, one must reconstruct his "origins" even if he must disguise it as a fiction taken on faith. In this decaying world about to enter the September of its life, the real fathers act upon a shared faith. They touch by immersing themselves in the life of the other. Once, in her yard, Maudie meets such a playmate who does not love out of a fear of rejection. And before her death she participates in a "mysterious communion":

> Then he turned and came toward Maudie. Up went the balls again; each vanished as he caught it: his hands were empty. They stood there looking at each other, and again there seemed to be something sad and mysterious in his gaze; he was like the old magician, old artificer from another country, and his eyes were black and tender: it was as if he had many secrets and somehow knew everything there was to know: not just those dancing balls, but the earth and sky, leaves and wind and falling rain; he knew their sorcery, knew their mysteries, and knew the secret heart of this girl he'd never spoken to. Bennie. Could he talk? He never said a word. There was something in him that understood love and death, entwined forever, and the hollow space of mindlessness: he gazed at Maudie and didn't smile, only reached out his hand and made a ball come out of her ear, another from her hair. (LDD, p. 223)

Bennie is a real magician, not a transformed image in the mirror of Helen Loftis's soul. His cheeks bulge, we are told, like those of a rabbit, and clearly identify him as the real father to Maudie whose surrogate is Milton Loftis, called "bunny" by Peyton. He is a real father because, like Daddy Faith, he both plays with and protects his children. Bennie is a variant of the harlequin who graced so much of the literature of the fin de siècle and emerges in

Picasso and Miro as the Pierrot figure. Combining life and art, Bennie lives his mask rather than uses it as a disguise. And like Daddy Faith, he recognizes that "love and death" are "entwined forever," as he enters the preverbal world of the child in the same way that the black preacher participates in the phylogenetic primitivity of his flock on the banks of the stream. Both have a freedom that is associated with "play." Early in his life, Milton Loftis's father had told him of those who have freedom: *"My son, most people, whether they know it or not . . . get on through life by a sophomoric fatalism. Only poets and thieves can exercise free will, and most of them die young."* Bennie, as a magician who makes juggled balls appear and disappear without getting entangled, is a combination of poet and thief. Daddy Faith takes four hundred dollars in contributions from the black domestics who run the Loftis household, and also speaks in the stentorian tones of a black Demosthenes—perfectly balancing the occupations of poet and thief. In keeping with the dichotomy of *Lie Down in Darkness*, one is the poet of silence and the other, the poet of excess.

To recognize that love, life, and death are all inextricably related is to recognize the nature of seasonal rhythms. Amidst all of the infidelities of this novel, only the truth of the earth remains constant. Helen Loftis sees her garden as the only constant in a world where changes mystify her:

> She wished she could tell Carey how much her garden meant to her. Whenever the dreadful depression came back, she would fly toward her garden as one dying of thirst runs toward water. She'd pluck and weed and pick, and as she knelt on the cool ground she felt, she said, absolutely rooted to something firm and substantial, no longer a part of the family. (LDD, p. 21)

Lie Down in Darkness has all the trappings of one of the ancient fertility myths, with everyone asking the same question, namely what will restore fertility to the kingdom of sterility. Except for the blacks, there are no children born in this novel, nor is there the prospect of any in the Loftis line. Everyone is afraid of giving birth; even for Helen Loftis the voices of children intrude into her dreams as a nightmare. If this novel is patterned upon the structure of ancient fertility rituals, then each person must ask of his oracle a painful question. All oracles, even from the beginning of time, have given the same answer: we can restore fertility only by being reborn, and that involves a confrontation with our own death. That would take place only if the funeral cortege bringing Peyton to her final resting place would encounter the baptismal raft of Daddy Faith. But it does not, instead opting for the detour—one more example of the circuitousness that pervades the lives of wanderers and travelers in the novel. All of the trappings of the fertility myths are there, including the beggar fisherman whom Peyton meets on her last walk, trying to catch coins out of a subway grate with a string attached to a pole. But there is no renewal for these people, because they cannot imagine death and life as part of the natural order of things, as Sir Thomas Browne well knew. Nor is there any cool, lifegiving shower, save for those blacks who immerse themselves in the stream's spray. The glare that has produced a spiritual desert continues to blind and suffocate the Loftises.

Peyton's last letter to Port Warwick, which arrives just before the news of her suicide, represents one last attempt to construct an individualized history of one who has no origins. For Peyton's letter is a sort of pseudoautobiography, a last confession. And it transforms us readers into would-be psychoanalysts who must listen with sadness and nod. In a world like that of Port Warwick at the end of World War II, in the process of transformation, there is no longer a "given" history, but each person must aestheticize his own past. Nostalgia is to memory as Peyton's last letter home is to the rest of the novel. Everyone in the novel—Dolly Bonner, Helen Loftis, Milton Loftis, the Reverend Carr, and Peyton—are confessing that they have been wrong. And yet, no one has been wrong. Peyton Loftis moves from the rural countryside to the city and discovers death. Daddy Faith at the end of each summer, moves out from the city and into the countryside, imitating the journey of the Apostles in bringing life. Port Warwick is both beginning and ending for two attempts at revival. But the people there are in an interlude between summer and winter, life and death, collective history and autobiography, in this August of 1945. As the train which moves through Whitman's "When Lilacs Last in the Dooryard Bloom'd" links Lincoln's death with the spring lilacs of rebirth, so Styron's novel is an elegy for a civilization that is a season, where trains at the beginning and ending link life, death, and love in a trilogy that is bound to the love of nostalgia:

> Perhaps now, upon reflection, it was only the season that had made her unhappy: this tail end of summer, the September mid-passage when the year seems sallow and emaciated like a worn out, middle-age countrywoman pausing for breath, and all the leaves are mildly, unsatisfactorily green. Everything then is waiting, expecting, and there is something in the air that promises smoke and burning and dissolution. One's flowers bloom gaily for a little while, but September is a quick, hectic month, bearing on the air seeds for burial and making people feel tired and a little frantic, as in a station just before the train pulls out. (LDD, p. 131)

Notes

1. *The Works of Sir Thomas Browne*, ed. Geoffrey Keynes (Chicago, University of Chicago Press, 1964), 1: 167–168. In the same paragraph Browne was to write that "the number of dead long exceedeth all that shall live." The significance of the epigraph is extensive, since in his five-chapter discourse, Browne attempted to show the folly of a civilization in attempting to participate in immortality while still on earth. As a survey of the various habits and customs of burial among the peoples of the world, it is a sort of parody of the ancient "Book of the Dead."

2. "The Editor Interviews William Styron," *Modern Occasions* 1 (1971): 503–504.

3. J. Hillis Miller, *The Form of Victorian Fiction* (Notre Dame, Ind., 1968), pp. 67–68.

4. This tendency of the so-called schizoid individual to participate in these patterns of potential or real rescue is a fruitful topic for further study. In *The Savage God* A. Alvarez has posed the question in the course of examining the history of suicide. Alvarez finds that a number of suicides actually wish to be saved and construct elaborate ruses in order to effect a

rescue. Yet, he too falls into the trap when he suggests that the late Sylvia Plath really did not want to commit suicide and hence labels her death "almost accidental." In a somewhat similar way Peyton Loftis tempts the inauthenticity of others by demanding rescue or affection as a way of insuring the maintenance of a fragile self. It is a way of enforcing love, even where none exists, so that the other cannot refuse. Again, it is the equation of love and need which prompts a bond sealed by negatives and double negatives rather than genuine affection.

IRVING MALIN

The Symbolic March

The opening paragraph of *The Long March* tells us much about
the symbols, themes, and characters of the entire novelette. Styron
begins with "noon," the hottest part of the day; the heat is as intense and extreme as the events—and the reactions to these events
—he will eventually describe. (Even *noon* is intensified by the
word *blaze*.) Then Styron introduces the human element: "eight
dead boys are thrown apart among the poison ivy and the pine
needles and loblolly saplings." The contrasts are vivid—the boys
are dead, wasted, "strewn"; the noon burns with energy. Several
questions leap to mind. How do men face extinction? What is
the role of accident or design? Can death be meaningful?

We would expect Styron to give us more information about the
causes of death, but he maintains the suspense. He simply informs
us in the next sentence that the boys, only "shreds of bone, gut, and
dangling tissue," look as if they had *always* been dead. Their past
lives have disappeared. The continuity between past and present
is shattered. (This theme is one of Styron's characteristic ones.)
But we do know that the accident occurs in the early 1950s under
"a Carolina sun" as the Marines train for service during the Korean War.

The mystery continues, but we now meet Lieutenant Culver,
the "center of consciousness." He is an alert, thoughtful observer
—he, like us, will have to put the pieces into some pattern—if only
to *survive*. It is interesting that his sentence is the longest one so
far; it contains so many qualifications, so many turns of syntax,
because he does not know how to get to the heart of the situation.
He cannot act simply; he must reflect at length. Thus his "how?
why?"—which occur at midpoint in the sentence—seem to capture
his thoughts. His question is said to buzz furiously; it is as active
as the "noontime heat" which is again mentioned. Culver identifies

with the "fifteen or so surviving marines" who barely escaped death; his questions are theirs as well. His initial response to the entire scene—to the "eight dead boys" and to the survivors—is perfectly natural: he vomits. And his vomiting, like his questioning, establishes our sympathy with him.

Styron tells us more about Culver. He gives us many details which demonstrate that our guide (through the "underbrush") is both a man of action and feeling. He is not a career officer; he is, on the contrary, an ironic commentator. He has the intelligence to ask the right questions about the causes of the training accident, even though he is "pulsing" with excitement. He does not, in other words, simply react without thinking about his reactions. His age clearly demonstrates that he is "no longer an eager kid just out of Quantico with a knife between his teeth." He is a tired thirty-year-old who seems to be out of place, having been called back for service during the Korean War.

There are many images which suggest the "unreality" of the entire situation. Culver sees among the "slick nude litter of intestine and shattered blue bones" some spoons—the survivors had been eating—which peek out "like so many pathetic metal flowers." What a strange description! We don't usually expect flowers to be metallic and, of course, we don't expect them to be "pathetic." Metal, abstract emotion, and nature—the three things are thrown together. It is up to Culver to define each, or better yet, to explore what is *truly human*. The description is metaphorically precise, but it also suggests that the lieutenant is a kind of visionary. He makes "odd," poetic connections.

I want to express the visionary qualities of Culver (which, by the way, make him an even more interesting guide). We are told that before he was called back to service during the Korean crisis, he experienced an "odd distress." He was dream-ridden; he was baffled by peace. But he enjoyed one recurrent vision of Sunday strolls in the park—he saw nature then as kind and calm (in contrast to the present "noon"). When Culver remembers peacetime, he thinks of the calm city heartbeat, the "pink-cheeked" people, the "sooty white tatters" of a recent snow, and these various images contrast sharply with the explosive, fragmented, and violent scene before his eyes. And in sharp contrast to the "pathetic metal flowers," he remembers two lovely little girls "like tumbling flowers." It is significant that the first part of the novelette ends with Culver's feeling that his last day before his return to service had been an "evil" one. He had to relinquish carefully defined pleasures for the renewed uncertainty of wartime service. The last sentence stresses blurring vision—he will have to see things differently; he enters strange coasts. He is adrift.

By the end of the first part, Styron has indicated the contrasts which he will develop throughout his narrative: peace and war; thought and action; "vision" and "reality"; design and accident; humanity and nonhumanity. It is Culver's fate to see distinctions clearly and to confront, if not artistically shape, them for his future well-being.

Part two begins again with the immediate past before the explosion and this time the warning signals are emphasized: a rustling of leaves; a "*crump crump*" noise. The contrasts between the "earth-shaking sound" and the relative silence of mealtime, between almost-cosmic interruption and daily routine, are vividly suggestive. They remind us of Culver's anxiety in the midst of peacetime—war always shatters things. And when Styron introduces the unease of a "clownish" radio corporal who is said to be usually "whimsical," we feel an "added dread."

Now we meet the colonel. His name is not mentioned at first; his rank (power) is all that is important. We are surprised that he receives the news of the explosion as if it were the most "routine of messages." He cannot feel dread. Although Culver recognizes that Colonel Templeton is probably "acting," he is irritated by the neat performance. Perhaps he would like to share the colonel's calm. (His own suspense throbs "inside him like a heart-beat.") We are not told. We sense, however, the growing conflict between them.

At this point Captain Mannix is introduced. His first word is "Jesus." This is the beginning of a later symbolic identification of the captain and Christ. (When we learn that he is a dark Jew aged thirty, we are not surprised.) Mannix is outraged by the meaningless explosion, but unlike Culver, he says something. He

[124]

demands to know and to punish the agents of destruction. What will Congress do about such accidents? He seeks meaningful authority which he can understand. Thus he will be able to fight "the sons of bitches" responsible for such accidents.

The stage is set for a close view of the three men. There is tension among them because they react so differently. Culver, still the "center of consciousness," stands in awe of the others. He observes; he passively notes things. He regards Templeton ironically as a prematurely aged "ecclesiastic," but he is afraid of the man's voice "which expected to be obeyed." The colonel represents "absolute and unquestioned authority." In Freudian terms Templeton is the father as lawgiver; surely his name and the religious metaphors (like "ecclesiastic") suggest an Old Testament wrath.

Culver is "in a constant state of half amusement, half terror," not knowing how to work out his tensions. He is a weak son. (We are never informed about psychological reasons for his attitudes.) He would like to be as rebellious as Mannix, but he cannot. Thus he thinks of him not as his "sibling" or partner but as another kind of superior being. Mannix is "*man*" as rebel against authoritarian commands; he is, oddly, as mysterious as Templeton (despite all his vocal complaints.)

Culver wants to sleep—to retreat from choosing between the alternatives of Mannix and Templeton. He dreams "fitfully" of home. But sleep, peace, and home no longer exist for a marine. And when the sergeant announces a "long walk tonight," we share his anxiety and gloom. Culver is trapped, recognizing that the long march may be as explosive as the real explosion, and he resents the sergeant. He pictures him "grafted to the system as any piece of flesh surgically laid on to arm or thigh." (Culver continually thinks of the body; he is keenly aware of mortality.)

Now Culver remembers that he heard of the march the night before. There is a flashback. He recalls Mannix and Templeton acting out their psychologically determined roles. Templeton is "solitary," aloof, and amused by Mannix's hot complaints. Both men (and also Culver) seem to be puppets. Culver is "the only one in the tent who could see, at the same instant, both of their expressions. In the morbid, comfortless light they were like classical Greek masks, made of chrome or tin, reflecting an almost theatrical disharmony." These lines are important. Culver is pictured again as solitary observer; he is caught between the two men. He sees more than either one, but he cannot forcefully act. He regards himself as audience. The irony is that he is "doomed" to his role as spectator—as much as the heroes on stage. By performing their habitual roles, Templeton and Mannix are non-human masks. They have lost some sense of choice; they apparently *must* act as they do. They are made out of "chrome or tin"; they perform mechanically. This is not to say that Culver fails to admire them. Using such words as *devout* and *religious*, he tries to be ironic—to shield himself from commitment (running up on stage)—but his admiration shines through his own ironic mask: he is oddly in awe of these extreme, godlike figures.

Mannix wears a mask of rebellion. He smiles toughly; he curses, saying "Christ on a crutch!" His gestures and remarks are "exaggerated." We are not told why. Does he choose his part? Or is it an overcompensation for chores forced upon him? The questions are important, but Styron does not answer them, except to suggest that Mannix is not a "regular."

Mannix, however, makes Culver squirm. Culver can no longer regard the march as an "abstraction"; he surrenders his theoretical view of life—at least for the time being. The imagery is significant here. Again Culver is the symbolist, finding that his surroundings "had shifted, ever so imperceptibly, into another dimension of space and time." He scrutinizes things in a dreamlike, lurid light: Mannix's "shadow cast brutishly against the impermeable walls by a lantern so sinister that its raging noise had the sound of a typhoon at sea"; he is in a "dazzling, windowless box"; he is upon a "dark and compassless ocean." The emphasis is upon exaggerated, neurotic visions of immobility and, strangely, movement. Culver lies *between* his superiors, between *all* the opposites of life. He dangles.

Culver may be an abstractionist, but he is controlled by his body. Indeed, he is afraid of it—he would like to get out of it (another windowless box?) and fly away or back in time—and we can recognize that the opening explosion is also a traumatic symbol of his psychological needs. There is a subtle interaction between the external event and the internal interpretation, a field of action. It is almost possible to say that the explosion would have to be "invented" (if it had not occurred) to satisfy Culver's imagination. He courts it as a reflection of his inner being.

Culver gradually becomes less of the careful observer we had taken him to be—he is a kind of sick symbolist, unaware of his resemblance to either Mannix or Templeton. As he broods about the forthcoming march—we are still in the lengthy flashback—he hears noises; he sees things; and he discovers meaning in the wails. The radio noises seem "like the cries of souls in the anguish of hell." We have once more the religious metaphors, but we don't know how to respond precisely to them. Why does Culver see (or hear) hell? Does he *believe* in an *actual* hell? Why should he use the word? Styron has not given us enough of Culver's background to establish the religious frame of reference. We are tempted to take the earlier words as ironic. Irony has given way—to what? Despite these questions, we are moved by the curious linkage of private and cosmic symbols, especially when Culver thinks of himself in a contained "universe" of sound.

One long paragraph makes his symbolist universe especially clear. Culver thinks of the captain as a fellow symbolist. Mannix is said to be a code maker, a creator of a different kind of language from the "secret language" of the military. In this respect he destroys such words as *hero* which means different things for marine and civilian. Mannix yearns for "pure" meanings. He tries to find these in his body scars. He is down-to-earth. What is fascinating for us, if not to either man, is that although both are symbolists, one is conscious (Culver) and the other unaware of his imaginative creations (Mannix).

There is a flashback *within* the flashback. Styron insists upon the "pastness" of events; he pictures time as an ever-receding point. The marines have to cope with a never-ending (indeed, always beginning) universe which can never escape from symbolic meanings.

We meet Mannix, Culver, and Templeton five months earlier —just after the reserves have been called back. They are slaves to a "horde of cunningly designed, and therefore often treacherous machines." *Peonage, renewed bondage,* and *oppressive weather* are some descriptive words used by Styron. Mannix is, as usual, the rebel, falling asleep during orientation meetings. He irritates the lecturers, but he also "inspires" Culver. Culver is off the center stage; he sits down "during the darkness of a lantern slide." But he does not feel entirely comfortable. Styron makes much at this point of *space.* The lecture "hall" is contrasted to the "Heaven's Gate" of the officers. Culver feels trapped by both. Although he should feel at home in the latter "pleasure-dome ingeniously erected amid a tangle of alluvial swampland, and for officers only," he finds little joy in this "playground" and, of course, less joy in the dark hall. Both places—like the marines and the body itself —trap him. He would like to "burn down the place" and assert his freedom from necessity.

One incident reinforces these symbols of imprisonment. Mannix recalls a past event—notice how we move even more deeply into time; our movement is, appropriately enough, a "long march" —and we see him drunk in a hotel room in San Francisco. He emerges naked from a shower and suddenly finds himself pushed out of the window by his buddies: "Imagine being that high upside-down in space with two drunks holding onto your heels. . . . I just remember the cold wind blowing on my body and that dark, man, infinite darkness all around me." The incident is perhaps the most explosive one so far described—with the exception of the opening explosion—because it strips Mannix (and Culver, his listener) of everything. He is "less than human"; he is alone with the sense of mortality. He dangles in space; he is out of control. But there are ironies. He realizes then that he is "human" and that no other person can help him get out of his condition.

Culver does not know what to make of Mannix, the survivor; he stares at him, but he cannot completely understand him. The peaceful scene—they are near the sea—blurs before his eyes. Instead of the "promenade of waves"—so unlike the possible fall into space—he sees the "substanceless night" in which he, and all slaves, move. Blood rushes to his head.

Suddenly we are wrenched back to the "noon" of the explosion.

Culver snaps awake. (But which is the dream? The past or the present?) He is, nevertheless, unable to tell where he is. Styron writes that "time seemed to have unspooled past him in a great spiral." Finally he realizes that he is listening not to Mannix but to the sergeant. He must still go on the forced march. In the jeep with Templeton and Mannix, he closes his eyes. He fights his visionary nature, not wanting to see the "ghosts of the bereaved and the departed" or the "motions without meaning." He longs for sleep.

The scene shifts. Styron moves from Culver's closed eyes to the closed eyes of one boy killed by the explosion. They are "brothers." Perhaps Mannix senses this identification (and his own) when he says in the last words of this section: "Won't they ever let us alone?"

Part three begins at twilight "just before the beginning of the march"; the time is appropriate because Culver is very unsure of his motives. The "noon" intensity has given way to dim vision. Mannix finds a nail in his shoe. The nail is, of course, an omen of doom—it functions as an almost-Greek "curse"—but it also serves to inspire his rebellious nature. He needs this "pinpoint of torture" as a kind of muse and, consequently, he refuses to listen to Culver's common sense.

What are we to make of Mannix here? He is far from the classical hero. He courts death in a "nervous and touchy way." He is "at odds with his men, to whom he usually had shown the breeziest good will." He twitches. He is, to use Styron's phrase, a bundle of "raw nerves." (The body imagery is never omitted.) But Mannix is a modern "hero" because he accepts the absurdity of things. He laughs painfully. He goes to extremes in an already extreme situation. He obsessively defies the marine obsessions of Colonel Templeton. He considers the nail as his private symbol—of "lousy luck" and also the lust for survival.

Culver recognizes the symbolic thrust of Mannix. He also sees Templeton as symbolic. When the colonel appears "neat, almost jaunty, in new dungarees and boots," carrying a ".38 revolver," the gun becomes Templeton's "emblematic prerogative." Note the contrast between the nail and the .38. Both objects are imbued with "power" by their owners; they become unreal and huge, carrying abstract meanings. It is also interesting to consider their metallic qualities. By surrendering to their symbolic objects, the men act mechanically—like the puppets mentioned once before.

Culver cannot explain his feelings, but he emphasizes his fears. He thinks of "helpless children," puny houses of "straw," "cataleptic sleep"—the recurring symbols capture his descent into panic. Surely Culver knows that he is involved in the march; he can no longer be out of view.

The march begins. Culver stares at the colonel who pushes "ahead in front of him with absolute mechanical confidence of a wound-up, strutting tin soldier on a table top." He cannot laugh at the metallic man. He is hopelessly involved with his own body —pains. The body, which had been pictured previously as a threatening, claustrophobic container, grows in symbolic importance. It is Culver's enemy. It forces him to do things he hates; he is thirsty; he is sweaty; he is faint. By insisting upon Culver's physical pains, Styron also makes us recognize that there is no way out of the body—symbolic meanings are physically earned: "And so it was that those first hours Culver recollected as being the most harrowing of all, even though the later hours brought more subtle refinements of pain. He reasoned that this was because during the first few miles or so he was at least in rough possession of his intellect, his mind lashing his spirit as pitilessly as his body." The "lashing," the "rough possession"—such words suggest that the master-slave relationship of Templeton and his men is mirrored privately in Culver. He cannot coexist with his body—except with great struggle. Thus before the "breather," he looks at Mannix and sees a "shape, a ghost, a horror—a wild and threatful face reflected from the glass." He identifies with him in this "absurd" universe of mirrors.

When they continue the march, Culver wonders how he will last. He is a fish under the sea—falling deeply (like Mannix in the hotel?). Then he is a "ewe who follows the slaughterhouse ram." His passivity asserts itself in such symbolic details. Consequently, when he sees Mannix limping, he shares his pain, and offers some advice. The Christ words are stressed here; both officers are in a state of communion, plagued by the crucifixions of the march (stations of the cross?).

Templeton appears to smile at them. He looks "like the priest in whom passion and faith had made an ally, at last, of only the purest good intentions; above meanness or petty spite, he was leading a march to some humorless salvation." He is the false father, hiding his intentions behind "solicitous words." He hopes to grind Mannix to dust with kindness. He tells him to *ride*, not to march any more: "Nothing could have been worse."

Culver hates Templeton not as Templeton but as "the Colonel, the marine." He considers him as the very symbol of all the "crazy, capricious punishment" imposed upon him. But he dimly understands that the colonel, like Mannix, is part of his own mind. The long march is within!

The march continues and becomes "disorganized." Styron plays with such notions as "organization" and "disorganization." One is as bad as the other. The former suggests Templeton, authoritarian principles, unquestioning allegiance; the latter hints at complete chaos. Styron apparently believes that one must be "loose," ironic, and aware of patterns or, better yet, able to shape patterns flexibly without yielding to either wildness or rigidity.

In the absence of Templeton (who has gone away in a truck), Mannix goes to extremes. He will endure the march; he will transform the pattern imposed upon him into his *own. He will create order*. What black comedy! The rebel becomes the complete organization man, despite his "terrible limp."

Styron is ambivalent about Mannix and his command. He admires—or at least Culver does—the captain's "perversity" and courage, but he suggests that he acts like a robot. (We find the same kind of situation in Ahab's "mad" march toward the whale, not knowing how to distinguish between "perversity" and "heroism.") Culver, like an Ishmael, wants to say to Mannix: *"you've lost; stop"*: "Nothing could be worse than what Mannix was doing —adding to a disaster already ordained (Culver somehow sensed) the burden of his vicious fury." But he cannot vent his own rage.

Culver recognizes that he is less of a man than Mannix. He lacks the power to rebel against him (as the captain did against

Templeton); he remains passive. Once more he thinks of "crazy cinematic tape, chaos, vagrant jigsaw images." He even dreams of cubed ice in a carnival tent. The machine, the performance, the box (tent)—all imply that Culver regards himself as an actor in someone else's confined script. He is no longer the reflective spectator watching classical masks; he is at center stage.

Templeton returns and demands that Mannix ride in the truck. Culver again recognizes the symbolic structure: when men cannot agree upon symbols (or words like *heroism, courage,* and *devotion*), they must battle. He tries vainly to separate the two men (and thereby act powerfully), recognizing that they have lost their manhood in loyalty to abstractions. And yet, in a perverse way, he is as rigid as they. All of them—not merely Mannix—are distorted, painted clowns.

The last line of this section is "What the hell," [Mannix] whispered, "we've made it." It is ambiguous. *Have they made anything? Have they,* on the contrary, *been made?* And "it"? What has Mannix won—except an insane, clownlike pattern? Styron does not permit Culver to respond here. The omission is especially interesting, suggesting that there are few final solutions or victories. Each man must believe that "he has made it"—if only to go on living—but he is finally alone without any listeners or critics. He is isolated in his symbolic universe.

Part five attempts to resolve the ambiguities. Culver lies in bed, trying to sleep. (Styron uses the contrast between the march and stasis.) He closes his eyes. But he cannot join the dead boys of the explosion because he is, after all, an aware survivor.

He keeps seeing visions—of open space and commingled "sunshine and darkness." These keep him in touch with reality; they will not permit him to drift away. The visions, like Styron's symbolic details, are full of commingled opposites. When Culver looks out of the window, he notices the officers' swimming pool ("grotto-blue") and "decorous" wives. (We think of their presence in contrast to the boys' strewn bodies.) But Culver moves beyond "Heaven's Gate"; he senses the "threatful beginnings of a storm." He knows that angry thunder lurks over "peace and civilization."

Culver feels a "deep vast hunger" for some transcendental vision which will *overarch* grottolike peace and threatening storm, dead boys and "lovely little girls with their ever joyful, ever sprightly dance." The vision finally eludes him because he is caught in time. He has seen too much—or not enough. Now he knows that as an anxious man—he has not been cured by the march—he can identify with all the others who must march to satisfy their symbolic longings. His hunger dies. He must live with the "hateful contraries"—with the "somber light" *and* thunderheads, with highs *and* lows (we see a "swan-dive" and a "skyward" glance), with war *and* peace.

It is fitting that Culver's victory, as tentative as it may be, should force him to move out of his room and meet Mannix. Both men have "won" victories; they "limp" to show their wounds. (Victory for Styron implies scars.) They are able to have one "unbroken minute of sympathy and understanding"—this is how long transcendental vision lasts—before their communication is destroyed.

Culver notices the Negro maid "employed in the place." She asks Mannix: "Do it hurt?" She senses his pain (and Culver's?); she has also lived in bondage. Before he can answer she says "Deed it does" (after the two of them share one "unspoken moment of sympathy and understanding").

It is at this point that Styron uses the symbolic device: Mannix's towel falls (he is going to shower); he is "naked as the day he emerged from his mother's womb." The nakedness is, of course, a comic "accident"—as opposed to the not-very-comic accident at the beginning—but it also reinforces Styron's insistence upon human frailty (mortality): man somehow dead (or at least dead tired) and alive, "clutching for support at the wall." Finally in the last words Mannix repeats: "Deed it does."

And Culver? He does not have the final word. He will, presumably, survive this scene to create his own pattern of meaning, to perform his solitary deeds. He will march again.

ROBERT PHILLIPS

Mask and Symbol in
Set This House on Fire

"We'll bring back tragedy to the land of the Pepsi-cola and the peanut brittle and the Modess," Cass Kinsolving, the hero of William Styron's third novel, proclaims in a speech which could be said to reveal the author's intentions as well. Certain critics have enjoyed the exercise of comparing Styron's works to classical Greek tragedy. Indeed in *Set This House on Fire* Styron appears to encourage such comparison. In one scene Cass is shown reading *Oedipus at Colonus* (a book he frequently quotes from within the novel, professing to be "as blind-drunk off of Oedipus as I was off of booze") in a cafe on the Boulevard Saint-Germain, and Styron skillfully contrasts Cass's cultured and civilized mentality with that of the gross American tourists at an adjacent table: "He was hemmed round by a sea of camera lenses and sport shirts; the noise of his compatriots assailed his ears like the fractious harangue of starlings on a fence." In this scene at least Styron intends to pit the nobility of Greek drama against the crassness which can turn even Paris into a Howard Johnson's.

While it is tempting to inflict a generic tragic interpretation upon the novel, such a reading strikes me as no more valid than some of the psychological, allegorical, and analogical interpretations which I shall also discuss before proceeding to my own. For Cass Kinsolving is surely no tragic hero. An artist of modest achievement, in his lifetime he has assumed no heights from which to fall. If he has a fatal flaw it is his solipsism, which leads him finally to the conclusion that hell is not giving of oneself. Yet his final encounter with the ultimate selfish man, Mason Flagg, ends in a murder which is more melodrama than a drama to inspire pity or fear. If there is a potential Oedipus figure in the novel, in fact, it is Flagg, who at least spiritually kills his father and loves his mother ("Wendy-dear"). Flagg is a possibly acknowledged bisexual, all of whose women seem to resemble his mother.

Yet Mason Flagg is not the hero of this novel. Cass Kinsolving is, and an Oedipal reading of the book is unsatisfactory. There is, incidentally, just as much "evidence" to support an allegorical reading based on Homer's *Odyssey*—with Luciano, the one-eyed menace and the threat who almost prevents Cass's/Odyseus's passage serving as Polyphemus (the Cyclops); and Saverio as one of the swine from the Island of Circe, described by Styron as a "ragged figure that approached us with a husky snuffling noise —a series of rich, porcine grunts." Later in the novel the narrator, Peter Leverett, calls Flagg "a swine" as well, and at one point Americans are called swine.

A third possible approach is to compare the novel with Malcolm Lowry's *Under the Volcano* (1947), which it resembles in an uncanny number of ways. Both novels pit an alcoholic protagonist against a Dantesque universe; the action of both focuses ostensibly on the events of one fatal day; the settings of both are exotic, foreign lands to emphasize the hero's alienation; and, most important, the common theme of the fall of man shared by both novelists is depicted in intensity and with the grandeur of a Melville or a Faulkner. Both Lowry's Consul and Styron's Cass are potentially tragic figures isolated in their own hells.

Such readings are fascinating, but seem to me to distort Styron's meaning beyond the intention of the novel's dream. To discover such parallels is to champion a preconceived notion at the expense of its subject, to be genre-ridden or (in the narrowest sense) idea-ridden, to move through the novel arbitrarily rather than letting the work's form and texture dictate its own discussion. *Set This House on Fire* does not seem such a willful work. Rather, it purposefully lacks sequence and order, like our own memories and dreams. The novel is so rewarding because there are many levels of meaning attributed to many acts and symbols, rather than a strict adherence to one- or two-leveled meanings.

What I hope to achieve, instead, is to follow Cass Kinsolving's observation on his own dreams: "What you've got to do is get behind the mask and symbol." For I maintain that to weave his rich tapestry, Styron has consciously or unconsciously drawn upon threads of many ageless myths and works of the imagination. Because his allusions and parallels are drawn from such a range of literature and experience, for the critic to insist upon one specific interpretation is to shortchange the author and the reader.

Before examining these masks, these symbols, let us begin with a statement of what the novel seems to be "about," and then examine the materials which support such a meaning.

Essentially *Set This House on Fire* is one man's search for inner freedom and his regeneration. When Cass Kinsolving takes his family to the Amalfi coast, he hates himself as much as he hates the America he has fled. (Of anti-American invective in the novel one could compile a small anthology; such invective perhaps reaches its apogee in the description of the United States as "an ashheap of ignorance and sordid crappy materialism and ugliness!") This hatred is primarily focused against what American public life does to man's private life—and Cass being an artist feels the invasion of private life more keenly than most.

After seesawing between the alternatives of living or dying, Cass redeems himself through two acts—personal sacrifice in attempting to save the dying peasant Michele's life and personal regeneration in succeeding in taking the life of the degenerate Mason Flagg. Cass's personal hell has been caused by his own self-centeredness. In risking his own health to save that of Michele, he finally gives of himself and propitiates a guilt of many years' standing, dating back to his southern boyhood when he unwillingly helped a companion destroy the contents of a poor Negro's cabin—a supposed test of Cass's manhood which he at first "failed" by protesting, then later "passed" by saving face and helping destroy the humble home. He feels he has been running roughshod over the lives of others ever since. Michele dies, however, and Cass must assume more guilt in feeling the man did not live because he himself did not give enough. The man's death is felt just as if one of Cass's children had died, and when Cass hears of it he echoes Macduff's speech, "All, then? *All?*" In failing to save

Michele, the attempt at salvation being Cass's one "creative" act for some months, Cass again experiences a failure of spirituality within himself. Yet the attempt to save the peasant was an act of life, not of death, and in doing so he directly defied the degenerate Flagg.

That guilt is minimal when compared to the burden Cass ultimately comes to feel over his unpunished murder of Flagg: "I've enough guilt about it to equip a regiment of Sumner's." Because the murder, allegedly in retribution for Flagg's rape of Michele's daughter, Francesca, in reality is a rationalization, a violent act intended to exorcise Cass's own evil. And when the police officer Luigi conceals Cass's crime from authorities, he robs the artist of the luxury of paying for it behind bars. ("You are a damnable romantic from the north," Luigi explains. "In jail you would wallow in your guilt.") Cass must instead accept the heavy burdens of freedom.

Cass's regeneration dates from this murder of his degenerate friend. It is a two-pronged salvation. In killing Flagg he has, first, struck a blow in defense of human dignity, which Flagg had violated in many ways: making Cass get down on all fours and perform like a seal is Flagg's symbolic mode of reducing man to the animal level, just as forcing Cass to paint pornography is an overt debasement of art. In the end Cass's commitment to humanity is greater than that to art; he steals pills from Flagg to save Michele, but it had never before occurred to him to steal back the pornographic painting till the search for the pills brings him inside Flagg's quarters. There is a paradox here. Cass has to remain tied to Mason in order to gain the financial means to save Michele and thereby free himself through achieving a state of selflessness. There is an additional irony in that the medicine which saves Michele is a product of and made possible by the American affluence Cass so disdains. More than even this, when Cass destroys Flagg's hold over him (achieved only by destroying Flagg), he attains the final triumph over self, which we know from one of Cass's Sambuco dreams "is to triumph over Death. It is to triumph over that beast which one's self interposes between one's soul and one's God."

[137]

The power of Flagg's hold over Cass cannot be overestimated. It is insidious and possibly homosexual in basis. (The Italian sergeant, Parrinello, makes a meaningful mispronunciation when he calls Flagg "Flogg.") Flagg is, as an individual, so totally unfulfilled that his only release can be achieved through violence, specifically the rape of Francesca. And since the peasant girl is Cass's beloved, Flagg in essence is raping Cass, either because he unconsciously wishes to do so through lust, or through revenge, since Cass is a true artist-figure and Flagg a mere pretender, a playwright who never wrote a play.

With Flagg eliminated, Cass's regeneration can be complete, and he returns to the America from which he had been alienated. In a way. In another way, the America to which he returns—the rural Carolinas—is the country of his childhood and not the noisy vulgar industrial nation he so despises. This leads to our first examination of Styron's use of names in the novel, the masks behind which his characters enact their roles. I suggest that when Cass strikes out against Flagg, he is also striking against the flag—the American flag. Early in the novel Styron gives us his epitome of American vulgarity, the so-called "palatial villa of Emilio Narduzzo of West Englewood, N.J., USA," which he describes as "a structure the size and shape of an Esso station", and which is "flaunting at its proud turreted roof half a dozen American flags." The flag here is a debased object, and Mason Flagg is a debasement of the American Dream. He is the man who apparently has everything—looks, money, women—and he is detestable. He is the embodiment of what Cass late in the novel calls

> the man I had come to Europe to escape, the man in all those car advertisements—you know, the young guy waving there—he looks so beautiful and educated and everything, and he's got it *made*, Penn State and a blonde there, and a smile as big as a billboard. And he's *going* places. I mean electronics. Politics. What they call communications. Advertising. Saleshood. Outer space. God only knows. And he's as ignorant as an Albanian peasant. (SHF, p. 392)

(It is one of Styron's ironies that, while Cass so detests the capitalist system as being dishonest, he depends upon his wife's trust fund for living.)

Mason's first name also carries symbolic value. He lived north of the Mason-Dixon line. To Cass, who is a southerner and returned from Europe to become a southerner again, Mason Flagg is the paradigm of the slick Yankee who embodies even more of the crass characteristics of the modern America he so despises.

Cass Kinsolving's revolt, then, is against the American way of life, which is no way of life for an artist. (For "artist" read any sensitive soul.) Cass's failure as a painter and as an individual are intended to be emblematic of the artist's failure in our society today. Read in such a manner, *Set This House on Fire* is totally consistent with Styron's central theme: that of the individual's revolt and outrage against the system.

The theme was first posited in *Lie Down in Darkness* in which the family was the institution against which the protagonist, Peyton Loftis, rebels. The theme was more overtly explored in *The Long March*. Here the military displaces the family as an odious system. Captain Mannix (representing Man) leads a protest against Templeton (the Temple, the Authority) and the latter's order of a thirty-six-mile forced march. Rather than dropping out of the system, as did Peyton in fleeing to New York and Cass by wandering across Europe, Mannix registers protest within the confines of the system. That is, he defies Templeton's expectations by having his men complete the long march. Mannix's injured foot is an outward and visible sign of his inner difference, his individuality, which in Cass the artist remains unseen. There is something to be said for Mannix's method of confronting the enemy head on. In fleeing, both Peyton and Cass seem not only to drop out of the system, but out of the human race as well. *The Confessions of Nat Turner* is of course Styron's most violent and outrageous dramatization of one individual's revolt.

There is a microcosm of the American macrocosm in each of these novels: the country club in *Lie Down in Darkness;* the officer's club in *The Long March;* the commissary in *Set This House on Fire;* and the plantation house in *Nat Turner*. These are all places in which false values are perpetuated (though some positive values are expressed and enacted at the Turner house, such as Samuel Turner's arguing against slavery, and Nat's being taught to read). Indeed, Flagg's endless trips to the commissary for steaks and whiskey function much as does Jay Gatsby's prideful display of his beautiful shirts in Fitzgerald's novel. Milton Loftis is as much a weak and self-indulgent American as Mason Flagg, however; both are men to be fled from. Both, pointedly, are alcoholics. Their excessive drinking is a manifestation of the American death wish. Cass Kinsolving's theory is that Americans drink so much because "drinking drowns the guilt over having more money than anybody in the world." Mannix's soldiers spending days uselessly chasing imaginary enemies also becomes a symbolic act for the way the majority of our countrymen waste their days pursuing an illusive American dream, whoring after false gods.[1]

Violation of the individual by the demands of institutions, then, is the heart of Styron's theme. Each of his books is a plea for man's dignity and individuality, a protest against the gradual deadening of conscience and sensibility to humane values for which we should all feel guilty. A good message for Americans to hear, in view of memorable official United States proclamations over the late Vietnam war: such as "In order to save the village we had to destroy it." Not that Styron had any particular political message to impart here; in his themes he manages to imagine deeply enough into human—and thereby national—characteristics that the subsequent manifestations of these ring true and strike a universal note. This universal theme of a national guilt is not restricted to recent events in *Set This House on Fire:* the narrator's father comprehends the enormity of our national guilt over slavery and ecological abuse. Peter Leverett himself evidences guilt over the Second World War ("I'm sorry, lady . . . I didn't bomb your home.")

Nor is it an accident that Cass's last name is Kinsolving. On one level the name is the same as that of a famous patrician family of American Episcopal clergy, and thereby evokes spirituality. But more important, Styron implies that it is through reaching out to our kin—our fellow human beings—that we can solve our own problems. This is the very lesson Cass learns so late in life, and Michele's physical illness is but a parallel to Cass's spiritual one. Cass comes to perceive that if the one could be saved, both could. To save Michele through giving of himself would be his own salvation, through earned self-respect and faith. (Styron emphasizes that Michele is not much older than Cass; they are brothers in the flesh.)

One final word on Cass's name: several times in the novel Flagg calls him "Cassius." This is exactly the kind of pseudointellectual word play Styron's Flagg would relish. But, like so much else in the novel, it too may have its irony. The Cassius of Shakespeare's *Julius Caesar* was the instigator of a conspiracy which ended in the death of a powerful dictator. It is easy to comprehend Flagg as a Caesar, Cass as Cassius, and the narrator Peter Leverett as Brutus. For several brief scenes, these are the masks the trio wears.

If the names Mason Flagg and Cass Kinsolving are so redolent with meaning, what of the symbolic implications of the others? I submit that Michele, the peasant gallantly dying, is a Saint Michael figure, one who must fight his personal dragon, tuberculosis. His daughter, Francesca Ricci, is possibly named after Francesca da Rimini, another unhappy and guilty Italian beloved. The family name of Ricci is cruelly ironic in view of Michele and Francesca's extreme poverty.

In contrast to the virginal Francesca is Vernelle Satterfield, a voluptuous figure from Cass's past who was quite literally vernal: springlike, youthfully fresh, and amazingly fecund and sexual. Fausto Windgasser's last name is farcical, his first classical, invoking the magus who sought worldly knowledge without help from God and who eventually sold his soul to the Devil. Of Styron's Faust, a hotel proprietor who thinks of nothing but revenue from the tourist trade, it is said, "on doomsday that guy will be scalping tickets for seats front and center, including his own." Fausto indeed. He is one of Styron's most pointedly archetypal characters.

Peter Leverett, the narrator, is a "square" who is repeatedly and significantly mistaken for a Levitt of the Levittown dynasty. Poppy, Cass's wife, is perhaps named for the associations of the flower by that name, which is said to be symbolic of consolation.[2] Then there is Luciano di Lieto, the indomitable victim, named not so much for Lucian, the second-century Greek satirist and wit, as Lucian, the chief character in *The Golden Ass* of Apuleius. In that early work Lucian is changed into an ass as a personification of the follies and vices of the age. Styron's Luciano has a similar function. His life is a triumph over blunders, and, as the director of nursing care says of him: "He will live to bury us all." Despite losing fingers and an eye, despite his streetcar and automobile accidents, his is the persistence of survival. He is like John Crowe Ransom's much beset Captain Carpenter and Lemuel Pitkin, the hero of Nathanael West's *A Cool Million*, both of whom are also disassembled in their daily contacts with what passes for reality. Luciano presents a near-comic spectacle of "the house" on fire: the human body plagued. After colliding with Cass, he is a mock *pieta* in the roadway, "flat on his back, asprawl in sacrificial repose . . . with his tangled sweet look of liberation and racking ecstasy." Like Styron's Ella Swan (the Loftis's black maid in *Lie Down in Darkness*), Luciano will prevail because he endures.

Finally, Styron peoples his novel with a cast of caricatures of recognizable American figures who have become types. Most notable are Burnsey, the tough-guy Hollywood actor (a ringer for "Bogey"), and the Reverend Dr. Ervin Franklin *Bell*, "the exemplary, prolific and optimistic Protestant clergyman" who is surely intended as a hit at Norman Vincent *Peale* and the demise of true spirituality. While these two caricatures further the novel's theme of degeneration, their presence somewhat jangles in the otherwise intense cast of characters. The scenes devoted to the Reverend Dr. Bell seem to be embarrassingly gratuitous flights of humor, and disturb, despite thematic relevance, the novel's tone.

The narrator encounters all these extraordinary people wearing masks from classical and contemporary mythologies. The mixed nature of their roles and symbolic intentions of their names deliberately add to the dreamlike quality of Sambuco, much in the way Tennessee Williams's mixed gathering of great romantics from all history—Casanova, Lord Byron, Don Quixote, even America's Kilroy—populate his drama enacted somewhere at earth's end, *Camino Real*. It is almost as if Leverett and Cass Kinsolving were projected into Hades and encountered there all the lost souls of the ages. Leverett's initial quest for knowledge of Flagg switches to a quest for knowledge of Cass, whom he originally saw as just another of Flagg's hangers-on, but whom he eventually comprehends, through his care of Michele, to be "this tormented, sad, extraordinary character." Cass's is the torment of hell on earth.

So much for personae. Styron gives Cass's torment symbolic dimension in several ways. The first is through the use of "psychescapes," interior and exterior landscapes as perceived by Cass in his confused and sickened state. A good example of the psychescape is Cass's encounter with "the sun, pitched close to its summit, [riding] like a heat-crazed van Gogh flower, infernal, wild, on the verge of explosion." Here we not only see the sun (flower) in the distorted way of Cass's hallucinating imagination, but we make a connection between him and the mind which first made such a sun tangible, the mad van Gogh. Elsewhere in the novel, the piazza of the town is said to be captured in "a dazzling noose of sunlight"—the noose shape summoning the menace everywhere attendant in Sambuco. Many of Styron's psychescapes are more subtle, as in the description of the "kind of shimmering jade light" which pervades Cass's Paris apartment. Symbolically, jade generally corresponds not only to the masculine yang principle, but to the dry element as well.[3] Paris was Cass's driest, most unproductive period. There is another paradox here: the more Cass drank, the drier he became.

The central symbol of the novel is that of the swallow which is trapped inside the palace, that bird "which swooped down among the fluted columns, then upward, and still beat its wings against the skylight in flight toward the inaccessible sun." This is, of course, a symbol for Cass's struggle to rise above the spiritual abyss into which he has fallen. Hindu tradition has it that birds represent the higher states of being, and folklore the world over generally interprets a bird as symbolic of the soul. (A more recent novel, *The Optimist's Daughter* by Styron's fellow southerner Eudora Welty, makes very similar symbolic use of a bird trapped inside a house.)

It is significant that Styron's bird flails upward in rooms where there is a frieze of "dingy nymphs," a contrast between Cass's hoped-for spirituality and Flagg's carnality, which must be transcended. The swallow, specifically, was a bird sacred to both Isis and to Venus, and served as an allegorical figure for spring (or rebirth). This swallow (Cass) must escape Flagg's palace for such a rebirth to occur. Late in the novel the imprisoned bird is still seeking freedom, only less frantically. Like Cass, it has been worn down. But still it tries to escape through "the moonlit fleur-de-lis of glass." The shape of the window is also suggestive. As an emblem, the base of any fleur-de-lis is an inverted triangle, representing water; above it is a cross (expressing conjunctions and spiritual achievement), with two additional and symmetrical leaves wrapped around the horizontal arm. The central arm is straight and reaches heavenward.[4] The symbolism is self-evident: an emblem of salvation, of illumination, and indeed of the Lord. Later yet in the book, the poor bird is still fluttering. But when Cass fights Flagg, "one single pigeon shot toward them, then veered aslant in fright with the faintest snapping of its wings." The struggling swallow is displaced by the descending dove, a benediction of the Holy Spirit. Release is at last achieved.

Other cohering symbols in the text include the figure of the tomcat with a mouse trapped between its paws (the mouse being at once both Cass and Francesca, whom Flagg has captured), and Poppy's symbolic act of donning a rain slicker indoors when it is not raining: an act which underscores her basic insecurity and need for protection. (Styron here echoes, perhaps purposefully, Temple Drake and her raincoat in *Sanctuary;* though both authors probably go back to Joyce's *The Dead.*) Another symbolic act is the death of Ursula, Poppy's Flemish-speaking parrot, which functions as a bad omen for Cass, as did the accident with Luciano for Leverett. The death of the bird is another death of the soul, like the trapped swallow. But why name the bird Ursula? And why have her die on the voyage to Sambuco? Of course, a part of Cass did die in Sambuco. But it is also perhaps not coincidental that in legend Saint Ursula was a Cornish princess, the course of whose voyage (and life) was utterly changed when shifted by adverse winds. She and her companions (and Cass traveled with family) were finally driven to Cologne, where they were destroyed by the Huns. As an omen, this legend is singularly appropriate. Instead of being undone at the hands of Huns, they meet their fate through an arch-representative of the "smart-Alex, soft-headed, baby-faced, predigested, cellophane-wrapped, doomed, beauty-hating, land."

To the catalog of masks, symbols, and symbolic acts which give meaning and dimension to this novel, one must add the many dreams which Cass and Cripps endure. As products of a character's fantasy—a mental process differing from that which supposedly governs their conscious thinking and behavior—they contain keys to their inner world. Yet I must state at the outset that I find the dream sequences to be one of the novel's failures. The dreams of Styron's characters seem all too literal, too much just another symbolic version of what already has been seen before. The Hollywood figure, Cripps, for instance, is said to dream that "a golf pro and a crooner and a drum majorette are all contesting for my soul." Cass's dreams are also too direct a transposition of his life's problems, as in the dream in which the face on a Polaroid portrait of a friend has been replaced by that of a monster. Of course Mason Flagg is a monster, a man who "would have sympathized with cancer if he thought it was à la mode." But this outward manifestation of his inner terribleness seems almost too facile. Flagg is more complex than that, and Styron is more to the point when he has the narrator, in full consciousness, declare:

> All the time I spent with Mason, I felt I never knew him, never could put my hands on him. He was like a gorgeous silver fish in a still pond: make a grab for him, and he has slithered away, and there you are with a handful of water. But maybe that was just the thing about him, you see? He was like mercury. Smoke. Wind. It was as if he was hardly a man at all, but a creature from a different race. (SHF, p. 446)

Three dreams are worth examining. The first is Cass's repeated fantasy of the three struggling old women in rags. These could be Styron's representation of the Moirae (called the Parcae in Roman mythology), the three Fates (Clotho, Lachesis, and

Atropos) with their spindles becoming sticks in Cass's dream. They are the traditional allegorical divinities for man's fate, and as Cass dreams of the wood-bearing women struggling and suffering, he sees before him the slow march of his own lot. Cass also dreams of beaten dogs, particularly of one whose body has been crushed yet whose head, miraculously, survives. In simplest terms this separation of body from head seems symbolic either of the split between the carnal and the spiritual which exists in Cass, or of his lack of feeling for others, which is not corrected till he begins to care for Michele. But Plato, in *Timaeus*, posited the thesis that "the human head is the image of the world." Thus, this graphic separation could also embody Cass as the body which has been crushed, with the surviving head being the reality which goes on without him, a symbolic alienation. (One is reminded of all the threats of decapitation in that masterpiece of alienation, Lewis Carroll's *Alice in Wonderland*.) Eventually the dream of the suffering dog and that of the downtrodden women with the sticks become one in Cass's mind. Then the dog being beaten by a pitying but incompetent doctor becomes an allegory for us mortals in the hands of God: "He is *beating* us, yet *mercifully*."

The third and less literal dream is that of Cass taking a shower in a stall in which giant spiders feast on struggling insects. This destructive act is related to the universal significance of spiders as symbols of the world of phenomena.[5] This significance, as explained by Marius Schneider, views spiders in their ceaseless killing and weaving, destroying and building, as symbolizing the endless alternation of forces on which the stability of the universe depends—and ultimately signifies the continuous sacrifice of man throughout his life. Cass sees himself as such a sacrifice, and Styron's vision is not unlike that of Ingmar Bergman's film *Through a Glass Darkly*, in which God is perceived as a giant spider. When Cass later suffers the DT's, it is a spider vision he sees.

One final device employed by Styron to add dimension to his novel is that of alternating narration (which in itself alternates between that of Leverett and Cass, between time present and time past) with Leverett's letters and quotations from Cass's journal. In the latter, Styron makes use of free association. A good example occurs in the entry in which Cass reports his son Timmy has just been bitten by a crab. Later in the same entry Cass writes: "I should have been brought up North in N.Y. suburbs Scarsdale or somewhere on that order, where I might never have learned the quality of desire or yearnings & would have ended up on Madison Avenue designing deodorant jars." For Cass, the pure artist, this is a vision of a very low estate to which one can sink. Is it, I wonder, all brought on by thoughts of Timmy's crab, a low creature, which leads to echoes of J. Alfred Prufrock's "I should have been a pair of ragged claws," which leads directly into Cass's "I should have been brought up North" and all that follows? This seems to reinforce our belief that Cass, and Styron, equate the North with insensitivity to true values. It is a possible free association. Styron echoes e. e. cummings earlier in the novel, stating Leverett's father "moved through dooms of love."

Poetic borrowings such as these, coupled with Styron's own considerable rhetorical gifts, sustain an emotional pitch seldom encountered in a novel of such length. Only occasionally does Styron flag (and the pun is intended), as when he persists in polysyllables such as *murmuration* instead of using the shorter *murmur*. Styron also allows his character Luigi to pontificate at excessive length about such good things as how "true justice must always somehow live in the heart," and how "this existence itself is an imprisonment." The points have been made long before.

The virtues of course outweigh the faults, and *Set This House on Fire* must be seen as a curiously neglected novel, one which was remaindered in hardback during its first year of publication and which has not, I take it, found a great following since. This is all the more curious because superficially read it could make a claim for popularity greater than the best-selling *The Confessions of Nat Turner:* for it is (nearly) a novel as mystery story. Constructed similarly to *Lie Down in Darkness*, it begins with a death the result of violence, then proceeds to present a slow unraveling of the events leading up to that death. By mystery story, of course, I am not implying the cheap thriller, or even the not-so-cheap thrillers of Ross Macdonald, Raymond Chandler, or Dashiell Hammet. Styron's is, unlike many others, a serious American literary novel with murder at the core. (One thinks also of Dreiser's *An American Tragedy* and Mailer's *An American Dream* and there the list seems to end.) Styron's use of murder, if it resembles anyone's, is like Dostoevski's—murder employed ritualistically as well as symbolically. And while early in this essay I rejected comparisons with Sophocles or Homer or even Malcolm Lowry, I will invoke Dostoevski.

For like Raskolnikov in *Crime and Punishment*, Cass Kinsolving is not morally hopeless, but merely tormented by his search for an object equal to his endless rationalistic striving, for some meaning to the world equal to his ceaseless tormented life of thought. Cass, like Raskolnikov, can have hope for the future, but only after repentance. Styron and Dostoevski alike share great sympathy for the poor and the defeated. (Some of Styron's best writing anywhere are the descriptions of the contents and smells of the Negro cabin and Michele's house, both in this novel.) Both writers are skillful in portraying abnormal states, and both write dramatic dialogues and passages of intensest introspection. Yet the quality Styron most shares with Dostoevski is his commitment to the novel of moral responsibility. Published in a decade when the heroes of so many novels were antiheroes—perverts and pushers, cowards and cads—Styron's book deserves comparison with that of a great writer if for no other reason than that he attempts something greater than most of his contemporaries.

Art, according to Thomas Mann, is the fusion of suffering and the desire for form. More than in the works of Updike, Capote, or Barth, for instance, Styron assimilates human responsibility and moral suffering, and gives them shape we can recognize. While he has not yet accomplished a *Crime and Punishment*, through his fusion of mask, symbol, and dream into a theme of great suffering, Styron does achieve in *Set This House on Fire* high art. Cass Kinsolving's choice of being as opposed to nothingness, "not for the sake of being, or even the love of being much less the desire to be forever—but in the hope of being what I could be for a time," is a message for the decades.

Notes

1. For this and other observations I am indebted to Louise Y. Gossett's admirable chapter on Styron in *Violence in Recent Southern Fiction* (Durham, N.C., 1965), pp. 117–130.

2. See *The Language of Flowers* by "F. W. L." (London, 1968), p. 22.

3. J. E. Cirlot, *Dictionary of Symbols* (London, 1962), pp. 153–154.

4. Oswald Wirth, *Le tarot des imagiers du moyen age* (Paris, 1927), as quoted in Cirlot, *Dictionary of Symbols*, p. 103.

5. Marius Schneider, *La danza de espadas y la tarentela* (Barcelona, 1948), as quoted in Cirlot, *Dictionary of Symbols*, pp. 289–290.

GEORGE CORE

The Confessions of Nat Turner
and the Burden of the Past

> We all have our simplifying image, our genius, and such hard
> burden does it lay upon us that, but for the praise of others, we
> would deride it and hunt it away—W. B. Yeats, *The Trembling
> of the Veil*.

The southern novelist must often awake, during the darkest hour
of the night, in a roil of tangled bedclothes and cold sweat. He is
haunted by a recurring nightmare—that he will be called *southern*
by his critics and that his work will be defined as gothic and grotesque—or that, worse still, the same fiction will be deemed a historical novel. In this nightmare the ghost of Sir Walter Scott presides, the shade of William Gilmore Simms lingers nearby, and
Edgar Allan Poe's apparition laughs knowingly in the wings.

There is a long foreground to modern southern fiction, a foreground dense with folklore, myth, and history which twentieth-
century novelists have not hesitated to seize upon; yet at the same
time they have shrunk from being styled historical novelists as if
admittedly using the form were the mark of Cain. Both Allen Tate
and Andrew Lytle have gone to incredible lengths to deny that
they or any other serious southern artists have written historical
fiction: indeed Tate has said that *Gone With the Wind* is a historical novel and that *None Shall Look Back*, *The Old Order*, and
The Velvet Horn are fiction as history, while Lytle has defined the
historical novel as costume romance.

Part of this aversion no doubt dates from the inevitable and violent reaction to Walter Scott after his great popularity in the South.
Everyone remembers Mark Twain's famous indictment of Scott
in part 2 of *Life on the Mississippi:*

The South has not yet recovered from the debilitating influence
of his books. . . . Sir Walter had so large a hand in making Southern character, as it existed before the war, that he is in great
measure responsible for the war.

If this particular diatribe has escaped the memory, then I will
recall for you the famous steamboat in *Huckleberry Finn*, a nest-
ing place of thieves and murderers, which is named the *Walter
Scott*; and when we last hear of the vessel it is rapidly heading
downstream to certain destruction.

I am not here to praise or to bury Walter Scott, but I will say
that although his example as novelist has been unfortunate in
its effects, at least to the extent it has been followed by *American*
imitators, Scott is a fine novelist, finer by far on the whole than
Mark Twain. But we can readily sympathize, I think, with the
novelists who have wanted to get out from Scott's long shadow,
for they have seen his effect on the nineteenth-century novel. It
has been persuasively argued that southern novelists today are
trying to get out from under Faulkner; in times past they have
attempted to move away from Scott's hegemony and the aura of
Simms, Cooke, and Page.

The modern southern novelist has then adopted a defensive posture about the historical novel, having forgotten for the moment
that a Russian count by the name of Tolstoy wrote a perfectly re
spectable historical novel entitled *War and Peace*. When a southern writer thinks of historical novels, he calls to mind Walter
Edmonds, Kenneth Roberts, C. S. Forester (whom freshmen invariably think is E. M. Forster's famous brother), John Masters,
and, especially, Margaret Mitchell. This habit of mind is by no
means limited to the South: when Richard Hughes's *The Fox in
the Attic* was published five or six years ago it was obvious most
reviewers do not know a historical novel from an etiquette book.
More recently Wilfrid Sheed has said that no historical novelist
has ever done more than put his own experience into fancy dress
and see how it works. The wonder is that the serious writer, in or
out of the South, continues to create historical fiction.

Which brings me to the case of William Styron—after a long

and circumlocutory introduction, for my allusion to Sheed is taken from his review of *The Confessions of Nat Turner*, a novel Mr. Styron has called a meditation on history. Although it can technically be called that, I will say flatly that Nat Turner's story, as Styron presents it, is a historical novel. Now the misunderstanding of the historical novel is one reason for the furore which has surrounded this book within the last year or so—and especially after the release of a rebuttal by ten Negro writers. The most unfriendly critics have said, often and vociferously, that Styron's novel is neither historically accurate in its general outline, that is to say in its depiction of Virginia society and chattel slavery in the early 1800s—nor in its specific instance of Nat Turner as embodiment of a shadowy historical character. These reviewers believe that although Nat has a black skin, he has a white heart—and that he is a straw man set up by William Styron in a new but ultimately transparent defense of the Old South. For these critics the novel is therefore a racist tract, a spurious piece of propaganda, meretricious in its original promise.

If there is any way to isolate the fire of racial unpleasantness from the brimstone of other controversial matters (and I doubt this), I would say that much of the real grounds for argument resides in the old misconception of the differences between fiction and history, a distinction Aristotle drew sharply some twenty-three hundred years ago: "the one describes the thing that has been, and the other a kind of thing that might be." Sir Philip Sidney agreed with Aristotle that poetry is "something more philosophic and of graver import than history, since its statements are of the nature rather of universals, whereas those of history are singulars." As Sidney put it, the historian is "captived to the truth of a foolish world." Yet fiction and history have much in common, and Macaulay felicitously expressed one aspect of this connection: "history begins in novel and ends in essay." One might respond to Richard Gilman by quoting Macaulay. Gilman recently said, in a review of *Nat Turner*, that "literature, as literature, has nothing to do with history, other than being able to draw upon it as it is free to draw upon anything." Robert Penn Warren has observed that the historian and the fictionist are both dealing with imagined worlds, but that the historian wants the facts about and behind that world while the writer must know the inside of his world. Here history and fiction meet on the same ground, in a complementary, invariable kinship, far from the relation Gilman posits.

In *The Confessions of Nat Turner* William Styron is primarily concerned about depicting his characters fictively, from within—against a setting which must be at once historical and contemporaneous. Styron brings to life both the larger, encompassing action (Tidewater Virginia in the early nineteenth century) and the main action—the conflict of Nat Turner and the society of which he is a part. The conflict is characteristic of the historical novel, in that the action represents the collision of two worlds, the one dying, the other struggling to be born. (One might argue, with some justification, that the old world is today still in the agony of labor.) Nat as protagonist carries the seeds of this struggle within: it is reflected time and again in his innermost feelings, attitudes, and thoughts as well as his outward behavior. Indeed the very tensions within Nat—the discrepancy between what he believes and what he is forced to do—are representative of his society.

Whatever else may be said for and against the novel it must be granted, I think, that the enveloping action is beautifully rendered. By this I mean the whole ambiance of the setting as Styron re-creates it for the reader through Nat is believable and moving. C. Vann Woodward has said that the novel "is informed by a respect for history, a sure feeling for the period, and a deep and precise sense of place and time." Even unfriendly critics have admitted this. Sheed, for instance, has said: "But if the book fails by default, as a novel, it does succeed in many places as a kind of historical tone poem. Styron's version of the old South is . . . place freshly imagined stone by stone." Quotations from the novel will not easily demonstrate this aspect: it is better to examine a representative scene and see what it will yield. The scene I choose is the visit at Turner's Mill by "a pair of traveling Episcopal clergymen—'the Bishop's visitants.'" The bishop is "awaiting some *providential wind* to guide us in the right direction," the priests intone solemnly. The providential wind must come from "the more *prosperous* landowners of the diocese," whom these unctuous

henchmen have been detailed to poll. The ensuing conversation between Samuel Turner, his alcoholic brother Benjamin, and the
priests throws the period attitudes toward slavery into a harsh,
clear light: Samuel Turner's sane voice—slavery "is a cancer eating at our bowels, the source of all our misery, individual, political, and economic. It is the greatest curse a supposedly free and
enlightened society has been saddled with in modern times, or any
other time"—is drowned out by his brother's drunken, hilarious,
and contemptible dogmatics: "A darky, gentlemen, is basically
as unteachable as a chicken, and that is the simple fact of the
matter."

So Styron begins his dramatic rendering of the failure of religion
in the upcountry Tidewater. The society revealed in the early
parts of the novel is what Allen Tate has called a "feudal society,
without a feudal religion; hence only a semi-feudal society." As
he has remarked, the Old South was incapable of creating an appropriate religion, appropriate for its way of life—the economy,
politics, and culture of the region. One might go further and say,
with Mr. Tate, that the god of the Old South was created by the
New World merchants of the sixteenth century. The mythology
of the Old South was therefore incomplete: the fabric of its life
was fatally marred by the divergence between the secular and religious impulses. Religion cannot be perfunctory and formalistic
in a traditional society, if that way of life is to survive.

The enveloping action of *The Confessions of Nat Turner* deals
in large part with this failure of Protestantism, and Styron makes
it perfectly clear the failure is principally due to the curse of slavery. In this respect—the comprehensiveness and credibility of the
picture of decadent Protestantism—Styron has outstripped other
southern novelists who have touched upon the same subject; and
this, to my mind, may be the most important historical and social
dimension to the novel—more so than its depiction of slavery.

Nat's masters are all religious in the trite mechanical sense,
and Samuel Turner (who is significantly not a church-going man)
is the most nearly Christian of them all. The mannered Episco-
palianism which Turner half-heartedly professes is replaced in
Nat's life by the backwoods fundamentalism of the Reverend

[154]

Eppes. In church Eppes whips his parishioners into a frenzy, whereupon they strip to their underwear and ride "each other bareback up and down the aisles." Later Nat is exposed to the callous Methodism of Margaret Whitehead's brother. When we last see this divine—prior to the onset of the rebellion—he is joining the posse to track down Will, "his prim lips vengefully set." It is ironic that a Baptist camp meeting gives Nat the chance to put his tactical plan into motion, and it is a mark of Styron's sure craftsmanship that the immediate foreground of both great turning points in Nat's fortunes—his transfer from the Turners to Eppes—and his rebellion (which begins with the murder of his first kind master since Samuel Turner)—are preceded by camp meetings. Nat misses the first when he inadvertently delivers his friend Willis to a slave trader; the second gives him the opportunity for the vengeance against all that has gone before in his life, for all the wrongs, real and imagined, including the sale of Willis, which he has carried in his heart.

But this is of course only half the story. The greatest irony in Nat's confessions lies in the fact that he is a more religious man than any of his masters, indeed more than anyone else in the novel; and his primitive Christianity is purer, more orthodox, than the Protestantism of the region, taken singly by denomination or as a whole. Yet Nat is separated from his spirituality when the rebellion begins, and the redemptive moment at the end of the novel, immediately before his execution, is a little forced.

Styron has said that *The Confessions of Nat Turner* is "a sort of religious parable and a story of exculpation. . . . It should be apparent that the book expresses the idea of Old Testament savagery and revenge redeemed by New Testament charity and brotherhood —affirmation." This is admittedly one aspect of the novel; but in giving us an allegorical explanation the author is unnecessarily limiting the meaning of his fable. As Andrew Lytle has remarked, "Whenever a writer talks about a story or a novel he has done, he is not speaking in his true voice. That voice has already been heard in the rendition of the action."

The Confessions of Nat Turner is more than religious parable —what some critics might call a modern-day version of *Pilgrim's*

Progress, with Nat as a negative hero caught in the throes of an existential agony like Camus's Stranger. Indeed Walter Sullivan has persuasively read the novel in terms not far removed from these. I believe, on the contrary, that the novel is generated by a deeply religious impulse which is not so simple as either Christian or existential parable would have it; for the story has that timeless, nonsectarian Christian dimension which one finds over and again in Hawthorne, Melville, Faulkner, and Warren. And it is all to Styron's credit that he has firmly resisted the perhaps strong desire to make his protagonist into a Christ-figure. The consequences of this almost-suicidal urge on the part of American novelists are too well known to bear repeating here, although I will ask rhetorically whether the appearance of a Christ-figure in any major piece of American literature since *Billy Budd* has been anything short of embarrassing to reader and author alike.

The point is relevant to my discussion because several critics have cited the historical Nat's retort to Thomas Gray's question about the failure of the rebellion: "Was not Christ crucified?" This piece of verbal heroics may be a "direct, simple and great flash" and "the most dramatic moment in the actual *Confessions*," as Herbert Aptheker has said; but a beginning student in fiction writing could tell Mr. Aptheker such a line doesn't belong in fiction. Judgment of this kind is unfortunately typical of the critics who have attacked Styron for his novel's lack of historicity. The critic who makes it—Stanley Kauffmann, Richard Gilman, Mike Thelwell, and Aptheker are typical—has no idea what George Saintsbury meant when he remarked, seventy-five years ago, that the great danger for the novelist is decanting too much history into his novel.

It is of course not enough for a novelist to be a good historian in order to make a fiction which will be read a century or even a decade after it is written. Were this so, Kenneth Roberts's work would not already be largely forgotten. Roberts is quite a good historian, but his talent for fiction is too limited for him to render novelistically the history he understands so well.

We come now to the vexed question of what a historical novel is—how it characteristically works—and why (a question that I do not intend to belabor). E. M. W. Tillyard has shrewdly argued that the historical novel is the lineal descendant of the epic —another literary form that is little understood today. In epic one is immediately confronted by the idea of myth and mythology— what the informing vision of a traditional society entails, as I have mentioned. In the epic and in the historical novel the dying traditional society has a shared way of looking at the world, a definite yet unstated ethic; and that ethic collapses in the face of pressures from within and without the society. The protagonist is of that society—yet apart from it, aware of change, and contending with change in the vortex of a historical crisis in which he is inescapably affected. The author uses history, then, as a frame for the central action, the inspiriting conflict which is his true subject; but the historical element is deliberately muted so far as particulars go: if it is not, then the novelist loses control and history takes over. In consequence the good novelist is careful not to put major historical figures in the center of the stage. In the same way, unless he is a superb craftsman who is utterly in control, he had best steer away from major historical events—from letting those events play too great a role in his fiction. That these dangers are real may be simply proven when we remember that a good novel has never been written about the American Civil War—or the Second World War.

There are two kinds of themes in the historical novel which the artist must seize and which he must bring together into firm unity: those that deal with the actual events and characters of the period he is writing about—the outer world—and those that concern the human life and its peculiar emotional gravity in this period and any other—the inner world. Since it is far easier to depict the outer world of fact as it can be historically reconstructed than it is to render the emotional life of the leading characters, the novelist must take pains to ensure that fiction is not subordinated to history; for otherwise what we get is history with a fictional subplot—the kind of work that Kenneth Roberts has characteristically written. The center of composition in a good historical

[157]

novel, as in any other kind of significant fiction, is provided by the fable, which is nothing less than the central action in miniature—the particular recurring pattern of life the author chooses—which can only be abstractly expressed through theme.

The rich density of Styron's fable in *The Confessions of Nat Turner* may be measured in large part by Philip Rahv's praise. He finds that the novel's creative success has come from the author's having caught "a substantial theme central to the national experience." That theme is expressed in various and similar ways by Judge Cobb, Samuel Turner, Margaret Whitehead, and Nat himself. Cobb puts it best when he cries out about the wrecked old dominion—Virginia. He sees the wasteland around him as having been caused by economic greed which sprang from Virginia's success with tobacco. The land has been literally ravaged by the reckless planting of tobacco; it has been figuratively cursed by the presence of slavery which now takes its most ominous form since Virginia has become "a monstrous breeding farm to supply the sinew to gratify the maw of Eli Whitney's infernal machine," as Cobb shouts to Nat.

The historical crisis eventuates in the breakup of Tidewater plantation society, and the personal reflection of this great transformation is instanced in Nat Turner's struggle to achieve selfhood. And so the historical, objective, logical plane of the novel—the larger action—is joined to the human, subjective, psychological level—the fable—by the common theme of the curse of slavery. Slavery, as Styron sees it, is the primary reason for the social, economic, and political changes which take place in Nat's world; whereas the failure of religion to provide a mythology shows the hollowness of its values, values which are prudential and expedient. The collapse of this society, Styron implies, is caused by its arrogant commercialism—and its inhumanity. Nat, like any other slave, is affected on both counts.

By showing how slavery affects every department of life and every stratum of society in Virginia in the early 1800s, Styron not only gives human embodiment and concreteness to his themes, but he brings to us a sense of the society as a whole and the interaction of the individuals who make up that society; for we are shown both religion and class through representative characters and actions. For instance, Travis, Nat's last master, is a mountaineer whose origins are similar to Thomas Sutpen's; McBride, the overseer who rapes Nat's mother, is a shanty Irishman; and so forth. In these ways Styron gives his novel the continuity of what George Lukács calls popular life, the life of the common people and the way history (as we know it from the vantage point of the present) impinges upon them.

Nat himself is essential to the unfolding action since he tells the story from beginning to end; and in examining his importance as a literary creation we are touching upon the nerve center of William Styron's novel. It is by now a commonplace that Styron's most daring strategy in *The Confessions of Nat Turner* is to present the action from the standpoint of a Negro when the author is a white man. Certain Negro critics have argued unconvincingly, I think—that a black man cannot be effectively rendered by a white author, especially a Virginian; by this reasoning we should throw out *Othello* and do away with any other work of literature in which an author of one race depicts the life of another race from within. (I know of no such cry from the Indians about *A Passage to India.*)

Technically, once Styron had "solved" the problem of his narrative point of view and of getting inside the mind and psyche of a complicated black human being, he really had little else to contend with. By this I mean that if you grant Styron his donnée and find it credible, you almost of necessity will find the novel convincing. Through this device the author has achieved a new simplicity which is not evident in his first two full-length novels, fictions which are enormously more complicated in a technical sense than *The Confessions of Nat Turner*. In his work Styron has exhibited the tendencies which Glenway Westcott sees as characteristic of contemporary fiction:

> My conclusion is that brilliancy of ego, headstrong and headlong display of intellect, powers of elaboration, poetical afflatus, and that frenzied and exalted artistry which is like drunkenness, play

an important part in literature; but as regularly as clockwork, most of the time, everything of that sort has to give way to a prosaic simplicity, to brevity and explicitness, and to traditional themes and immemorial symbols and images.

If I may be permitted to display an old chestnut, it is clear that William Styron has used "technique as discovery" in this novel more than most novelists can or will—and yet technique by no means becomes preeminent. He has followed the examples of Ford Madox Ford, Faulkner, Tate, and Warren in his strategies; and on the whole these have worked. The chief one involves point of view, as I have said; and here Styron has used a convention, one immediately recognizable to anyone who knows how to read fiction. The author invests Nat with a sensibility and intelligence and range of knowledge which are doubtless greater than he in fact possessed as historical personage, but this is possible because so little is known of the actual Nat Turner. If we knew more about him, the very recalcitrance of the facts that were the man might prevent his becoming an important fictive creation. This is true of Lee, for example. Warren once said of him: "Who cares about Robert E. Lee? Now there's a man who's smooth as an egg. Turn him around, this primordial perfection: you see, he has no story. . . . It's only the guy who's angular, incomplete, and struggling who has a story."

Having given Nat Turner considerable complexity Styron must render it; and he does so by providing Nat with two voices—the one is a received, standard nineteenth-century southern rhetoric which has much in common with the similar language of Faulkner, Wolfe, and Warren; the other is plantation Negro dialect of the same period, this last being more enduring and less literary, and it may still be heard often today. The problem is how to account for two radically different forms of speech coming from the same person. The first voice approximates the written word, the way Nat would have set down his story himself; it is a stately rhetoric, one appropriate for the occasion of his confessions to Gray and the world—and a form of speech in keeping with the language of the educated southerner. The second voice is that of the spoken word, caused by necessity—Nat's need not to antagonize his masters and his equal need to communicate with his fellow Negroes. That such bifurcation ordinarily exists between written and spoken language could not be proven, not even by the histrionics of a transformational grammarian; but there is a basic distinction between language as we write it or otherwise employ it formally—and language as we use it conversationally, especially with folk whom we presume to be more ignorant than ourselves. Styron has grounded his convention on that solid and indisputable foundation.

Some critics have objected that no one ever talked as Judge Cobb and Thomas Gray and Nat Turner do in the course of the narrative. To this argument one might answer that nobody (even Thomas Wolfe himself) ever spoke the mellifluous idiom of Eugene Gant, and that no one in conversation ever used the baroque periods of Mr. Compson or Gavin Stevens. The related objection that Styron has written the novel directly in his own voice will not stand inspection, even though Styron has testified against himself in this respect. The language of *The Confessions of Nat Turner* is not the language of *Lie Down in Darkness* or *Set This House on Fire*, and the difference is not simply a matter of artistic change and maturity.

Styron has deliberately fashioned a southern, biblical language for Nat which is complemented by a level of definite Latinity, of Miltonic sonorities, as George Steiner has remarked. The deeper current of this prose, Steiner tells us, "relates the novel to other moments in American consciousness and prose in which the syntax of the Jacobean Bible, compressed by Puritan intensity or loosened and made florid by political rhetoric, served to define the new world. From Cotton Mather to Faulkner and James Baldwin, biblical speech has set a core of vision and public ornament inside the American language." The deliberately archaic quality of the language therefore has a range of powerful effects. The style reflects the religious themes, the sacramental dimension which is part and parcel of the novel.

We turn now to the character of William Styron's Nat Turner. Nat is haunted by three obsessions, each bound to the other: repressed sexuality, the possibility of escape from servitude through violent overthrow of his white masters, and religious fanaticism. It is the quality of his religiousness that gives Nat his deep humanity and complexity, not his sexual urges, which Styron has used quite plausibly as an alternative means for the modern reader to understand Nat and the condition of his servitude. Ultimately Nat's spirituality exceeds his religious fanaticism, and his sexuality is also sublimated. Stanley Kauffmann, in a perverse and brilliant misreading of the novel, has suggested that Styron left his religious parable unfinished by not presenting Nat as a Christ-figure but that, having so failed, he could have still "saved" his fiction by presenting the "psychosexual drama" in a more believable, less hackneyed fashion, rather than being "glib and reductive." Kauffmann really wants Freudian tragedy, I suspect. He misreads the character of Nat Turner as Styron reveals it: Nat is a sensitive man who is wholly possessed by his humanity and by his sacramental way of looking at the world: this in the end leads to his undoing as a revolutionary leader and to his redemption as a man. Indeed one might say that the tragedy of Nat Turner is caused by his humanity against the general inhumanity of his time, and that in the moment of crisis he was unable to stifle that humanity.

Now I would not argue that *The Confessions of Nat Turner* is a flawless novel in a technical or a substantive sense, as I will doubtless be accused of doing. I would only say that its critics have on the whole seriously misjudged its virtues and defects through a misreading not only of the novel but of southern history. For example, Styron's slight departures from the text of the original *Confessions* are beside the point, because in a fictive sense and in the larger historical perspective it makes little or no difference who taught the actual Nat how to read, or whether he or his father ran away, or whether Will was a homicidal maniac, or whether slaves helped quell the rebellion. What is of essential importance is Nat's stature as a man as Styron renders it—and his place in the society which produced him. I wholly agree with Louis Rubin when he says, "It is my belief that when the smoke of controversy blows away . . . the best critics . . . will recognize how fine a characterization, and how great a man, William Styron's Nat Turner is."

The defects of the novel result principally from the author's use of a single, restricted post of observation and his decision to write a tour de force. Nat's presence becomes a little tedious at times, even though the shifts from panoramic summary to scenic presentation work well on the whole. His commentary on the natural setting as it reflects his own visions tends to strain our credulity, despite our awareness that the pathetic fallacy in such instances is part of the prophetic mode. What Styron sacrifices in his choice of point of view is typical of tragedy and epic—that quality which Yeats calls the emotion of the multitude—the choral effect. Styron's method lets us see life as a whole in the historical situation he has chosen to illuminate, but that method is necessarily a little too schematic in the treatment of slaveholders, as some critics have complained, and, to a lesser extent, in the anatomy of Protestantism. In limiting the action to one post of observation Styron has lost the advantage of the multiple point of view: greater comprehensiveness, objectivity, and credibility might have inhered in a different treatment; and I think it undeniable that more reflectors would have provided another analogy for the action. As it is the action has but two dimensions—the larger historical frame which may be called overplot, and the main action which embodies the fable. So *The Confessions of Nat Turner* lacks an underplot, and Nat's recurring dream of the mysterious "white building standing on its promontory high above the shore" is not a satisfactory alternative for a fully realized analogy to the action. An underplot would have given the kind of random, indeterminate quality of felt life itself, had it been used properly. If *Hamlet* and *Bleak House* and *War and Peace* are too stern in the examples they offer, one can cite appropriate instances from Faulkner and Warren. Lacking this dimension the plot seems a little contrived, too neat in short.

I have purposely been applying the highest standards, because even though *The Confessions of Nat Turner* does plainly fall short of greatness, it does not miss by much being a novel

of the next rank—the place occupied by *The Sound and the Fury,
Light in August,* and *Absalom, Absalom!* It will not be said,
I hope, that my implication is that technique is everything—that
by a mere change of strategy here and there Styron might have
produced a masterpiece, a southern *War and Peace.* Certainly
no one would argue this who knows anything about the historical
development of the novel—nor would he agree with Richard Gilman that with a " 'subject' such as Nat Turner . . . you either
advance fictional art or set it back." (Gilman and Kauffmann both
suggest that Styron needed to create a new novelistic form: to
this the most appropriate answer is Dr. Johnson's—"Ignorance,
sheer ignorance.") Technique in the end is merely a way of seeing
the job at hand and getting at it; the informing vision of the artist
and the spreading field of possibility it affords him and the reader
are something else again. This brings us to a consideration of the
most abiding aspects of the novel at hand—and indeed of any good
historical novel about the South.

The balance sheet reveals that in *The Confessions of Nat Turner* William Styron has clearly and ably used those strategies
which Scott made available for the historical novelist; but Styron
has worked not so much deliberately as intuitively, I would think.
He did not set out to write his novel along the lines of the classic
formula I have sketched—quite the contrary. The book would
seem to have come, as Warren tells us, out of a long and painful
"brooding, an activity deep, personal and at any conscious level,
aimless, the process of finding a self for the story and story in the
self." That this is evident strikes me as unarguable: one need only
look at Styron's response to Herbert Aptheker in the *Nation,* or to
his opening remarks at a Southern Historical Association panel
discussion. In both places he quotes at some length from George
Lukács's brilliant study of the historical novel. Obviously Styron
read this book after writing Nat Turner's story and getting em-
broiled with Aptheker and others in defending it. He encountered
Lukács with a shock of recognition and realized his methods in the
novel were classically correct. In speaking of Lukács rather self-
consciously, Styron is erecting a defense for his novel which is far
more substantial than his earlier random remarks which I have

alluded to on several occasions—remarks which have tended to undercut his art by oversimplification. Today Styron would not be embarrassed to admit that *The Confessions of Nat Turner* is a historical novel—and, having discovered this, he may now be content to let the novel stand on its own. There is an obvious moral to be drawn for the southern novelist, but I will spare you that; for I want to look once again at the novel—this time in a slightly different perspective.

"Things reveal themselves passing away," someone remarked to Yeats; and this comment holds not only the largest significance of *The Confessions of Nat Turner* but of the historical novel generally. In this novel we see the destruction of feudal society in Tidewater Virginia, and its death throes produce a Nat Turner, one of those specters who appear in the darkening gloom when a way of life is coming to an end. Nat as we know him historically is a symptom and little more: indeed Edmund Wilson is being metaphorical in calling him a black John Brown. In bringing Nat to life as a complex, deeply human person of tragic dimensions, Styron has given us what Lukács calls the sine qua non of the historical novel—a concrete prehistory of the present. Now this does not mean the past is simply a preliminary to the present, and that it is distorted from its proper shape to become congruent with the apparent configuration of the present: it is to say that Styron shows the transformations of history as the changes in common life—life not only in early nineteenth-century Virginia but in our own time, because these social disruptions and transitions are essentially alike: they always are. As Lukács says, "Without a felt relationship to the present, a portrayal of history is impossible." The trick is in "giving poetic life to those historical social and human forces which . . . have made our present-day life what it is," without distorting the past.

William Styron has dramatized a significant moment in the southern past—the Nat Turner rebellion, and in illuminating that moment through the informing power of fiction he has revealed to us what may be seen as the first important crossing of the ways that radically affected the established southern social fabric. The early decades of the nineteenth century in the upcountry Tidewater reveal a serious breach in the feudal complexion of southern society; and if the old squirearchy of Virginia is here passing away to be reincarnated in the plantations of the Deep South (a story told in *The Long Night* and *Absalom, Absalom!*), the same pattern of disruption and accommodation recurs in more obvious, cataclysmic proportions in the Civil War and its aftermath. It is not being too fanciful, I believe, to suggest that John Brown's raid as prologue to the war is a repetition of the Nat Turner rebellion in some respects: in this sense Wilson's analogy holds true. The later crossroads in southern history—the end of Reconstruction and the birth of the New South, the First World War, the depression years, and finally the decades since the Second World War (a period of which we are so much a part as to be partially blinded to whatever truth it may hold)—have a good deal in common with the 1820s and 30s in upcountry Virginia. To this extent, then, *The Confessions of Nat Turner* is a paradigm of the present: William Styron has used memory and imagination for a liberation—ours and his—from time future as well as time past. Nat's ultimate redemption, Styron suggests, is our own, since as Eliot says,

> A people without history
> Is not redeemed from time, for history is a pattern
> Of timeless moments.

Styron shows us the past in the present in this novel, but his fiction does not compress and refract all time to the eternally present. We are therefore redeemed from time, if only briefly, by our understanding of a moment in history as it bears upon the present and our own experience. In this sense *The Confessions of Nat Turner* is very much a novel of our day.

Through our understanding of the past, whether it is made possible by fiction or history—by a William Styron or a Vann Woodward, we are liberated from the old atavistic and disabling southern preoccupation with the past, but we are by no means freed entirely from it. On the contrary, we simply come to terms with the past and the present and therefore ourselves and the predicament of being human in a time of terrible stress and disrelation. The collective experience of the southern people, Woodward has shrewdly observed, is the most distinctive and enduring feature of the South—not the legends, shibboleths, and apologias which have derived from it. If we as southerners are ever entirely freed of our awareness of a common past—if we ever give up our attempts to understand that past in the light of all the knowledge and compassion which we can bring to bear on it, the South and the southern identity will no longer signify; and the region east of the Mississippi and south of Mason and Dixon's line will simply be a part of the national geography.

The southerner is uniquely himself by virtue of the South's history, his feeling for that history and the place which that history affords. For him, as Faulkner said, "The past is never dead. It is not even past." A novel such as *The Confessions of Nat Turner* reconciles past and present without confusing either. And in consequence of the renewed awareness of the southern experience which William Styron makes possible for us—an awareness that this experience is itself a great image of the human condition, we can more easily assume the burden of the past.

SEYMOUR L. GROSS & EILEEN BENDER

History, Politics, and Literature: The Myth of Nat Turner

Up until a few years ago Nat Turner as a figure of history was not known to many Americans, although there is evidence that the name of "old Prophet Nat" had been kept alive in black oral tradition. But with the publication of William Styron's *The Confessions of Nat Turner* in 1967, and the sensational and far-reaching reaction to the novel by much of the black intelligentsia, the relative obscurity of this leader of a slave rebellion in nineteenth-century Virginia is itself a thing of the past. Now he belongs to all of us. But it will be the intention of this essay to show that he belongs to us as he has always belonged to those who used him—as a myth, as an imagined configuration of convictions, dreams, hopes, and fears. This is as true of the insanely religious fanatic of Thomas Gray's *The Confessions of Nat Turner* in 1831 as it is of the Black Power militant of Addison Gayle's "Nat Turner vs. Black Nationalists" in 1968, in which the meaning of Turner's life is seen to "negate the absurd and nonsensical philosophy of Martin Luther King."[1]

The rhetoric of accusation and vilification with which black writers and critics have responded to Styron's novel, of which *William Styron's Nat Turner: Ten Black Writers Respond* is but the most formal,[2] has many of the unpleasant intellectual characteristics of party discipline carried over into literary studies. It is reminiscent not only of the vulgar Marxist criticism of the 1930s but, ironically, of the deliberately mounted attacks on *Uncle Tom's Cabin* in the white South of the 1850s as well. With the notable exceptions of John Hope Franklin and James Baldwin, those black critics whose initial reaction to Styron's novel was favorable, Poppy Cannon White and Gertrude Wilson, for example, found it incumbent upon them to recant.[3]

Much of the black criticism of *The Confessions of Nat Turner* has taken the form of tactical insult of its author and distortions of the novel: Styron is "an unreconstructed southern racist" suffering from "moral senility," who deliberately "dehumanizes every black person in the book" for the criminal purpose of legitimatizing "all of [the white] myths and prejudices about the American black man"—and so on.[4] Like the white schoolchildren in South Carolina at the turn of the century who had to take an oath never to read *Uncle Tom's Cabin* because there was no truth in Mrs. Stowe, present-day blacks are being similarly assured that they can safely despise Mr. Styron's book without having to read it. One index of how successful this programmatic onslaught has been is the fate of the motion picture based on the book. According to Styron, "irrational" and "intentionally false" charges by black militants that the book was racist so intimidated Twentieth Century-Fox that it severed Styron's connection with the film. As of now, the movie is "shelved."[5]

A less dramatic but perhaps more disturbing result of the war on *The Confessions* is to be found in the case of Ralph Ellison. Ellison, as all who have followed his career know, has always been his own man in cultural and literary matters concerning the Negro in America and has written what many readers think to be the most powerful treatment of the black experience in our country. Nor has he escaped abuse for this stance ("I am known as a bastard by certain of my militant friends because I am not what they call a part of the Movement"). It is therefore distressing to note that Ellison has recently admitted that "after the controversy I deliberately did not read [*The Confessions of Nat Turner*]," although he seems to have read *Ten Black Writers*.[6] Surely this is an evasion; and if such a man as Ralph Ellison is evading, then it would seem as if, indeed, the black campaign against Styron's novel has had just about complete success. After asserting that Styron "invited the kind of attack he received," Stephen E. Henderson, with evident satisfaction, concludes, "one can be fairly certain that the next white writer will think twice before presuming to interpret the Black Experience."[7]

One of the essays in *Ten Black Writers* is entitled "You've Taken My Nat and Gone." The "My" in this title—as throughout the volume—is meant to refer to the "real," the "true," the "historical" Nat Turner, the meaning of whose life Styron has deliberately attempted "to steal." For these black critics, there is neither ambiguity nor haziness nor complexity in the figure of Nat Turner. *They* know him—know him not merely as a racial symbol but as an historical fact. And the historical fact which Styron has "distorted," "manipulated," "rejected," "emasculated" is the "true story" of an authentic militant hero and revolutionist, a nineteenth-century version of H. Rap Brown or Stokely Carmichael.[8] Now this may indeed be the truth of the matter, but how do these twentieth-century critics think they know this? They know this, they tell us, because *history* has told them so. And what is this history? It is, for the most part, the 1831 *Confessions* ("the basic historical document"), the full text of which is appended to the volume to serve, presumably, as a starkly historical repudiation of the "vile racist myth" of Styron's "faked confessions." Although some reservations about Gray's pamphlet are voiced (most particularly by John Killens), and some other nineteenth-century historical writings are referred to, it is "the astringent report of Lawyer Gray," as Vincent Harding puts it (p. 29), which is for these black writers the basis of "the real history." "It should be noted," remarks Lerone Bennett, "that Nat Turner was served better in many instances by Thomas Gray, the avowed racist, than by William Styron, the avowed liberal" (p. 5). "Gray . . . gives [Turner] to history, unrepentant, courageous, sure of his act and his eventual vindication" (p. 16). This needs some looking at.

The year 1831 is a highly significant one in the annals of American Negro history. In January of that year, William Lloyd Garrison began publication of *The Liberator*, an abolitionist newspaper considered so dangerous that the Georgia legislature offered a reward for his capture. In his first issue, Garrison presented his readers with this piece of melodramatic emancipatory rhetoric:

> Wo if it come with storm, and blood, and fire,
>   When midnight darkness veils the earth and sky!
> So to the innocent babe—the guilty sire—
>   Mother and daughter—friends of kindred tie!
> Stranger and citizen alike shall die! [9]

Seven months later, as if to prove Garrison's verse prophetic, a grandly mad or a madly grand slave—which, we shall perhaps never know—named Nat Turner led a band of some sixty Negroes in a bloody massacre of some fifty-five whites, mostly women and children, in Southampton, Virginia. Some of the rebels lost their lives battling federal and state troops, some were deported, some were hanged. Others were let off because they were considered mere dupes of Turner, thereby obviating the injustice of punishing the "innocent" owners of only semiguilty property. Turner himself escaped capture for about ten weeks; he was tried on 5 November 1831, and hanged six days later, but not before he presumably gave an account of himself, "fully and voluntarily," to one Thomas R. Gray, who had it published in Baltimore in an edition of thousands of copies as *The Confessions of Nat Turner, The Leader of the Late Insurrection in Southampton, Va.* (1831).[10] Although, according to Gray, Turner had killed but one person, Margaret Whitehead, he was universally considered by whites as the sole "author of their misfortune." According to a later account, William Drewry's *The Southampton Insurrection* (1900), Turner's body was skinned by physicians and a spiritual progenitor of the Bitch of Buchenwald had a purse made from part of the hide.[11]

There had been slave unrest before 1831, most frequently expressed in individual rebellion or escape, a phenomenon which southern psychology handled by attributing it to a disease— *drapetomania,* from the Greek words meaning "runaway slave" and "insanity." Then, too, there were two large-scale revolts led by Gabriel Prosser in 1800 and Denmark Vesey in 1822, both, however, aborted through betrayal by one or more of the leader's black followers. Nevertheless, despite their failure, both insurrections contributed to the shattering of the relative tranquility with which white southerners customarily contemplated their peculiar institution, a tranquility in no small part dependent upon a conspiracy of silence. During the Denmark Vesey scare, for example, a Charleston lady wrote that twenty-five hundred whites were under arms but cautioned her correspondent that "it is a subject not to be mentioned . . . say nothing about it."[12] Governor Monroe of Virginia writing President Jefferson of the Prosser revolt calls it "unquestionably the most serious and formidable conspiracy we have ever known of the kind," and says that he tried to keep it "secret" for as long as he could.[13] But it was the success of the Turner insurrection, Prosser and Vesey's contemplated murders accomplished, which broke the secret and unleashed a widespread fear of a general servile war. That slaves would rise up in the night to butcher their masters in what George Fitzhugh was to characterize as "civilized and virtuous" Virginia, where "negroes . . . love their master and his family, and the attachment is reciprocated,"[14] this could hardly help causing a shock of horrified bewilderment to pass through the mind of the white South. Here, then, were the materials for a crisis in the stereotyped white perception of the slave-master relationship. The place was not Mississippi or Arkansas where mind-and-body-killing practices could drive slaves to the measures of despair. "No one has dreamed of any such event happening in any part of Virginia," the astonished Richmond *Enquirer* lamented two days after the revolt.[15] Nor was the slave himself, even by his own admission, ill-treated. How, then, could it have happened?

It would be difficult to exaggerate the psychic toll which the Turner massacre exacted from the southern mind. As is evidenced in the ritualistic desecration of Turner's body, the event had cut through to the lower layers of the psyche where the nightmares are transacted. The Richmond *Enquirer* quotes one reader as saying "there it is, the dark and growing evil at our doors. . . . What is to be done? Oh! My God, I do not know, but something must be done."[16] A contemporary in Richmond wonders if the Turner rebellion might not "excite those to insurrection that never thought of such a thing before." A southern lady judges the situation to be "like a smothered volcano," is afraid "that death in the most horrid form threatens us," and asserts that some have already "become deranged from apprehension since the South Hampton affair." A Virginian writes a friend in Ohio: "These insurrections have alarmed my wife so as really to endanger her health, and I have not slept without anxiety in three months. Our nights are sometimes spent listening to noises. A corn song, a hog call, has often been a subject of nervous terror, and a cat, in the dining room, will banish sleep for the night."[17]

Considering the psychological investment that the white southerner had made in a life based upon the institution of slavery, it is not surprising that when confronted with an event that cried out for a reassessment of the presiding assumptions upon which that institution was based, he turned in wrath toward combating the effects and in righteousness toward preventing its recurrence, rather than in doubt toward scrutinizing its causes. Vigilante committees were hurriedly formed to kill and terrorize Negroes and state legislatures met in emergency sessions to pass laws which would further inhibit the freedom of slaves and discourage manumission. "We have," one Virginia lawmaker affirmed, "closed every avenue by which light might enter their minds. If you could extinguish the capacity to see the light, our work would be completed: they would then be on a level with the beasts of the field, and we should be safe."[18] This is precisely the specific moral that Thomas Gray was to draw from the Turner insurrection: "It is calculated . . . to demonstrate the policy of our laws in restraint of this class of our population, and to induce all those entrusted with their execution, as well as our citizens generally, to see that they are strictly and rigidly enforced."

The attacks on Styron's novel generally take it for granted that Thomas R. Gray was not much more than a recorder of Turner's words and that therefore his *Confessions* is a reasonably reliable source for our knowledge of Turner and his motives. Aptheker, for example, uses Gray's pamphlet as the base in reality from which to attack Styron's novel as a "consequential distortion" of the truth.[19] Our impression, however, is that Gray was anything but a blank-faced scrivener; that he was, on the contrary, a very

[173]

shrewd man who knew precisely what he was doing and why; and that his pamphlet is a political document in the most basic sense of the word.

We ought, first of all, to remind ourselves just how much of the pamphlet, despite its title, is Gray's. It is Gray who structures the work so that Turner's words are sandwiched between his own interpretation of the event and his horrified eyeball-to-eyeball confrontation with the black murderer; it is Gray who decides when to quote and when to paraphrase; it is Gray who ends the document with the lists of murdered whites and sentenced Negroes. Moreover, it is also well to remember that we have only Gray's word for it that the section of the pamphlet entitled "Confession" is in fact the "faithful record" of Turner's statement "with little or no variation." It is certainly true that a lot of effort went into authenticating the document—some might feel too much. Five justices of the peace certified that the confession was read to Turner who acknowledged it "to be full, free, and voluntary," and then the county clerk certified the judges. But considering Turner's position at the time ("covered with chains") and what we know of eliciting confessions from prisoners, one can be pardoned for not accepting all the legal paraphernalia as prima facie evidence of the authenticity of the *Confessions*, especially when certain internal evidences, which we will come to in a moment, also lend themselves to doubt.

Gray's pamphlet is an exercise in reassurance—on two levels. Most explicitly, it attempts to lay to rest the "thousand idle, exaggerated and mischievous reports" which had so "greatly excited the public mind." Because the specter of a mass uprising of slaves had been somewhere back in the shadows of the white southerner's mind ever since the successful revolt in Haiti in the 1790s, rumors inflated the extent of the uprising in Southampton to frightening proportions. Accordingly, Gray assures his readers that the insurrection was purely "local," and that Turner's "designs" were "confided but to a few, and these in his immediate vicinity." Gray tells us that when he questioned Turner about an insurrection occurring in North Carolina about the same time, "he denied any knowledge of it."[20] What Gray calls "the first instance in our history of an open rebellion of the slaves" has proved to be a purely parochial phenomenon.

More interesting, however, is the way the pamphlet confronts what Gray recognizes as the deeper psychic disturbance inherent in the "conspiracy." Although Gray usually keeps the level of his discourse safely above the sinister with such psychologically innocuous phrases as "public curiosity," he is keenly aware of the "deep impression" that Turner's rebellion has made "not only upon the minds of the community where this fearful tragedy was wrought, but throughout every portion of our country, in which this population [slaves] is to be found."[21] He knows that unless he can satisfactorily explain (or, rather, reassuringly explain away) "the origin and progress of this dreadful conspiracy, and the motives which influence[d] its diabolical actors," his pamphlet will have failed in one of its essential purposes—the removal of "doubts and conjectures from the public mind."

With the word *diabolical* Gray signals his primary strategy— a deliberate attempt to depict Turner as a possessed, deluded, religious maniac so as to short-circuit any disturbing thoughts about the institution of slavery which might tend to issue from the insurrection. *Ferocious, dark, remorseless, corrupted, warped, perverted, fiendlike, inhuman*—these adjectives thread Gray's framing remarks and point the direction of his characterization. The "fearful tragedy," Gray assures his white contemporaries, "was not instigated by motives of revenge or sudden anger" against slaveholders. It was rather the result of a "bewildered and overwrought mind" in whose "dark recesses" religious enthusiasm had turned to homicidal mania. "Fiendish," "inhuman," "hellish," the massacre was, but only in the sense that it emanated from "a mind . . . endeavoring to grapple with things beyond its reach." Religion "bewildered and confounded, and finally corrupted" Turner's naturally intelligent mind until he was left outside the pale of humanity, "a complete fanatic." How else, Gray asks, can we explain that of all the insurrectionists only Turner made no attempt "to exculpate himself," but frankly and without remorse acknowledged his monstrous acts?

Gray has looked into the pit, but it is, after all, he assures his

readers, a psychologically manageable one. Gray has attempted
to make his readers feel what we feel when we read in a newspaper that a man has killed his entire family because God had commanded him to do so. We may be appalled but we are not involved.
Murder for passion or money or freedom—these are capable of
implicating us as social creatures, or individuals, because we can
identify with such murders humanly. But religious madness leaves
us safely on the outside: nothing we do or do not do can affect
it.[22] What we are suggesting, then, is that even as Gray recounts
the ghastly details of the massacre, he is supplying his readers with
the means for removing it from the structure of the slave-master
relationship. The white man's self-fulfilling prophecy—his selec-
tive inattention to all aspects of slavery save those which reenforced
his stereotyped response—has been left intact.

The self-portrait which emerges from the section of the pamphlet entitled "Confession" dovetails with the "argument" in
Gray's framework. It breaks into two almost equally discrete parts:
a rhetorically pressured account of the origin and progress of
Turner's communion with supernatural forces, followed by a matter-of-fact resumé of the massacre. The contrast between the passionate sense of divine election and the dispassionate murder of
human beings is, as we are certain it was intended to be, grotesque.

As a child of three or four, Turner astounded his family by relating events which occurred before he was born. The mysterious
ease with which he learned to read (he had no recollection of
learning the alphabet) and his capacity for knowing of things
even before he learned they existed, convinced Nat that he was
not like other men. His superior knowledge ("perfected by Divine
inspiration") set him above and apart from the other slaves, who
looked to him for leadership. But having discovered himself "to
be great," he must appear so: "[I] therefore studiously avoided
mixing in society, and wrapped myself in mystery, devoting my
time to fasting and prayer—." One day at prayer the "Spirit" spoke
to him, saying, "Seek ye the kingdom of Heaven and all things
shall be added unto you." (When Gray asked him what he meant
by "Spirit," Turner replied, "The Spirit that spoke to the prophets
in former days.") After two more years of prayer, the Spirit spoke

to him again and "fully confirmed [him] in the impression" that he "was ordained for some great purpose in the hands of the Almighty." At this point Turner, knowing the influence he had over his fellow slaves, who attributed his widom to "the communion of the spirit," began to prepare them for "the great promise that had been made to [him]." In 1825 Turner's destiny was made manifest in another vision: he saw white and black spirits locked in mortal combat in the sky, from which blood flowed in streams while the sun darkened and thunder rolled through the heavens. "Such is your luck," he heard a voice say, "such you are called to see, and let it come rough or smooth, you must surely bare [sic] it." He withdrew even further into solitude until one day a voice promised him that it would be given to him to know the whole nature of the cosmos: "the knowledge of the elements, the revolution of the planets, the operation of tides, and changes of the seasons." Turner then sought even more strenuously the state of "true holiness," and when he was made "perfect," he saw the light from Christ's hands stretched across the skies. He prayed for certainty and in answer he discovered blood upon the leaves, which, in "hieroglyphic characters," represented the figures he had seen in the heavens. The Holy Ghost revealed himself to Turner and explained that the blood which Christ had shed on earth had ascended to heaven and was now returning to earth—"the great day of judgment was at hand." On 12 May 1828 the Spirit again appeared to Turner, telling him to prepare to fight the "Serpent," for the day when the last shall be first was approaching. (At this point Gray asked him if he felt himself now mistaken, to which Turner replied: "Was not Christ crucified [?]") The sign which the Spirit had promised appeared in February 1830, in the form of an eclipse of the sun, and Turner communicated "the great work laid out for me to do" to four of his most trusted fellow slaves. They hoped to begin "the work of death" on 4 July 1831, but were unable to arrive at a suitable plan; when another sign appeared in August, they delayed no longer.

It may be objected at this point that Turner's charisma is not so unusual since it was the customary practice of nineteenth-century Negro rebels against slavery to relate their advocacy of rebellion to Christian morality and biblical precedent. But a comparison of Turner's "explanation" with, for example, the use made of Christian ethics and terminology in Frederick Douglass's *Narrative* (1845) or David Walker's *Appeal* (1829) shows a difference of such degree as to be a difference in kind. Whereas Turner unequivocally asserts the literal presence of supernatural phenomena in his life, Douglass only quietly indicates his faith in Providence, of which the following remark is typical: "I may be deemed superstitious, and even egotistical, in regarding this event [his being sent to Baltimore] as a special interposition of divine Providence in my favor. But I should be false to the earliest sentiments of my soul, if I suppressed the opinion."[23] And whereas Turner locates the command "to begin the work of death" in divine signs specially communicated to him, Walker evokes divine sanction for his holy crusade more as metaphor than as fact: "The man who would not fight under our Lord and Master, Jesus Christ, in the glorious and heavenly cause of freedom and God— . . . ought to be kept with all of his children or family, in slavery, or in chains."[24] Douglass exhibits the modulated faith of a Christian in the rectitude of his cause; Walker accommodates the rhetorical force of a readily available analogy to his political intention. But Turner—the Turner of Gray's pamphlet—is simply God-mad.

The mystical origin of the insurrection covers about five pages; the progress of the revolt and Turner's capture about six. Whereas the first part, as we have already suggested, is primarily directed toward discounting any socio-political implications in Turner's actions, the second both substantiates the religious madness of the leader and justifies the repressive measures which resulted from "this unparalleled and inhuman massacre." This section conveys the impression that only a man whose connection with humanity has been totally severed could recount murder in such chillingly prosaic terms. Each death is flatly stated as a statistical fact, without so much as a hint of emotional involvement. "The murder of this family, five in number, was the work of a moment"; "there was a little infant sleeping in a cradle, that was forgotten, until . . . Henry and Will returned and killed it"; "we entered, and murdered Mrs. Reese in her bed"; "Will immediately killed Mrs.

Turner, with one blow of his axe"; "I struck her several blows over the head, but . . . the sword was dull"; "they . . . had not been idle; all the family were already murdered"; "I killed her by a blow on the head, with a fence rail"; "Having murdered Mrs. Waller and ten children, we started for Mr. William Williams'— [and] killed him and two little boys that were there."

If these are indeed Turner's words, then he has given us a devastatingly effective self-portrait of a man who, through a sense of divine mission, has rendered himself unavailable to normal human feelings. Gray, however, seems not to have trusted wholly to this technique. His editorial prompting is not only evident in interspersed parentheses (which the careless reader might take for Turner's), but can perhaps also be discerned in several remarks supposedly made by Turner. For example, in the opening paragraph of the "Confession" Turner says that his early childhood "laid the ground work of that enthusiasm, which has terminated so fatally to many, both white and black, and for which I am about to atone at the gallows." Since Turner was convinced of the supernatural support of his insurrection, we would hardly expect him to characterize his religious commitment as "enthusiasm" since by the nineteenth century the term had only derogatory connotations, as is clear from Gray's later use of the word. Moreover, how can we possibly reconcile the idea of his having to "atone" for his "enthusiasm" with his response to Gray's query concerning Turner's feelings of guilt—"Was not Christ crucified?" *Atone* implies a sense of personal wrongdoing; the identification with Christ implies rectitude and holy sacrifice. They are scarcely reconcilable.

Other places in the *Confessions* betray additional signs of Gray's editorial hand. Considering Turner's rhetorically matter-of-fact method of recounting the murders, it is jarring to come upon stock locutions which italicize in the manner of sentimental fiction. It is difficult to conceive of Turner speaking of sending Richard Whitehead "to an untimely death," or crying out "Vain hope!" in response to a door shut by a white family against the invaders, or declaiming that Mrs. Reese's "son awoke, but it was only to sleep the sleep of death." Equally unbelievable is Turner's gothicized self-portrait of himself as viewing "the mangled bodies . . . in

[179]

silent satisfaction" or searching for "more victims to gratify our thirst for blood." The real Nat Turner, or even the Nat Turner who cold-bloodedly narrates the details of the slaughter, may indeed have *felt* something like this, but the language is as clearly Gray's as is its intention.

Near the end of the pamphlet Gray quotes the sentencing speech of the presiding judge in which Jeremiah Cobb remarks to Turner, "Your only justification is, that you were led away by fanaticism." And therein, Gray makes clear, is the central explanation. "It has been said," Gray earlier commented, "he was ignorant and cowardly, and that his object was to murder and rob for the purpose of obtaining money to make his escape." He was neither ignorant nor cowardly—a stereotype the white southerner could identify—nor did he kill for money with which to escape, Gray replies. The truth, dramatically embodied, Gray gives his readers in that last glimpse of the two of them sitting in "the condemned hole" of the prison: "The calm, deliberate composure with which he spoke of his late deeds and intentions, the expression of his fiend-like face when excited by enthusiasm, still bearing the stains of the blood of helpless innocence about him; clothed with rags and covered with chains; yet daring to raise his manacled hands to heaven, with a spirit soaring above the attributes of man; I looked on him and my blood curdled." Driven by God-madness beyond all human definition, even that of the black human, Nat Turner has soared beyond the problem of slavery. Gray, then, despite recalcitrant materials, managed to do the job which John Calhoun demanded of southerners—"We must satisfy the consciences, we must allay the fears, of our own people. We must satisfy them that slavery is of itself right . . . that it is not an evil, moral or political."[25]

It may be, as Aptheker says, that Gray's 1831 pamphlet must be the main source for our understanding of the Turner revolt—though we have already indicated our reservations—but its place in the nineteenth-century creation of a Turner legend is far from unambiguous. It is to be expected that around its relatively meager details would swirl an enlarging body of folkloristic matter such as predictably accompanies any event of shocking magnitude, especially when, as is the case with the *Confessions*, the account does not satisfy one's imaginative sense of the drama. Such matter almost immediately achieved the status of fact in Samuel Warner's rumor-ridden and "almost wholly inaccurate"[26] *Authentic and impartial narrative of the tragical scene which was witnessed in Southampton County . . .* (1831). Then, to further complicate matters, subsequent reprintings of Gray's *Confessions* silently deleted significant portions of Gray's framework or, with equal silence, added spurious portions to it, or did both. An 1861 reprint, for example (as well as the version in the November 1859 issue of the *Anglo-African Magazine*), inserts, after Cobb's sentencing speech, a section entitled THE EXECUTION, an account of Turner's last moments.

> —Nat Turner was executed according to sentence, on Friday, the 11th of November, 1831, at Jerusalem, between the hours of 10 A.M. and 2 P.M. He exhibited the utmost composure throughout the whole ceremony; and, although assured that he might, if he thought proper, address the immense crowd assembled on the occasion, declined availing himself of the privilege; and, being asked if he had any further confessions to make, replied that he had nothing more than he had communicated; and told the sheriff in a firm voice, that he was ready. Not a limb or muscle was observed to move. His body, after death, was given over to the surgeons for dissection.[27]

This material was to be used repeatedly by pro-Turner writers as if its source were the original Gray pamphlet.

It is perhaps impossible by now to unscramble all but the most salient facts of the Turner insurrection from the legendizing matter which has been spun around it, to, in Louis Rubin's words, "reconstruct anything resembling the real Nat Turner."[28] What is of interest, then, is how these "facts" were used by subsequent writers. The bloody fiend with his manacled hands raised blasphemously to heaven gave the proslavery mentality its basic image of the demonized alien; but the very power of the portrait, aided by additional materials, evoked for opposing points of view moral shapes quite the reverse of what Gray intended.

Thomas Gray's interpretation of Nat Turner had a long life in the South. Turner's kind master coupled with the rebel's imagined communion with the supernatural made the motiveless malevolence explanation all but irresistible. Perhaps, as several scholars have suggested, Poe's nightmare vision of white men trapped in a fiendish black world—the Tsalal episode of *Arthur Gordon Pym* (1837–1838)—takes its motive force from the southern view of Turner's insurrection. Under the mask of kindness of disposition and docile accommodation, the blacks lure the white men into a wholesale slaughter, literally tearing them to pieces in "brute rage." These blacks, Pym relates in horror, "for whom we entertained such inordinate feelings of esteem," were, in reality, "the most wicked, hypocritical, vindictive, bloodthirsty race of men upon the face of the globe." More directly, John Esten Cooke in his *Virginia: A History of the People* (1884) asserts that "Turner's motives remain unknown." The "plausible theory," he goes on, that Turner reacted to "cruelty is not supported by the facts." It is, says Cooke, the simple case of "a negro of feeble person [i.e., mind]" being driven mad by "passions and superstitions," the result of which was "a frenzied desire to shed blood, without further aims."[29] Even as late as 1941, a writer for the Virginia WPA saw the Southampton debacle as "an orgy of butchery" brought into bloody being by a religious maniac who had "exhorted into frenzy" his fellow-slaves.[30]

The only change of note rung on the Gray thesis was the accusation, utterly predictable and without any foundation in fact, that Abolitionist propaganda had driven over the brink a mind already unbalanced by superstition. In his "The Morals of Slavery . . ." William Gilmore Simms attributed the Southampton insurrection to "the secret workings of the abolitionists,"[31] and W. S. Drewry found abolitionist incitation a useful explanation for an event which seemed to him rationally opaque—a well-treated slave leading a murderous insurrection.[32] Something of the same thing is to be seen in *The Old Dominion; or, The Southampton Massacre* (1856) by G. P. R. James, an Englishman whose four years' residence in Virginia as consul at Norfolk evidently made him sympathetic—at least partially—to the southern view of Turner. Sir Richard Conway, the hero, has inherited a plantation close to the one on which Turner is a slave. His first meeting with Turner jars his conception of the Negro as a happy-go-lucky child of nature utterly devoid of intellect. Sir Richard is initially impressed by Turner's apparent metaphysical cast of mind, although Turner's idiotic laugh upon catching a fish gives the Englishman pause. In subsequent meetings Sir Richard acknowledges that Turner is a superior specimen, but that even he has "almost all the peculiar weaknesses of the African race"; he is cunning, superstitious, conceited and, as Sir Richard discerns, capable of ruthless cruelty. The real villain in the piece, however, is a nefarious northern abolitionist, the Reverend Mr. M'Grubber, who duplicitously incites Turner to his disastrous insurrection and is given his just deserts when he becomes the first man Turner kills. "I have come to the conclusion"—says Sir Richard's "acute friend"—"that the abolitionists are the very worst enemies of the slaves themselves."

Of far greater interest are the responses in the North to Gray's proslavery apology. Unwittingly, the *Confessions*, directly or indirectly, set in motion a process of reverse mythologization by giving the antislavery intellectuals a romantic symbol which they could recreate in terms of their own most passionate convictions. Although the emphases vary, these writers changed Turner's purpose, his motivation, the quality of his mind, the character of his religion, even his appearance. The maniac became messiah; the Black Beast became the Black John Brown; mad murder became moral symbol.

When the nonresistant abolitionist William Lloyd Garrison read Gray's pamphlet, he acidly remarked that a bounty should be put on Gray's head, for his pamphlet would "hasten other insurrections," a method of emancipation to which he was strongly opposed. Mrs. Stowe also read the pamphlet as creating a slave-hero; but because she saw slavery as primarily a religious problem, her response to Gray's Turner was not Garrison's. That Turner had aligned himself with the Savior—"Was not Christ crucified?" —was for Mrs. Stowe the decisive fact. In *Dred* (1856), to which she appended the *Confessions*, presumably for the purpose of authenticating her portrait, the title character, although nominally the son of Denmark Vesey, is really Nat Turner. Like Gray's Turner, Dred has learned to read with mysterious ease, has seen bloody "hieroglyphics" on the leaves and the crucified Christ in the heavens, and is consumed by his sense of an apocalyptic destiny. But the proslavery Turner is, of course, turned 180 degrees —from a "warped and perverted" demon to a sacrificial prophet of emancipation. "Nat Turner—they killed him," Dred exclaims, "but the fear of him almost drove them to set free their slaves! . . . Die? Why not die? Christ was crucified."

When Thomas Wentworth Higginson, a brave champion of the black man's rights, turned his attention to "Nat Turner's Insurrection" in 1861,[33] he did so with something more than a scholarly interest in his subject. His sources were contemporary newspaper accounts, "legends" and what he calls "a small pamphlet, containing the main features of the outbreak" (not Gray's, he admits). His essay, however, is an imaginative construct as well, for it was Higginson's intention to contour a portrait which would validate his claim that "beside the actual Nat Turner," Mrs. Stowe's "Dred seems dim and melodramatic."

Higginson's Nat Turner suffers the indignities and injustices of slavery. He has a wife whom he cannot protect from sexual "outrage," scars on his body which may have come from white hands, and a band of blacks that "had been systematically brutalized from childhood" and who "had seen their wives and sisters habitually polluted" by white ravishers. More important, Prophet Nat has the strength of character that comes of rectitude, such as had John Brown, to whom he is compared. He confesses his crimes but pleads not guilty; meets his death "with perfect composure," signaling the sheriff "in a firm voice that he was ready"; and at his execution "not a limb nor a muscle was observed to move." (The source for these facts, it will be noted, is the passage which was later spuriously added to Gray's Confessions.)

But what is most significant in Higginson's portrait is his handling of the mystical pronouncements of Gray's Turner. Higginson acknowledges them, to be sure, quoting whole passages. As "religious hallucinations," he remarks casually, they are "as genuine as the average of such things, and are very well expressed." As Higginson begins to deploy them, however, it be-

comes clear that he views them as rhetorical strategies for revealing the intensity of Turner's commitment to freedom for his
people, a commitment so passionate that it needed the vocabulary
of apocalypticism to be adequately exposed. Even Thomas Gray,
in Higginson's reading, when vouchsafed a symbolic glimpse into
"the heart of this extraordinary man . . . who devoted himself soul
and body to the cause of his race" (in the manacled hands to
heaven scene), rose, despite himself, "into a sort of bewildered
enthusiasm." It was no religious fanatic, then, who fell like an
"earthquake on the doomed community around—and who . . .
took the life of man, woman, and child, without a throb of com-
punction, a word of exultation, or an act of superfluous outrage."
It was, rather, in Higginson's final words, "a symbol of retribution
triumphant."

Two years earlier, the preface to a heavily edited reprint of
Gray's *Confessions* in the *Anglo-African Magazine* for 1859 made
a somewhat different use of the Turner insurrection. "Emancipation must come, and soon," the black writer pronounced, and in
only two ways could it be effected—the way of John Brown or the
way of Nat Turner. Whereas John Brown believed that emancipation could be accomplished without blood by making the two
races equal, "Nat Turner's terrible logic could only see the en-
franchisement of one race compassed by the extirpation of the
other." Had the order of events been reversed, the writer went on
to say, "had Nat Turner been in John Brown's place . . . the soil
of Virginia and Maryland and the far South, would by this time
be drenched in blood." If John Brown's method of emancipation
be not soon adopted, "then Nat Turner's will be by the enslaved
South." Here Turner is neither maniac nor messiah, religious
fanatic nor symbol of retribution. His insurrection is seen, rather,
as the inevitable recoil to historical injustice, which, if not soon
obviated in a rational manner, will leave the American slave with
no choice other than Turner's "wild and sanguinary course."
Which shall it be, the editorial concludes, Brown's way of reason
or Turner's way of mass blood-letting? (p. 356).

William Wells Brown, who himself had at one time been a
slave, devoted sixteen pages of his *The Black Man, His Anteced-*

ents, His Genius, and His Achievements (1863) to Nat Turner,[34] almost half of them direct quotation from some version of Gray's pamphlet. Brown clearly had a fertile imagination: at one time or another he put forward three different autobiographical versions of his parentage and childhood. His novelistic bent (he was the author of *Clotel*) served him well in his dramatization of the progress of Nat Turner from a child "of an amiable disposition" to the gloomy man who "was never known to smile," thus fleshing out those "private . . . wrongs" which Higginson said we could never know. Detailed anecdotes, minutely observed settings, and long speeches give the impression that Brown was there (as a novelist is "there") and bring Turner much closer to the reader than he is in Higginson's account. Brown gives no sources for his sketch except for Gray, who, he says, "had known Nat from boyhood," thus perhaps implying that Gray is the source for Brown's stories of Turner's childhood, which he is not.

It is in the context of the southern view of the Southampton insurrectionist that Brown's opening assertion that "the American people are not prepared to do justice" to Turner is to be understood. Accordingly, Brown sets out to trace the "circumstances" which changed an intelligent young slave of "kind and docile" disposition into one who was wracked with "the most intense hatred [for] the white race." Brown begins with two as-the-twig-is-bent incidents. When still a boy, Turner was "severely flogged" by two "patrolers," Whitlock and Mull, for being off his master's plantation without a pass; a few months later, a gang of white boys cruelly pelted Nat, who had "no right to retaliate," with snowballs. No Sambo, Nat responds to these incidents with a burning desire for revenge. With Tom Sawyer–cleverness, Nat tricks the two patrolers into an accident, Mull suffering a dislocated shoulder and a severely lacerated face, and Whitlock a broken wrist and a bashed head; a concealed Nat repays the gang of boys for their snowballs with accurately hurled rocks. Both incidents, as Brown-the-novelist shapes them, not only serve as motivating factors but also as symbolic prophecies of the central action of Turner's life, thereby contributing significantly to that sense of wholeness and continuity in his subject's life which all mythicized figures must possess.

Growing ill-treatment causes Nat to withdraw more and more into himself and into communion with his visions. "Being hired out to cruel masters" (in Gray, "placed under an overseer"), Nat runs away for thirty days but returns, his only explanation being the biblical injunction "Return to your earthly master, for he who knoweth his Master's will, and doeth it not, shall be beaten with many stripes." (Brown omits the rest of the quotation which in Gray concludes with "and thus have I chastened you.") The final meeting before the insurrection takes place in a "wild and romantic" swampland "upon which human feet seldom trod, on account of its having been the place where a slave had been tortured to death by a slow fire." Turner's final speech, which is "quoted" directly, certainly attempts to normalize the insurrection. It concludes: "Remember that we do not go forth for the sake of blood and carnage, but it is necessary that in the commencement of this revolution all the whites we meet should die, *until we shall have an army strong enough to carry on the war upon a Christian basis* [emphasis added]. Remember that ours is not a war for robbery and to satisfy our passions; it is a struggle for freedom. Ours must be deeds, not words. Then let's away to the scene of action." Then follows the account of the progress of the insurrection from Gray, and Nat's conduct at his execution from the interpolated paragraph already referred to.

An interesting addition to the legend is Brown's expanded characterization of Will, who here functions as a contrast to Turner. In Gray, all we learn of Will is that he joined the conspiracy without invitation, was willing to die for freedom and earned the title of "executioner" for his work during the slaughter. In Brown, however, Will joins the revolt "as much to satisfy revenge, as for the liberty he saw in the dim distance." His scarred body and face, testimony to his intractableness (he "scorned the idea of taking his master's name"), and the memory of "a dear and beloved wife sold to the negro trader" turn him into the most "bloodthirsty and revengeful" of the insurrectionists. His dying words were, "Bury

my axe with me," because, Brown explains, Will "religiously believed that in the next world the blacks would have a contest with
the whites, and that he would need his axe." Here, then, we can
see how some of the religious madness of the proslavery image of
Turner has been shifted to one of his lieutenants.[35]

Brown concludes his portrait with a conscious attempt to evoke
Turner's mythic status—and a warning. Turner had predicted
that the sun would refuse to shine at his death, and so it was that
Southampton suffered the most "boisterous" storm in its history
on the day of his execution. He is dead but his acts "live in the
hearts of his race, on every cotton, sugar, and rice plantation at
the South." For the present generation of slaves there is magic in
his name and a belief that in another insurrection "Nat Turner
will appear and take command." In the midst of the crisis of the
Civil War, in which "the negro is an important item," all eyes are
"turned towards the south, looking for another Nat Turner." And
this should curdle the blood of the slaveholding states as Turner
himself had curdled the blood of Thomas Gray, for "a negro insurrection, in the present excited state of the nation, would not
receive the condemnation that it did in 1831."

Brown's omissions are of interest and worth speculating upon.
He omits Turner's identification of himself with Christ (from
Gray) perhaps because it smacked too much of religious mania;
he makes no mention of the baptizing of the white man, Etheldred
T. Brantley (also from Gray), perhaps because it would jar the
black-white antithesis he works with—there are no good white
men in the sketch; and he does not acknowledge the wife Higginson says Turner had (Brown had read Higginson's essay) because he may have felt that such a human connection would have
destroyed his portrait of a lonely, isolated figure enveloped in
"a gloom and melancholy that disappeared only with his life," one
married solely to a desire for "freedom for his race."

The Nat Turner in George Washington Williams's magisterial
History of the Negro Race in America (1883)[36] is essentially that
of Wells Brown, much of which he quotes and paraphrases. The
same items are omitted and the portrait is similarly directed toward presenting a "Black John Brown," whose image "is carved

on the fleshy tablets of four million hearts," although because legal slavery was no more, Williams does not add the threat of further insurrections. Williams's contribution to the evolving image of Turner resides primarily in the extent to which he regularizes Turner's religion, making him even less of a religious freak than he was in Brown (who considered Turner's visions "wild" and the man himself, at least partially, though not crucially, "a victim of his own fanaticism"). Williams who was himself, amongst an impressive variety of accomplishments, a Baptist minister, considers Turner "a Christian and a *man*." Nat's early background made a religious emphasis inevitable. His parents, though unlettered, were very pious people, the father a preacher and the mother "a mother in Israel." From a very early age Nat was "set apart to the Gospel ministry by his father, the church, and visiting preachers." Turner's orthodoxy is revealed in his severe denunciations of such pagan practices as " 'conjuring,' 'gufering,' and fortune telling." It is to his well-meaning mother that Nat owed his sense of mission: "she would sing to him snatches of wild rapturous songs and repeat portions of prophecies she had learned from the preachers of the times." To these exciting tales the impressionable youngster "listened with reverence and awe, and believed every thing his mother said." His grandmother, too, "a very old and superstitious person [Brown called her "ignorant"] encouraged him in his dreams." His death is a set piece of Christian sentimentalism: "He died like a man, bravely, calmly, looking into eternity, made radiant by a faith that never faltered."

By the time Turner comes to William J. Simmons's massive biographical dictionary, *Men of Mark* (1887),[37] all mention of the bizarre aspects of Turner's religion has disappeared. Turner is now a Baptist preacher ordained by his father; his eyes "shone with the brightness of diamonds" whenever "he spoke of the Scriptures or the wrongs of his race." On Sundays he would come to the plantations to preach to the slaves and then go back to the mountains "to brood over the condition of his burdened people." Naturally, Simmons remarks (with justice), some racists have tried to demean this "Spartacus of the Negro race" by calling "him a religious fanatic." "When men of other nations have arisen and used whatever means they had at their command to liberate their people, it has been called heroism; with the Negro it is brutality." Simmons's clear-eyed "bold emancipator" has come as far from Gray's "gloomy fanatic" as it is possible to come: the counter-myth is complete. Simmons's most imaginative addition is his expansion of the story of Turner's having run away for thirty days. Where before Turner simply leaves, here he strikes the slave breaker to the ground and leaves him tied in ropes.[38]

As we hope the above survey makes clear, Styron's novelistic attempt, in his words, "to re-create and bring alive that dim and prodigious black man" is not, as hostility would have it, a "libel-ous" deviation from history into myth. It is, rather, very much a part of a tradition. Styron has "used" Nat Turner as Gray, Hig-ginson, Wells Brown, and, indeed, the accusing critics themselves have used him—reading into him, and out of him, those usable truths which seemed to him to coalesce about the image he was contemplating. Styron's hostile critics may not like what his imaginative search has turned up; they may even in the free coun-try which is literary study denigrate his motives and try to deny him the right to his subject. But they can scarcely attack his "meditation on history" from some supposedly unassailable ram-part of historicity. There is no such lofty redoubt from which to hurl down upon the head of the author of *The Confessions of Nat Turner* a barrage of shattering historical facts with the killing aim these ten black critics imagine they possess, as the following ex-amples will illustrate.[39]

"In real history," says John A. Williams, "Will was almost as patient and self-possessed as Turner" (p. 48). Mike Thelwell strenuously takes exception, as does Aptheker, to Styron's depic-tion of Will as a bestial, hate-ravished, scarred-up "half-nigger, half-beast" (Williams's words—p. 88). It is quite true, as Thel-well contends, that the Will in Gray does not suggest dementia or frenzy. It is difficult, however, to see the efficient killer whom the Turner in Gray refers to as "the executioner" as being "patient," if Gray's pamphlet is what Williams means by "real history." But more to the point, William Wells Brown (whom Thelwell quotes approvingly, though he calls him James Wells Brown and cites the wrong book) tells us that Will, a battleground of physical and mental scars, has indeed been driven nearly mad by his life under slavery. Brown's Will joined the insurrection "as much to satisfy revenge, as for the liberty he saw in the dim distance"—which is to say more immediately for revenge than for freedom. Having been tormented beyond endurance, Will turns out to be the most "unfeeling of the insurrectionists," the most "bloodthirsty and revengeful" of the conspirators, and his dying wish to be buried with his axe so as to be ready for the race war in the afterlife is a moving revelation of hatred becoming psychotic. If the accounts of Will in William Wells Brown and George Washington Williams (they are similar) are historical (and Thelwell says "Mr. Brown . . . was, after all, writing history, not fiction"), then Styron's Will is equally so. If they are not, then Brown and Williams also deserve the "racist" label for having turned Will into a "black beast stereotype." Considering the little we learn of Will from Gray's pamphlet, Thelwell's view of Will as an "archetypal destroyer" is quite as "imaginative" as Styron's portrait of him as a slavery-maddened killer.

The outraged critical objection to the form which Will's desire for revenge takes in Styron's novel—murder and rape are twisted in his mind into a single cathartic act—is admittedly more problematic. No sexual incidents seem to have occurred during the insurrection, and Styron depicts none. The absence of sexual molestation seemed remarkable enough to later commentators to be worth noting. Higginson, for example—who is approvingly cited by various of the critics on other historical matters—mentions a report that some of the conspirators "were resolved on taking white women for wives, but were overruled by Nat Turner." "If so," he goes on to say, "he is the only American slave-leader of whom we know certainly that he rose above the ordinary level of slave vengeance" (p. 176). Considering the well-documented fact that servile vengeance (and not just black) often takes the form of murder and sexual outrage, and that Higginson gives us some reason for believing that the Turner insurrection was not *wholly* eccentric in this regard, then Styron's decision to characterize Will as he did is not an utter historical "perversion," as has been asserted, although there is no *biographical* justification for the portrait. With the exception of Turner himself, no other conspirator is so individuated in the historical record as is Will; his ferocity made him the logical choice to act out an authentic modality of slave life, without which the depiction of that wretchedly peculiar institution would be that much the more incomplete. In this connection it is instructive to glance at Arna Bontemps's *Black Thunder* (1936), the novel which has been repeatedly flung in Styron's face as an example of how a slave-revolt novel should be written.

The sexual undertone of Gabriel Prosser's revolt reverberates effectively all through *Black Thunder*. Bontemps's handling of the one murder in the insurrection is a splendid dramatization of what Harold Cruse in *The Crisis of the Negro Intellectual* has described as "that racial drama of love and hate between slave and master, bound together in the purgatory of plantations." As Criddle, one of the insurrectionists, crouches outside a white farmhouse, he derives

> an unaccountable pleasure from the thought of thrusting [his scythe-sword] through the pale young female that stood looking into the darkness. . . . Yet she looked flower-like and beautiful to him there. . . . She reminded him of a certain indentured white girl in town, a girl who made free with slaves. . . . That wasn't the kind of cutting he was up against tonight, though. Yet and still, there *were* similarites. . . . He held his sword arm tense; the scythe blade rose, stiffened, stiffened and remained erect. "I'm going to start in right here, me."[40]

Such explicit use of sexual imagery to crisscross and complicate the desire for murder during an insurrection by a black novelist in no way vitiates black critical enthusiasm for this "tremendous and perceptive novel." But when one of these critics contemplates a similarly imaged scene of sex and death in Styron's work, he contemptuously dismisses it with, "it looks as if nigger-beast has struck again" (p. 89).

Styron assigns Turner's education to his white master, but the critics insist that he was taught by his parents, citing the 1831 *Confessions* as evidence; they interpret this transfer as part of Styron's plot to create, as Bennett puts it, "a proper ADC slave family" (p. 9). Aptheker, who likewise sees Styron working in terms of "the so-called Moynihan thesis," puts the matter square-ly: "Turner tells us that his parents taught him to read—though he adds that he has no memory of just how early this occurred" ("A Note on the History," p. 375). This is not *quite* what the pamphlet says. First of all, "Turner" does not tell us that his parents taught him to read. In that part of the *Confessions* in which he is presumably speaking in his own voice he says, "the manner in which I learned to read and write . . . had great influence on my mind, as I acquired it with the most perfect ease, so much so that I have no recollection whatever of learning the alphabet." More-over, his parents could hardly have taught him because when he demonstrated his ability, it was "to the astonishment of the fam-ily." It is *Gray*, speaking in his own voice, who later, in corroborat-ing Turner's literacy, adds parenthetically "(it was taught him by his parents)." The matter, then, is not as unambiguous as these critics would lead us to believe. It is interesting to note, in this connection, that none of the later sympathetic accounts of Tur-ner ascribes his learning to read to his parents, evidently pre-ferring the more romantic explanation. When William Wells Brown, for example, quotes the passage in which Gray's paren-thesis appears, he drops it out without a sign, having already chosen to go with the averred legend that "a full knowledge of the alphabet came to him in a single night" (pp. 72, 61). Only the proslavery accounts—those which had a vested interest in em-phasizing the dangers of slave literacy—ascribed Turner's educa-tion to his parents.

There is nothing particularly "corrupt" historically about Sty-ron's having rejected both explanations—the familial and the mys-tical—and having chosen to have Turner taught to read by a white master. After all, that prototypical slave-rebel, Frederick Doug-lass (whose autobiographical writings are one of the "sources" of Styron's novel), was similarly served by a white owner. The rejection of the mystical explanation is part of Styron's intention —which, as we have seen, was *the* intention of the nineteenth-century pro-Turnerites—to eliminate Turner's most fanatic face, that religious warrior-freak who, Gray and Cooke knew, would be hard for the slaveholder or racist to recognize. This led him to omit as well the descriptions of Turner "praying at the plow," the bizarre "hieroglyphic characters . . . in blood," the manacled-hands-to-heaven scene in which Turner becomes "a spirit soaring above the attributes of man," and the literal identification of himself with Christ—which Mrs. Stowe found so apt but which the later black historians downgraded. Since Styron intended a representationally human victim of the tragedy of slavery, the critical accusation that he refused "to confront the man who talked to God and who heard God order the destruction of the enemies of God and man" (p. 12) could hardly strike him as telling. It may be, as Bennett asserts, that Turner's visions "are obviously genuine [since] Thomas Gray was hardly up to inventions of that order" (p. 5), but it is interesting to note that in the preface to the 1968 reprint of *Black Thunder* Arna Bontemps tells us that one of the reasons he chose *not* to write on the Turner insurrection "was the business of Nat's 'visions' and 'dreams.' " Not quite knowing how to take this "trance-like mumbo jumbo," and, like Styron, distrusting Gray, he turned to Gabriel Prosser, for "freedom was a less complicated affair in his case" (pp. xii–xiii).

Styron's decision to have Samuel Turner teach his intelligent slave to read, although without specific justification in the historical record, is part of his intention to expose one aspect of the relationship of the well-meaning slaveholder to the institution of slavery. That is, it functions in the service of revealing that well-validated historical insight which Styron in the novel calls "the central madness of nigger existence": that the more humanely the slave was treated the more he rebelled against the inhumanity of his condition. Samuel Turner, the benevolent slaveholder, it will be remembered, is the only man for whom Turner felt a gaggingly intense personal hatred, and who, more than anyone else in the novel, impelled Turner to his final decision to make white blood flow "in a foaming sacrament." The truth of this apparently paradoxical insight was first testified to by Frederick Douglass, who repeatedly asserted that kind treatment intensified rather than lessened the slave's desire for freedom. Higginson, remarking on "the extreme felicity of [Turner's] position as a slave" (in Gray, Turner acknowledged that his last owner "was to me a kind master [of whose treatment] I had no cause to complain") also pointed to the paradox that "in all insurrections, the standing wonder seems to be that the slaves most trusted and best used should be most involved" (p. 186). It is therefore puzzling in the extreme to discover that these critics, for whom Gray, Douglass, and Higginson are historically valid touchstones (Higginson and Douglass are repeatedly cited), consider this aspect of Styron's novel another instance of his lack of historical understanding "of the psychology which makes slaves rise up and cut their oppressors' throats from ear to ear." For Charles Hamilton, such a portrayal denies Turner "his basic revolutionary temperament" and shows "Styron join[ing] that school of thought which believes that the kinder you treat the subjects, the more likely they are to rebel" (p. 76). And Loyle Hairston reads the slaveowner's kindness in the novel as Styron's attempt to show how "benign" the peculiar institution was, to prove that Turner's insurrection was only "the vengeful ingratitude of a literate, pampered slave for his benevolent masters, an ingratitude which turns, unprovoked, into hatred and murder" (p. 67). This not only demonstrates a lack of knowledge of the historical tradition in which Styron is working, but a penchant for malicious misreading as well.[41]

Among the other "historical discrepancies" of which Styron is accused is his handling of Turner's grandmother and his omission of Turner's reputed wife.[42] In Gray, Turner says of his grandmother only that she encouraged him in his sense of special destiny and that he was "much attached" to her. Later accounts either drop her or characterize her as "ignorant" or "superstitious" (Brown and Williams), part of that fundamentalistic religious ambience which helps to explain Turner's "belief that he had seen visions, and received communications direct from God." Since Styron deemphasized this aspect of the received legend, Turner's grandmother (even in memory) functions in a quite different historical way. In one of the most moving scenes in *The Confessions of Nat Turner*, Nat at age thirteen thinks of his grandmother dead at thirteen, as he stands gazing at the decaying orthography of the Negro cemetery. Destroyed by a Christian civilization, Turner's grandmother lies in a grave marked by a monument of poignant irony:

"TIG"
AET. 13
BORN AN
HEATHEN
DIED BAP-
TISED IN CHRIST
A.D. 1782
R.I.P.

Turner has never laid eyes on his grandmother, though he has "heard about her and her kind"; in his mind's eye he can see the pregnant, terrified Coromantee child-woman, paralyzed at the approach of her white owner, who to her was "white, white as bone or skulls or deadwood, whiter than those ancestral ghosts that prowl the African night," and who she believes is about to eat her. Having been "driven crazy by her baffling captivity," she tries to tear to pieces her newborn baby, Nat's mother, and dies in a stupor a few days later, having refused to eat. Why should Thelwell, who knows something of the history of slavery, be so contemptuous of this portrait of, as he snidely puts it, "a mute, catatonic, culturally shocked Coromantee wench" (p. 83)? True enough, there is no historical source, narrowly construed, for the portrait; but, typologically, it is unassailably historical, and, more important, its presence in the novel makes the evil of human bondage reverberate in a far wider historical context than it would if it were limited to just the actual life of the protagonist.

In making Turner derive from a Coromantee (we do not know from which tribe or tribes he actually derived), Styron has placed his insurrectionist in the tradition of African rebellion. For, as he would know from his reading of Mannix and Cowley's *Black Cargoes*, the Coromantees were the most frequent leaders of slave mutinies. The Jamaica House of Assembly, for example, in describing a series of slave revolts in the mid-eighteenth century, reported that "all these disturbances . . . have been planned and conducted by the Coromantin Negroes who are distinguished from their brethren by the . . . martial ferocity of their dispositions."[43] Moreover, the shocked response of Nat's grandmother is not historically absurd. Many Africans believed that the white men were malevolent spirits who planned to eat them. Oloudah Equiano (or Gustavus Vassa), who was enslaved about the time of Nat's grandmother and who was also sold to a Virginia planter, tells in his memoirs of the terror he experienced at first encountering his white captors. Their strange complexions and language terrified Oloudah into believing that he had fallen "into a world of bad spirits"; and when he saw the boiling copper cauldron on ship and the chained slaves in a state of dejection, he was convinced that he was "to be eaten by those white men with horrible looks," and, "quite overpowered with horror and anguish," he fainted away on the deck.[44] Other slaves, less resilient than Oloudah, suffered the fate of Nat's grandmother, as witness this contemporary account: "Many of the slaves we transport . . . to America are prepossessed with the opinion that they are carried like sheep to the slaughter and that the Europeans are fond of their flesh; which notion so far prevails with some as to make them fall into a deep melancholy and to refuse all sustenance, tho' never so much compelled and even beaten to oblige them to take some nourishment; notwithstanding all which they will starve to death."[45]

Styron makes no mention of Turner's having a wife. This omission particularly infuriates the black critics because, as they see it, it is part and parcel of the white novelist's plot to depict Turner as a brute nigger lusting only after white women. Drawing upon Higginson (who probably got it from Warner's highly questionable pamphlet), they uniformly assert that the real Turner had a slave wife, the unequivocal evidence for which Styron deliberately ignored in pursuit of his "project" to destroy "the vitals of the historical personage named Nat Turner" (pp. vii, 11, 20, 40, 63). "Why is not the author," Alvin Poussaint asks pointedly, "able to 'imagine' that Nat Turner had a young, feminine, beautiful, and courageous black woman who stood by his side throughout his heroic plan to revolt against slavery!?" (p. 21). One might begin by answering that the very source which Poussaint cites as evidence for the existence of such a woman (Higginson, p. 174), says that "Nat Turner's young wife was a slave [who] belonged to a different master from himself," so that it would have been rather difficult for her to be by his side all through the lengthy planning stages for the insurrection. More apposite, however, is why if Turner had a wife did he not mention her in Gray? He mentions the rest of his family. (Given our position on Gray's document, we could argue that the presence of an emotional motivation for the revolt —the splitting up of families—would militate against Gray's portrait of motiveless malignity; but these critics take the document rather straight, so they cannot avail themselves of such an explanation.) Anna Mary Wells's explanation for Turner's failure to mention his wife in Gray's *Confessions* as an attempt "to spare her further suffering" is extremely far-fetched since it assumes that Turner believed that no one knew he had a wife, which, considering the composition and size of the society in which Turner lived, is rather unlikely. Miss Wells may have had this explanation suggested to her by Daniel Panger's novel, *Ol' Prophet Nat* (1967), in which Nat doesn't write the name of his wife in his diary (found by the narrator in a present-day junk shop) for fear that "the raging white men might blame her for some part in my doings." And finally, if, as Miss Wells says, at the time Higginson wrote the existence of Nat Turner's wife "had then never been questioned,"[46] then why did William Wells Brown, two years later, make no mention of her, especially since the ripping apart of husbands and wives was one of his explanations for the insurrection? Nor did any of the other nineteenth-century black historians mention her. Even Aptheker, who formulated the pattern for the critical attacks-from-history, omits the detail of a wife from his catalog of Styron's historical "distortions." All this is to say, then, that Turner may indeed have had a wife, but there is no reasonable way to assert it as an unequivocal fact and then to use it as evidence of Styron's racist imagination.[47]

The charge of total historical irresponsibility has also been leveled at Styron in the matter of slaves helping to put down the Turner insurrection. For Aptheker the references in the novel "to masters arming loyal slaves to resist the rebels are made up of whole cloth; there is no evidence of this whatsoever . . ." ("A Note on the History," p. 376). Thelwell concurs: "Mr. Styron, contrary to any historical evidence, has Turner's ultimate defeat coming as a result of the actions of loyal slaves who fought in defense of their beloved masters" (p. 90). This is too unequivocally put. But first, to set the record straight, Styron does not attribute Turner's *ultimate* defeat to the loyal slaves: his Turner says only that "the black man had caused my defeat *just as surely as* the white" (italics mine); moreover, there is no indication in the novel that the slaves fight their racial brothers out of love for their masters: we are told that they fight with "passion and fury," which need hardly imply love but only repressed assertiveness which welcomes any kind of outlet, even the tragic one of slave killing slave.

A lack of black solidarity, although not encountered with the frequency that a proslavery mythology would have had us believe, is nevertheless one of the sad facts of history. According to the black social historian E. Franklin Frazier, "faithful house-servants were often bound . . . to their masters by close emotional ties and common interests" and "in Jamaica and Brazil, where Negro revolts were generally more successful [than in the United States], it was always a faithful slave who revealed a conspiracy."[48] Both the Prosser and Vesey plots were, as already remarked, betrayed by loyal blacks. William Wells Brown tells us in his *Narrative* that "twenty-one years in slavery had taught me that there were traitors, even among colored people,"[49] and the escaping hero of his *Clotel* of 1853 acts out the lesson his author learned in life by not daring to "go amongst even his colored associates for fear of being betrayed" (p. 227). In Gray, Turner tells us that although he begged two Negroes to conceal him from the whites, he knew from their responses that "they would betray me."

At the slightest rumor of an uprising, John Hope Franklin has written, "All whites—loyal Negroes, too—were expected to do their share to prevent death and destruction from stalking through the land."[50] Although there is no justification for the "great numbers" that are mentioned in the novel,[51] there is also no justification for the allegation that Styron has made up the situation out of whole cloth, "contrary to any historical evidence." Higginson, in recounting a touching story of a slave who had saved his master's life during the insurrection and then asked to be killed because he could no longer live in bondage, remarks that the master must be one Dr. Blunt—"his being the only plantation where slaves were reported as . . . defending their masters" (p. 181). Brown tells something of the same story but in his version the master is one Captain Harris. Whether this indicates another plantation on which slaves helped their masters or whether it is the same story with a different cast of characters, it is impossible to tell. At any rate, buried in the records of the 1832 Virginia legislature is this partial corroboration of Higginson: "The Assembly received five petitions on the part of persons who had lost eight slaves in the suppression of the Insurrection, praying that they might receive the value of their negroes. More justifiable was the petition for compensation for a slave killed while actually in arms in defense of Dr. Blunt's house."[52]

Several other alleged historical discrepancies deserve at least brief attention. John Killens wonders "why did not Styron use Walker's *Appeal* as part of Turner's motivation?" "Surely," Killens thinks, "Nat had read and been inspired, yes, inflamed by David Walker's *Appeal . . . to the Colored Citizens of the World But in Particular and very Expressly to those of the United States*," and concludes that Styron was trying to give the impression that there was very little unrest among the slaves and that therefore Turner "was some kind of freak" among his brother slaves (p. 41). The kind of motivation Killens wants, as we have already seen, was that suggested by several proslavery writers on Turner, but is without historical foundation. Aptheker, after surveying the possibilities of a literary stimulus, concludes, "The fact is that never has an iota of evidence been submitted to show any abolitionist propaganda, of the Walker, Garrison, or milder type, had any connection whatsoever with bringing on the Turner revolt" (*Nat Turner's Slave Rebellion*, p. 42). Killens also objects to Turner's comparing himself to Napoleon in the novel ("Lord, how I strove to drive the idea of a nigger Napoleon into their ignorant minds!") —"why did not Nat think to inspire them with an example of black militancy in the person of black Toussaint?" (p. 42).

Comparisons to the white John Brown are ubiquitous in the pro-Turner literature, but to Toussaint L'Ouverture not at all. There is no more evidence for believing that Turner was influenced by Napoleon than by Walker or L'Ouverture, but Wells Brown did at least find an analogy between Turner and Napoleon (p. 59). There is, at any rate, an unsuspected irony in Killens's approval of Gabriel Prosser's having compared himself to George Washington in contrast to Styron's Turner having compared himself to Napoleon: a Virginia slaveholder as model seems even less appropriate than the French "man of destiny" (pp. 39, 43).

One of the more astonishing moments in Gray's pamphlet is Turner's story of having converted and baptized a sinful white man, Etheldred T. Brantley. Of Brantley personally we know almost nothing, except what we can reconstruct imaginatively from between the lines.

> About this time I told these things [the coming Day of Judgment] to a white man, (Etheldred T. Brantley) on whom it had a wonderful effect—and he ceased from his wickedness, and was attacked immediately with a cutaneous eruption, and blood oozed from the pores of his skin, and after praying and fasting nine days, he was healed, and the Spirit appeared to me again, and said, as the Saviour had been baptised so should we be also—and when the white people would not let us be baptised by the church, we went down into the water together, in the sight of many who reviled us, and were baptised by the Spirit—After this I rejoiced greatly, and gave thanks to God.

Higginson adds only the fact that Brantley was "poor"—as of course he must have been; the later nineteenth-century commentators drop him.

Styron portrays Brantley as an impoverished, physically repulsive, ignorant homosexual, whose pleading presence fills Turner with "pity and disgust." But it is just because Brantley is so agonized, so helpless, so enslaved by nature and circumstances, almost—Turner thinks—"as wretched and forsaken as the lowest Negro," that Turner agrees to "save" him. Styron follows Gray in the matters of Brantley's ghastly dermatological eruptions, the unsuccessful attempt to have the baptism take place in a church, the sacramental immersion in a natural body of water, and the outraged response of the crowd of whites who watch the baptism. Brantley's "wickedness" Styron concretizes into drunkenness and sexual deviationalism. Thelwell and Harding consider Styron's portrait as "demeaning" Nat Turner, as "diminishing [his] power," since only "a pariah-like" white man is shown as being "drawn to Nat Turner's religious teachings," only a "degenerate . . . is shown associating with slaves on anything that looks like simple human terms" (pp. 27, 87).

Therefore, when the critics condemn Styron's portrait as having no justification in the historical record, they can mean only the form that Brantley's "wickedness" takes in the novel. Yet Thelwell himself admits that Turner's baptizing a white man was "an event unprecedented in Tidewater Virginia of the time." What then must have been the depths of self-loathing and shame that drove a white man, even the most wretched of poor whites, to seek the help of what he would have thought of as a nigger preacher rather than some religious of his own color? Perhaps, too, something of Brantley's moral state can be induced from the suddenness and severity of his dermatitis, which, in Gray, sounds suspiciously psychosomatic. Brantley's physical affliction, if indeed it is psychological in origin, would be consonant with some guilt far more terrible than a merely generalized feeling of sinfulness or just drunkenness. It is precisely because Panger's Brantley is only a drunkard in *Ol' Prophet Nat* (with a consumptive wife and sickly children) that the entire interlude is so unconvincing. The encounter is handled so casually that even the baptism comes off without the presence of reviling spectators. We shall never of course know if Brantley's wickedness was pederasty, as Styron has it; but surely it, or something like it, is needed to explain the extraordinary behavior of Etheldred T. Brantley. But perhaps the truth, as we suspect, is that the objection is not so much to the characterization of Brantley as it is to the fact that Turner warns him of the coming holocaust. Nat Turner in Styron's novel finds himself the victim of his own humanity: he cannot do to whites what whites have done to blacks—reduce them all to an abstraction. For these critics, however, this is a betrayal of the historical Nat Turner, who, in their view, was committed to a revolutionary ethic that made no distinctions. It hardly needs to be pointed out, however, that even in "the basic historical document," Gray's pamphlet, Turner does treat a white man with a kindness that betokens a certain vulnerability to humane considerations.

It seems clear to us that the widely disseminated charge, believed even by some critics whose interest in *The Confessions of Nat Turner* is not politically motivated,[53] that Styron is guilty of distorting the facts of history is itself not supported by the facts. It has been the intention of this essay to try to free Styron's novel from the coffle of propagandistic criticism masquerading as historicity so that its achievement can be more justly evaluated. For us, that achievement is appreciable—and not only because as the great black historian of slavery Benjamin Quarles has suggested, in Styron's "pages Turner emerges as the man he must have been in real life."[54] Of greater importance is the fact that Styron's literary imagination, working with the fragments of a dynamic legend—which is all there is—has brought to life truths of the national ordeal of slavery which reverberate from 1831 to the present. Our survey of Nat Turner in the American imagination from Thomas Gray to William Styron has led us to believe that at least in this instance Macaulay's dictum should be reversed: History begins in the essay and ends in the novel.

Notes

1. *Liberator* 8(1968): 6.
2. John Henrik Clarke, ed. (Boston, 1968).
3. White's columns are in the 25 November and 9 December 1967 issues of the *New York Amsterdam News*, Wilson's in the 21 October and 30 December 1967 issues of the same newspaper.
4. The quotations are respectively from pp. 56, 72, viii, and 34 of *Ten Black Writers*.
5. Detroit *Free Press* (UPI), 13 March 1970.
6. Ralph Ellison, William Styron, Robert Penn Warren, C. Vann Woodward, "The Uses of History in Fiction," *Southern Literary Journal* 1 (1969): 74, 87.
7. Mercer Cook and Stephen E. Henderson, *The Militant Black Writer* (Madison, Wis., 1969), p. 74.

8. The connection between Turner and Carmichael or Brown is made throughout the book, sometimes explicitly (e.g., pp. ix, 32, 36), sometimes implicitly by reference to present-day Black Power advocates. A 1968 anthology of militant writings, *The Black Power Revolt*, includes a section from Gray's *Confessions*.

9. Quoted by W. P. Garrison, *William Lloyd Garrison* (New York, 1885), 1: 229.

10. All quotations from Gray's *Confessions* are from a facsimile copy of the 1831 edition in the William L. Clements Library of the University of Michigan.

11. This grisly fact is supported by John Cromwell, whose 1920 article reports that "there still lives a Virginian who has a piece of [Turner's] skin which was tanned." ("The Aftermath of Nat Turner's Insurrection," *Journal of Negro History* 5 [1920]: 218.)

12. Quoted by T. W. Higginson, "Gabriel's Defeat," *Atlantic Monthly* 10(1862): 337–45.

13. S. M. Hamilton, ed., *Writings of James Monroe* (New York, 1898–1903), 3: 201. The letter is dated 5 September 1800.

14. *Cannibals All!* (reprint ed., Cambridge, Mass., 1960), p. 200.

15. Quoted by Herbert Aptheker, *Nat Turner's Slave Rebellion* (New York, 1968), p. 58.

16. Quoted in C. G. Sellers, Jr., "The Travail of Slavery," *American Negro Slavery*, A. Weinstein and F. O. Gatell, eds. (New York, 1968), p. 179.

17. Aptheker, pp. 59–60.

18. Quoted in W. L. Katz, *Eyewitness: The Negro in American History* (New York, 1967), p. 104.

19. "Styron's Nat Turner . . . A Note on the History," *Nation* 205 (16 October 1967): 375–376.

20. What Gray is probably referring to is the *report* of an extensive slave conspiracy in eastern North Carolina in early October 1831. (See Hugh T. Lefler, ed., *North Carolina History Told by Contemporaries* [Chapel Hill, N.C., 1934], p. 265.)

21. An example of the perturbation caused by the Turner insurrection was the reaction in Murfreesboro, North Carolina, as reported by the *Baltimore Gazette* (16 November 1831): "Fear was seen in every face, women pale and terror stricken, children crying for protection, men fearful and full of foreboding, but determined to be ready for the worst" (Stephen B. Weeks, "The Slave Insurrection in Virginia," *Magazine of American History* 25 [1891]: 456).

22. "The case of Nat Turner warns us [that] no black man ought to be permitted to turn a preacher. . . . the law must be enforced—or the tragedy

of Southampton appeals to us in vain" (*Richmond Enquirer*, 30 April 1832).

23. *Narrative of the Life of Frederick Douglass* (reprint ed., Cambridge, Mass., 1967), p. 56.

24. Milton Meltzer, ed., *In Their Own Words: A History of the American Negro* (New York, 1967), 1: 26.

25. Quoted in Katz, p. 104.

26. Aptheker, p. 116

27. *The Confessions of Nat Turner* (1861, reprint ed., Miami, Fla., 1969), p. 12; *The Anglo-African Magazine* 1 (reprint ed., New York, 1968): 396.

28. "William Styron and Human Bondage: *The Confessions of Nat Turner*," *Hollins Critic* 4(1967): 6.

29. (New York, 1884), p. 487.

30. *Virginia: A Guide to the Old Dominion* (New York, 1941), p. 473.

31. *The Pro-Slavery Argument* (Charleston, S.C., 1852), p. 223.

32. William S. Drewry, *The Southampton Insurrection* (Washington, D.C., 1900), passim.

33. *Atlantic Monthly* 8(1861): 173–187.

34. (Reprint ed., New York, 1969), pp. 59–75.

35. It is interesting to compare the characterization of Will here with Brown's characterization of one Picquilo in his earlier account of the Turner insurrection. In *Clotel* (1853), Brown speaks of Picquilo (who is nowhere else mentioned in the literature of the revolt) as "one of the leaders of the Southampton insurrection"; this figure, from "one of the barbarous tribes in Africa," of "stern and savage countenance," from revenge imbrued his hands in the blood of all the whites he could meet" (*Clotel* [reprint ed., New York, 1968], pp. 59–60).

36. (Reprint ed., New York, 1968), 2: 85–90.

37. (Reprint ed., New York, 1968), pp. 1035–1039.

38. Until the appearance of Styron's novel and the critical recoil it occasioned, the twentieth century added little to the image of Nat Turner. Two plays—Randolph Edmonds's *Nat Turner* (1934) and Paul Peters's *Nat Turner* (1944)—are well intentioned but essentially unimaginative treatments of the Black Moses. Daniel Panger's novel, *Ol' Prophet Nat* (1947), to which we make reference further on in the text, is a rather pedestrian fictionalizing of Higginson's essay, which is its primary source. Those twentieth-century black historians who have devoted some attention to Turner's insurrection—Carter Woodson, E. Franklin Frazier, Saunders Redding, Benjamin Quarles, and John Hope Franklin, for example—have stayed pretty close to the slim historical record, content to describe what happened in objective terms.

39. We address ourselves only to criticisms of the novel premised on Styron's purported historical distortions of the facts. Objections to style or other formalistic matters, psychological credibility or wholly "made-up" characters or situations, we have mostly passed over as lying outside the focus of this study, although not, of course, as lying outside legitimate areas of defense.

40. (Reprint ed., Boston, 1968), pp. 90–92.

41. The ubiquitous association of Styron with the views of U. B. Phillips throughout *Ten Black Writers* is a depressing example of how when politics is in possession of a reader he can make himself believe anything he wants to, even to the point of fantasy.

42. The accusation in Ten Black Writers that "Styron has eliminated the troublesome black father" (p. 9) and that Turner "has no knowledge of his father" (p. 82) needs little to rebut it. It is simply not true. What is significant about Turner's father is that he was a proud man, who, when slapped by his owner, escaped into freedom for good. This action has left a decisive mark on Turner's memory and consciousness and is part of his evolving rebelliousness. That the father's escape takes place in the novel before Nat's birth rather than, as the legend has it, after, would seem to make no difference since even the child who was alive when it happened would have to think of it as an adult before its meaning would emerge for him.

43. Daniel P. Mannix and Malcolm Cowley, *Black Cargoes: A History of the Atlantic Slave Trade* (New York, 1965), p. 17.

44. *The Interesting Narrative of the Life of Oloudah Equiano; or, Gustavus Vassa the African.* Written by Himself (1791), excerpted in Meltzer, ed., *In Their Own Words*, 1: 3–4.

45. *Black Cargoes*, pp. 48–49. Cf. also pp. 85–86.

46. Miss Wells's remarks appear in "An Exchange on 'Nat Turner'" (*New York Review of Books*, 7 November 1968, p. 31), an exchange of letters between several black writers and Eugene Genovese, whose "The Nat Turner Case" (*New York Review of Books*, 12 September 1968, pp. 34–37) attacked the "ferocity and hysteria" of *Ten Black Writers*.

47. It is interesting to consider the black writers' claim that Styron has "reduced history to sex," comparing his view of an intense, celibate revolutionary with Bontemps's Gabriel in *Black Thunder*. Gabriel has just such a black woman by his side as Poussaint wanted for Turner—the "tempestuous" Juba. "She sat astride Araby's bare back, her fragmentary skirt curled about her waist, her naked thighs flashing above the riding boots . . . and felt the warm body of the colt straining between her clinched knees" (p. 80); "She could still feel Araby twitching and fretting between her clinched knees. Lordy, that colt. . . . Almost as much fun as a man, that half-wild Araby" (p. 114). One can easily guess what Styron would have

been accused of had he depicted the "courageous black woman" who stood by Turner's side in these terms!

48. *The Negro in the United States* (New York, 1949), p. 91.

49. *Narrative of William Wells Brown, a Fugitive Slave* (Boston, 1847), pp. 95–96.

50. "Slavery and the Martial South," *Journal of Negro History* 37 (1952): 42.

51. In an interview in the *New York Times Magazine* the week after his novel's publication, Styron admitted that there was no historical fact behind his image of "Negroes in great numbers with rifles and muskets . . . firing back at us"; in creating that episode, he claims, he was sensing what might lie between the lines of Turner's recorded agony.

52. Quoted in T. M. Whitfield, *Slavery Agitation in Virginia, 1829–1832* (Baltimore, 1930), p. 123. Panger in *Ol' Prophet Nat* has "ten or more" of Dr. Blunt's slaves firing back at Turner's band: they had been beaten so often that they had become "willing beasts." Being fired upon by black men leaves the insurrectionists "shaken, our spirits badly dampened" (pp. 151–152).

53. Richard Gilman, for example, in support of his literary attack on Styron's handling of Turner's sexual desire, remarks with unjustifiable certainty, "he was in fact married which Styron ignores" ("Nat Turner Revisited," *New Republic* 158 [27 April 1968]: 26).

54. *Social Studies* 59 (1968): 280. In addition to John Hope Franklin and Benjamin Quarles, a third black historian, Saunders Redding, also finds *The Confessions of Nat Turner* "very perceptive and true" (*American Scholar* 37 [1968]: 542). In contrast to these three professional historians, Darwin Turner, a black English professor, dismisses the novel as the product of Styron's "sick and bigoted fancies" (*Journal of Negro History* 53 [1968]: 185).

NORMAN KELVIN

The Divided Self: William Styron's Fiction from *Lie Down in Darkness* to *The Confessions of Nat Turner*

William Styron is a novelist in search of unity, and in his effort to achieve it he attempts to invoke a romantic vision out of realistic details. From *Lie Down in Darkness* to *The Confessions of Nat Turner*, we find opposites striving for union through conflict or love. But to note this is to note curious defects in Styron's technique and procedure as a novelist. The materials for conflict or love are realistically observed; the experience or act is, however, rendered in a manner intended as romantic but unsuccessful as such: one in which heightened awareness, or an intensification of the spiritual, is attempted but unattained.

Moreover, this attempt and failure contribute to making the resolutions within his novels evasive. The opposites, which are inadequately joined, are the halves—or fragments—of divided characters. Styron, too often, tends to lose control of these, to lose sight of which self or part is striving to combine in conflict or unite in love with the external: with a cause, an idea, or simply another character.

Related to these technical problems, and at the same time encompassing and transcending them, is the theme that Styron, for novelistic purposes, has made his own: the meaning and action of evil. In each of the four novels that have appeared so far, Styron prepares himself to confront evil, to take fire in pursuit of it, to ignite the moment when convergence occurs. But when the moment arrives the flames are often spurious, and what remains, as they expire, is sentimentality.

And in Styron's novels sentimentality is also, unfortunately, the weak bond holding together opposites that are intended to unite but cannot because they are either fragmentary or unrelated to each other. The result is a haphazard design in which evil is set forth in an unstable pattern, one that ultimately falls into disarray. To write about evil, to hold it in sustained focus in a novel, one must be free of sentimentality in matters relating to it. This Styron is not. The form that sentimentality takes in his work is an analytic view of the spectrum of pain. All manifestations and experiences of pain are as a result seen as equal, and whatever depth there is beneath any one of them is never fully explored.

Sentimentality affects the tone of Styron's writing too. Its analytic genesis causes, in fact, a number of disparate tones which seldom reconverge into a greater whole; which seem, rather, to work against each other. We hear in Styron's prose the voices of tortured, divided characters yearning to be whole, and despairing. We hear these characters impatiently, arrogantly, and futilely attempt to dismiss each other. We hear the would-be voice of reason. We hear the incantation of leaden spirits desperate to take flight. But these voices, though emanating from characters who are nominally aware of each other, seem oddly unrelated. They are never heard together, either in harmony or discord, but seem dutifully to succeed each other in often aimless progression.

It is a curious fact that Styron's novels elude the attempt to see them whole in the mind's eye. Nor do they create the impact of calculated discontinuity that would mark the intention behind them as modernist. The impression that remains in retrospect is that many trails have been trod, that all—in promise—were to converge upon truth in an open space, and that all of them end in areas of low-lying scrub, where further revelations are simultaneously named as possible and discounted so far as any search in the work at hand is concerned.

There is another regrettable consequence—a stylistic one—to Styron's ambitious and praiseworthy attempt to convert evil into the matter of fiction. It is a regrettable consequence, that is, of the ways in which the attempt falls short. There is a heavy reliance upon clichés in dialogue. Presumably they are to suggest the haplessness of Styron's characters in a world hostile to their search for identity. But when even the central characters depend upon such clichés in their efforts to communicate, not only is the truth of evil rendered doubly safe from capture by the word. Love and conflict also remain beyond its reach. This is because the dialogue which is part of their process is fretted with words that restrict all movement to parallel tracks: tracks, moreover, that are all too visible ahead.

Styron's difficulties with style and technique lead to further problems of uncertainty of manner and substance. In *Lie Down in Darkness* Dolly Bonner's banal, insipid comments, really no better than Pookie's, make Milton Loftus's ability to sustain the relationship for years without sex, then have sex, then leave Dolly, then return to her, implausible. That Helen each time drove him to Dolly may be credible. But surely Milton would need extraordinary powers of forbearance, a heroic capacity to sustain boredom, if Dolly, in all the intimate and ordinary moments in which we do not see or hear her, speaks the same deadening platitudes that she does when the focus is upon her. Yet there is nothing in Styron's characterization of Milton to suggest that he has the qualities necessary for a continued relationship with Dolly. Styron, so good at suggesting pain, particularly the pain of conflict, has in fact sentimentalized the whole idea of a sexual affair in Milton's life by giving insufficient counterweight to the moments, years, in which Dolly, rather than Helen, is the woman with whom he lives.

Sentimental for other reasons is Styron's characterization of Harry Miller, whom Peyton Loftus marries in preparation for her tragedy. Harry is Jewish. He is a New Yorker. He paints. He is a veteran of the Spanish Civil War. He has a "spot on his lung" which keeps him out of World War II and thus makes it possible for Peyton and him to begin married life in Greenwich Village, even though the year is 1943. When driven to distraction by Peyton's inability to sweep under beds or balance bank accounts, as well as by her jealousy and infidelity, Harry's anger, though streaked with sorrow, is expressed in words that are meant to let Peyton know that all is over between them. They are words which constitute one of the immediate reasons for her suicide. Yet when Harry speaks, his words sound not like bitter, harsh, or sorrowing anger, but like the murmuring of a hurt child who cannot express either the depth of his pain or the nature of the evil that is occurring. The whole conception of Harry Miller is awkward in the extreme. It is reminiscent of Jewish secondary figures of the Hollywood films of the forties and fifties: the one-dimensional paragons of goodness and manliness sent forth to refute the prejudices of populist anti-Semites.

And it is this sentimentalism, this inadequately realized romanticism, in the characterization of Harry that makes Peyton's death curiously less tragic, less meaningful, less absurd even (in the existentialist sense) at the conclusion of the novel than it seemed at the beginning—during the superbly written and realized opening scenes, when we knew only of Peyton's death, Milton's grief, Helen's tortured imprisonment within herself, and nothing of Harry.

In *Set This House on Fire*, Styron's second full-length work of fiction, Cass Kinsolving, the central figure, discusses evil. He reflects that neither "the plague" nor the "sickness" theory will do. Both "are as evil as the evil they are intended to destroy and cure." But Cass concludes, "Yet for the life of me I don't know of any golden mean between the two." The phrase is a key to much of Styron's difficulty in attempting to convert the idea of evil into the matter of fiction. Too often the lack of a "golden mean" causes the idea of evil to fall between whatever two stools have been set out and to disappear forever from clear view.

This is too bad, for what Styron is best at creating is the pain of being a divided person. In *Set This House on Fire*, Cass Kinsolving is believable when he writes: "Sometimes the sensation I have that I am 2 persons & by that I mean the man of my dreams & the man who walks in daylight is so strong and frightening that at times I am actually scared to look in the mirror for fear of seeing some face there that I have never seen before." The dream and the face of the stranger in the mirror are, in fact, continuous motifs in Styron's writing and they help to convey in an impressive manner an emotion closely associated with pain, namely, fear: the fear of nonexistence, the fear of losing one's identity to another or to circumstances.

Yet to say even this is not to say, unfortunately, that the expert realization of pain and fear means that the characterizations of which they are a part are wholly successful. Since pain and fear in Styron's novels indicate split, fragmentation, the diminished self, they require the controlling and sustaining power of point of view to maintain the presence of character. But although this power is exercised from time to time in Styron's writing, it lapses too frequently. And the effects are all the more apparent because of Styron's preference for a first person narrator. The writing, apparently so open, confounds the reader's attempt to relate with fair continuity to the viewpoint. It is as if the eye wanted to look continuously at the moon but was prevented from doing so by frequent passages of clouds over its face.

Furthermore, recognition of the viewpoint in Styron's work (and particularly in *Set This House on Fire*) is necessary to interpret tone: an essential source of the mood and moral comment. But the tone heard—and especially again in Styron's second novel—is muffled, as if it came from a distance or from beneath a partially insulating surface. It is melancholy, flat. It doesn't vary enough with shifts in character, event, or idea. It lacks intensity.

The Long March, although it was the second of Styron's works to be published, in some ways seems to belong after *Set This House on Fire*. Insofar as Styron's fiction explores moral ideas, it is the least ambitious of his first three works. Because it is a novella, however, it is free of some of the difficulties that beset the longer form. Its brevity prevents the dissipation of character, prevents the fading of tone and point of view. The dialogue is better than it is in *Lie Down in Darkness* or *Set This House on Fire*, perhaps because the situation prevents the drift toward soliloquy that occurs too often in the novels. The speech of two of the Marine officers—Colonel Templeton, who has ordered the march, and Captain Mannix, who is Jewish—and the narration of Lieutenant Culver, who is an observer of the action, a kind of silent first person narrator, are properly terse and direct and aid the characterization.

Captain Mannix is forced by his own needs to prove himself: his pride in his Jewishness and his fear and anger at the possibility of giving credence to any of the assorted, unspoken prejudices in the colonel's implied conventional anti-Semitism. But as so often in Styron's writing, there is an attempt to make a detail epitomize moral and psychological experience and the attempt fails. In this case, the detail is a protruding nail in Mannix's boot. During the long march, the nail causes his foot to swell into a painful balloon, but Mannix refuses to drop out. There are, presumably, two reasons for this.

The first is his need to prove himself as good a man, American, and marine as Colonel Templeton. Since Styron successfully describes and creates Mannix's physical pain and in part succeeds in suggesting his psychological distress, the mere narrative fact that Mannix does limp and stagger on to the end of the march makes authentic and credible the existence and demand of the need.

But the theme is meant to be more complex. Mannix's need to prove himself is a need to compete with Templeton. In theory this is certainly an interesting possibility, a promise of fresh psychological connections in the creation of character and conflict. But though the possibility is present in Captain Mannix's literal actions, it is not always successfully conveyed by the tone or mood in which even these are narrated.

Once again we feel it necessary to try to locate the difficulties that tone—the need for appropriate tone—creates in Styron's work, particularly in *Set This House on Fire* and *The Long March*. It might help to say that just as the intention in *Set This House on Fire* to keep a split character buoyed up and in motion requires the kind of urgent, supportive tone that we hear in the novels of Virginia Woolf, so the thesis that Captain Mannix needs to compete with Colonel Templeton demands tone and mood of the sort that in the writing of Ernest Hemingway convey the mannered, muted, intensity of competition. The shifts of tone in *The Long March* suggest some attempt to contain its larger ideas. But again, what is needed in treating the theme of competition is something like Hemingway's single focus on the code and on the idea that fate may be inevitable but not unattractive.

In an attempt to add this larger meaning to Captain Mannix's stubborn endurance, Styron causes Lieutenant Culver to observe an exchange between Mannix (as he drags himself from a shower room at the base camp at which the long march has ended) and a black woman employed as a maid at this camp:

> "Oh my, you poor man. . . . Do it hurt? . . . Oh, I bet it does. Deed it does." Mannix looked up at her across the short yards that separated them. . . . Culver would remember this: the two of them communicating across that chasm one unspoken moment of sympathy and understanding . . . before, almost at the same instant, the towel slipped away and fell to the floor. . . . He seemed to have neither the strength nor the ability to lean down and retrieve the towel and so he merely stood there huge and naked . . . and sent toward the woman, finally, a sour, apologetic smile, his words uttered, it seemed to Culver, not with self-pity but only with the tone of a man who, having endured and lasted, was too weary to tell her anything but the truth. "Deed it does," he said. (LM, pp. 119–120)

Thus *The Long March* concludes. What are the themes? One, it would seem, is that the dispossessed recognize each other's pain and can thus communicate. But what does Mannix's nakedness signify? Perhaps that the identity of the naked self is weariness. And what again of Mannix's need to compete with Templeton? If that idea has found some final expression in the concluding scene, it has managed to do so while remaining silent and invisible.

This conclusion is a touchstone for a number of our concerns. By linking Mannix with the woman rather than with Templeton, Styron has not only left the central confrontation uncompleted, but he has also denied *The Long March* the richness of meaning that such a confrontation, properly developed, would have revealed.

To glimpse the possibilities that have been missed, it has to be remembered that the event which constitutes the story of *The Long March* is a training exercise, that is, a game. Its distinguishing characteristic, as such, is that it is not played to the death. This means that pain is experienced without any accompanying fear of physical obliteration. Indeed, the game, if played successfully, will provide Mannix with a role, an identity, that will give him a chance to be proof against even psychological danger. For in the game the psychological threat is loss of face, humiliation, which is fatal only if it is willed to be such.

The situation is properly absurd. Whatever dangers in the real world Templeton might have signified, in the game Templeton is the player who can cause only humiliation for Mannix. To say even this is not wholly correct. Templeton provides a potential: he can become a psychological danger to Mannix only if Mannix permits him to become one; only if Mannix elaborates a full motive, for conduct and feeling, out of the potential made available by Templeton's presence. In brief, Mannix is dependent on Templeton for the conditions of his own internal struggle.

The questions this situation raise are existential. Because the training march is a game, Templeton's anti-Semitism does not operate as a social given, as a deterministic force. It does not dictate moral resistance or counterattack as it would in an objectively real world. As has been suggested, such resistance is chosen, and it has been chosen for the sake of identity, of internal coherence, not in the hope of stopping the Templetons in the real world. In these terms, Styron's characterization of Mannix is successful. Within the game, he is integrated. He converts the show of evil signified by Templeton into a morally neutral reason for playing out his own role effectively. And by morally neutralizing evil, while retaining it as a motive for action, he converts evil into the force of pure competition: of the kind of competition that properly characterizes a game.

But the confrontation between Mannix and the woman subverts all this. It arbitrarily brings a real world into the story. The woman signifies the existence of social injustice, of its victims. And as Styron has used the implications of social injustice, of victimization, there is nothing to suggest that the process is existential. It seems absolute and objective.

The result is that Mannix is unnecessarily turned into a divided character. During the balance of the story, he is organized to function in an absurd situation. At the very end, he is called upon to declare kinship with those who must resist an uncontained, objective social evil. It is as if Styron were dissatisfied with the degree of control of evil he had achieved for fictional purposes, the degree of control evident so long as Mannix struggled against himself: a self mobilized by the idea of Templeton. It is as if, having discovered in himself the intention to move his story into the larger world, Styron found it necessary to invoke in the characterization of Mannix a dormant possibility, a theoretical aspect of Mannix that might indeed be realized in a world subject to external reality. But it is an aspect of Mannix that belongs to a different story, not to *The Long March*.

Had Styron kept the focus on Mannix's struggle with the concept of Templeton, he might have seen that by giving his story the structure of a game, he had conquered evil: that he had internalized it within the mind and feelings of his main character. Any larger questions remaining would then have been seen to concern the relation of the game to the world of social reality, to what happens to evil when it is, in fact, a condition of life, a determinant of social forms and conduct, rather than an imprint on the imagination that can be divorced from its external cause and made a motive for action in an internalized struggle. But in *The Long March* there would have been no need or expectation of answers to such larger questions.

Through these observations we arrive at Styron's most recent novel, *The Confessions of Nat Turner* (1967). This time, it would seem, the delayed confrontation with evil—the conversion of this confrontation into the matter of fiction—will be made. For *The Confessions of Nat Turner* is about the obscenity and evil of black slavery in America. Slavery, "an abomination and a horror," as Styron has called it elsewhere, makes special demands upon the novelist. The perimeters—place, immediate time, many of the details of daily existence under slavery—are the données of history. The free novelistic imagination must therefore be able to create characters whose experience does not violate these perimeters, does define the nature of the abomination and represent magnitude as an essential dimension of the horror, and does indictate the presence of energy and will that balance the force of the abomination and horror; and of energy and will that can, in the world they define, preserve character identity.

But in the act of converting the idea and institution of slavery into fictive character and event, Styron misses his opportunity. The theory of evil suggested by the search for a missing "golden mean" between "plague" and "sickness" seems to be present in the novel and to exercise a diversionary effect. In addition Styron's propensity to create divided characters who never heal but who attempt to confront other characters with only a part of themselves, or to pursue their destinies with only a fragmented self, is much in evidence.

The missed opportunity is all the more noticeable in that Styron's initial source, Thomas Gray's 1831 pamphlet, *The Confessions of Nat Turner*, achieves in its own brief compass both historical power and literary effect. Nat Turner led a slave revolt in Virginia in 1831. Then, while in prison awaiting execution, he purportedly dictated these confessions to Thomas Gray. The Nat Turner that emerges from Gray's pamphlet is a man of extraordinary intelligence, character, and energy, a man of remarkably clear vision and purpose.

Styron recognized this, but his needs as novelist required that he unravel the possibilities inherent in Gray's portrait and reweave them into an extended work. The results are less than successful, in part, because the extended pattern does not justify itself; indeed, it calls itself into question. In the design that Styron has rewoven, the theme of evil—the power of the evil of slavery to oppose all other imaginative forces that in this novel create character and event—appears vividly at first and then intermittently disappears and reappears as the design develops. The threads that interrupt the strand of evil only succeed in interrupting the pattern promised by the character of Nat Turner and by the nature of slavery; they do not seem effectively to re-create this pattern in the intended larger form.

This can be seen in Styron's attempt to make moral distinctions among the characters who are slaveholders. At one point in the novel, Styron has Nat Turner say, "I think it may be seen by now how greatly various were the moral attributes of white men who possessed slaves . . . how different each owner might be by way of severity or benevolence. They ranged down from saintly (Samuel Turner) to the all right (Moore) to the barely tolerable (Reverend Eppes)." These are all but one of the slaveholders to whom Nat Turner was in bond at various times. The omission is the final one in the series, Joseph Travis. He has been omitted, presumably, for purposes of plot, and perhaps to create moral ambiguity.

Joseph Travis, early in his career, commits one of the more outrageous crimes of slavery that occur in the story. He sells the wife and small son of Hark, Nat Turner's fellow slave, friend, and, finally, lieutenant. Nat Turner simply comments: "Joseph Travis was at bottom a decent and sympathetic man." Thus the evil that is slavery and that might, for fictional purposes, have been profoundly realized in the characterization of Travis, prepares instead to take wing in a dozen different directions. That the evil in the immediate sequence comes into focus again is, strangely, one of the results of the scatter as it passes by. Joseph Travis had, we are reminded, "committed the unpardonable: he had sold Hark's wife Tiny and their little boy south, preferring to endure Hark's reproachful glances and sullen grief than to be faced with two extra mouths which it might have been a strain but hardly a killing sacrifice to feed."

There is something surreal in the inadequacy of the references to Hark's "reproachful glances" and "sullen grief." Given all the undermining and dehumanization that slavery could accomplish —and Hark is not characterized by Styron as thoroughly undermined or dehumanized—surely the fictional character and moment have engendered feelings larger and more profound than reproach and sullen grief. Surely, too, Styron has left undeveloped the implicit pathology in his characterization of Travis. If slavery drove slaves insane, Styron's words suggest that it even more effectively induced a profoundly pathological character in slaveholders: as Styron has told it, there is an element of calculated, methodical sadism and unbalance in Travis. Presumably having asked himself the hideously wrong question—would it be a "killing sacrifice" to supply food for Hark's wife and son—and within this catechism having supplied himself with the answer that is supposed to prevent him from selling the woman and child, he then proceeds to sell them.

But as the bits and pieces of the characterization of Joseph

Travis jostle for attention, we get, instead of a study in the pathology induced in slaveholders by the institution of slavery, something that comes dangerously close to farce. Nat Turner is made to speculate that it may have been Travis's "mountain heritage, his lack of experience with Tidewater ways, that caused him to do something that no truly respectable slaveowner would do." And, in the peroration, all the possibilities of the relation between the pathology and the evil of slaveholding go up at once in the smoke of generality and irrelevance. Styron's Nat Turner intones: "It had become plain to me that white men reared outside the tradition of slavery often made the most callous taskmasters—what hordes of corrupt and ruthless overseers hailed from Connecticut and New Jersey!"

There will be a return to Travis. As Hark prepares for the rebellion, he will tell us again what Travis has done and will say that as a consequence Hark will be able to kill.

Finally, the confrontation between Nat Turner and Joseph Travis will be transposed to a religious plane, where pathology will disappear and evil will become evasively transcendental. One reason proposed in the novel is that Nat Turner is a visionary and that in his vision he has been called by God to shed blood to redeem mankind from the sin of slavery. Thus, early in the novel, Styron scrupulously follows Thomas Gray and has Nat Turner say (as Gray actually wrote): that at the time of the rebellion, "I had been living with Mr. Joseph Travis, who was to me a kind master, and placed the greatest confidence in me; in fact, I had no cause to complain of his treatment to me." When, in the novel, Gray asks for an explanation of how Nat Turner could have killed Travis, Nat says he can give no reply, and adds in his meditation: "And I couldn't—not because there was no reply to the question, but because there were matters which had to be withheld even from a confession, certainly from Gray."

The apposite scene in the novel occurs near its conclusion, indeed, as the rebellion begins. Following Gray (and logic) Styron selects Travis as the first to be attacked. It is night. Nat Turner and his men have mounted the stairs to the room where Travis and his wife are asleep. And later—that is, at the time of narrative present when Nat Turner in his cell is recalling his life—he says, remembering Travis:

> I realized with wonder that this was the first moment in all the years that I had been near him that I had even looked directly into his eyes. . . . I had known his presence like that of a close kin [but] my eyes [had] not once encountered his own. It was my fault alone, my primal fear—but—no matter. Now I saw that beneath the perplexity, the film of sleep, his eyes were brown and rather melancholy, acquainted with hard toil, remote perhaps, somewhat inflexible but not at all unkind, and I felt that I knew him at last. . . . It was as if by encountering those eyes I had found the torn and long-missing fragment of a portrait of this far-off abstract being who possessed my body; his face was complete now and I had a final glimpse of who he might truly be. Whatever else he was, he was my man. (NT, pp. 387–388)

The image completed by the missing piece is presumably one that Nat Turner has seen in his vision. What, then, has happened to the specific and particular details concerning Hark's wife and child—details which are not in Gray's pamphlet and which Styron presumably has introduced to make the idea of evil concrete? What, in brief, has happened to characterization as the vehicle for Nat Turner's confrontation with evil? What were the reasons that deterred him from answering Gray's question? Was it because Gray would not believe or understand the religious theme or that Gray would not see that what Travis had done was a symptom of the basic evil of slavery? If both, was there also a third reason for Nat Turner's silence—Margaret Whitehead, the white girl whom Styron has linked with Nat Turner, and whom Styron makes the central reason for the course that the rebellion takes?

There is no answer to these questions in the words or pattern of Styron's novel, but there is a suggestion of something else. *The Confessions of Nat Turner* would have been a better novel had it been briefer, had Travis been more fully developed as a character, and had the confrontation between Nat Turner and him been the scene and the moment in which the truth of evil and its consequences were fully realized. There was even room for mystery. In Gray's pamphlet the blow from Nat Turner's hatchet glances from Travis's head, and Travis is killed by Will, a slave who, in the novel, is depicted as maddened by slavery but who, in Gray's pamphlet, is the most profound in vision among Nat Turner's followers. Had Styron, in developing Will, made the most of the stature hinted at by Gray, the contrast between Nat Turner's failure to kill and Will's success would not have been so readily—and so simplistically—attributable to Margaret Whitehead's influence on Nat Turner.

Another opportunity missed by Styron, one that would have been preparation for the confrontation between Nat Turner and Joseph Travis, is that the historical Nat Turner seems to have been not only extraordinarily intelligent but also more intelligent than any of the slaveholders. In the course of creating other characters and of relating them to Nat Turner, Styron seems to intimate this. But he ultimately leaves undeveloped a large idea implicit in these characterizations and relationships, namely, that slavery induced in slaveholders not only pathological character traits that expressed themselves as evil, but also a form of stupidity that manifested itself as evil.

Specifically, if Samuel Turner, who is described as the most benevolent of the slaveholders with whom Nat Turner lives and who is the preparation for Joseph Travis, had been explored with depth and focus, the essential horror into which the context of slavery converts his good intentions might have been realized. Nat Turner as a youth is promised freedom by Samuel Turner. Given that all these events and possibilities are being seen in retrospect, to say nothing of Nat Turner's already manifest knowledge at this point in the novel of his own intellectual capacities, what is he—or the reader—to hear when Samuel Turner says: "You are the walking proof that young darkies like yourself *can* overcome the natural handicaps of their race and at least acquire such schooling as will allow them to enter into pursuits other than the lowest menial labor." If this is meant as historical realism—if Samuel Turner's words express an enlightened early nineteenth-century view, if it is theoretically possible also that slavery could make a slave receptive to them—there is nothing either in Gray's pamphlet or in Styron's basic use of it to suggest that Nat Turner would have felt complaisance or remembered with tranquillity whatever he felt when Samuel Turner spoke of his "natural handicaps." At the very least Styron's own Nat Turner, had he been consistent with much of the rest of the characterization, would have found Samuel Turner's pomposity and paternalism attenuated but authentic forms of evil.

Similarly, the would-be joviality that accompanies Samuel Turner's promise of eventual freedom is, in fact, clumsiness at best. "I shall only stipulate," he says, "that you return to Turner's Mill for a visit every blue moon or two—with whichever young darky girl you have taken for a wife." Leaving aside the claim by some that the historical Nat Turner had been married by 1831, the impression that it makes no difference whom Nat Turner will marry, the absence of any tone that would evoke an authentic individual, even if an unknown one, results in a curiously flat note. It is flat because what is unclear, what is unheard, is the tone that Nat Turner hears in the words spoken and thus that the reader is to hear.

Margaret Whitehead has been mentioned. In no way does Styron so obfuscate his own tale of evil and its fated course as by introducing Margaret Whitehead and assigning her so large a role in determining Nat Turner's conduct during the two days of his revolt, his life leading up to it, and his meditations after it. Styron's inspiration is the fact that in the original confessions Margaret Whitehead is the only one named by Nat Turner whom he had himself killed. For Styron, this suggests that Nat Turner wielded the hatchet to murder what he loved.

Yet the manner and the time of Margaret's death muddle even the dubious meaning given to her. Killing her, in the novel, is an act forced upon Nat Turner by Will, who has challenged Nat's authority. Styron makes Nat's ability to keep control of his forces dependent upon killing Margaret. It is as if Styron, the moment before Margaret's death, had emphasized that Nat Turner's rebellion was in fact a military undertaking, only to turn the emphasis into a vapor flash to be seen no more. Yet when Nat Turner does kill Margaret Whitehead and loses all heart for the rebellion, we perceive no link between the scenes before the rebellion, in which he is driven to sexual despair by a Margaret Whitehead whom Styron depicts as an intolerable tease (in her enthusiasm for Nat she is a complement, in fact, to Samuel Turner) and the manner or circumstances of his killing her. Whatever liberties Styron has taken with the character of Will as it is suggested by Gray, what we do see in the novel is a credibly realized and fateful conflict between Nat Turner and Will. Margaret's death is the result of that conflict, but neither Margaret nor her death, as the novel is actually written, is related in any other significant way to the causes or conduct of Nat Turner's rebellion.

In death, Margaret does serve another doubtful purpose. She makes ambiguous once more the theme of evil. When all is done, Nat Turner, in prison, begins to wonder whether he did wrong in God's sight. As he searches for an answer, the uneasy spirit of Margaret, which has been hovering about in search of a completion to its destiny, floats into Nat's meditation and helps him find the answer. Merged with the voice of the jailer who has arrived to conduct him to the hangman, it is the voice of God that Nat hears calling him, and he says: "Yes, I think just before I turn to greet him, *I would have done it all again. I would have destroyed them all. Yet I would have spared one. I would have spared her that showed me Him whose presence I had not fathomed or maybe even known.*"

Mention has been made at the opening of this essay of the flawed romanticism in Styron's novels. Nat experiences a final, onanistic yearning for Margaret. The accompaniment perversely conjures up thoughts of *Wuthering Heights*, of Heathcliff responding to the imperative call of the spirit of Catherine. "Her voice is close, familiar, real," Nat Turner says, "and for an instant I mistake the wind against my ear . . . and I turn to seek her in the darkness." The voice of the jailer, calling "Come!" blends also with the voice of Margaret: "*We'll love one another*, she seems to be entreating me, very close now, *we'll love one another by the light of heaven above.*" The insistent echo of *Wuthering Heights* and its inappropriateness to Styron's intentions in *The Confessions of Nat Turner* merely help to pose once more the danger he continually runs of turning tragedy into something other than itself.

What of Nat Turner's war? It has ended in mutual forgiveness, in charity on Nat Turner's part. This would have been plausible enough if the character of Margaret and the role assigned to her had been effective. But they are not. Her late entry in the story serves not to advance but to change it—and this only momentarily—from a story concerning Nat Turner and Joseph Travis. This story is left unfinished when Styron turns his attention to Margaret, and this fact points both to a technical problem and to its implicit solution.

For once again in Styron's work, the unmet requirement of form has interfered with meaning, and it is form that suggests the needs of both. Had the novel been much briefer, its length would have served Styron better; and the theme he chose might have been better served by him. At the center of the story Styron has written are Nat Turner and Joseph Travis, and in a supporting role, Samuel Turner. Had all three been developed with proper magnitude—the magnitude required by the enormity of the idea of slavery—the story that at times Styron seems intent on writing might have been given effective form and adequate substance. In the scene in which Travis is killed, there is time and space for all that has gone before to be given meaning and for revelation and conflict that would justify a theme as large as slavery and Nat Turner's rebellion against it. As in the terse lines of Gray's account, as in Styron's own novel, when Gray at first seems more aware that Nat Turner has "killed" Joseph Travis than that he has killed anyone else, the death of others, including Margaret Whitehead's, should have served only—or primarily—to give number and extension to the event. The image of Nat Turner in prison presented by Thomas Gray—the image of Nat Turner, defiant, "daring to raise his manacled hands to heaven"—suggests a more meaningful conclusion than does the voice of Margaret calling to Nat to join her in heaven. Gray's image suggests the confrontation of great human purpose with the energy of evil: the true embrace by life of death in the final moment of conflict between human purpose and evil. The voice of Margaret Whitehead does not.

The reason is that Styron has once again turned his central figure into a divided man, and has done so arbitrarily. In a way the problem is the reverse of the one unnecessarily created at the conclusion of *The Long March*. Nat Turner has lived in a real world, one that takes its shape and its moral imperatives from the nature of slavery. By invoking Margaret, Styron has reached out for a realm of experience not so much opposed to the world of slavery as incommensurable with it and irrelevant to it. By attempting to link Nat Turner to Margaret, Styron is attempting to link an obligatory world to a constructed one by revealing allegedly transcendent grounds for sympathy between the two characters.

Styron's intention, apparently, is that Nat Turner is not to be seen primarily as a divided or double self, but as a man whose better self becomes attached to the idea or memory of Margaret. But only unwarranted inconsistency is apparent in the development of Nat Turner, because Margaret, as a result of much of Styron's characterization of her, is in fact linked to Samuel Turner and to Joseph Travis. For Nat Turner to yearn for a transcendent union with Margaret is therefore for him to yearn also for union with that part of her that is common to all three: with those modes of perception of the slaveholder, shared by all three, that deny him his identity.

This is a fault in the characterization of Nat Turner. A consequence is that it seems to have caused Styron to overlook the fact that he had, in his novel, the materials to show that beyond the complexity of the evil of slavery is its grim simplicity. That the institution of slavery directs to a single end the would-be kindness of Samuel Turner, the adolescent reveries of Margaret, and the subhuman conduct of Joseph Travis points to the single evil that they all help to sustain, despite their differences as characters. For all three, slavery is a necessary condition for their own being. Within the context of slavery, the expression of the expansive feelings, of the affections, testifies only to the existence of Sartrean bad faith. Samuel Turner and Margaret Whitehead help to forge Nat Turner's chains as inevitably as does Joseph Travis.

To return to the final scene of the novel, it would seem that Styron's intention is for us to see, metaphorically, that Nat Turner's chains, charmed by the voice of Margaret, have dropped away. But once again, had Styron persisted, had he explored and revealed the evil linking Samuel Turner, Margaret Whitehead, and Joseph Travis, the appropriate image would have been the one contained in Gray's pamphlet—the image of Nat Turner defiantly raising his manacled hands to heaven.

Had Styron maintained his focus, had he insisted on making her a major figure, Margaret would not have risen to trouble Nat Turner in prison. Linked to the ghosts of Samuel Turner and Joseph Travis, the spirit of Margaret, weighted down by artistic logic, would have absented itself. A blank and voiceless heaven would then have suggested itself at the conclusion and would have been better. It would have been seen as a mask covering, as it encompassed, the many faces of a single evil. And heaven as a blank mask would have measured the magnitude of what Nat Turner opposed, and, through active conflict, matched. Confronting such a mask, a heaven of such meaning, the figure of Nat Turner would have realized the stature and the moral coherence promised at the beginning of the novel.

ROBERT K. MORRIS

In the Clap Shack: Comedy in the Charnel House

In the Clap Shack, William Styron's first full-length play, seems on the surface a rather surprising work to follow on the heels of *The Confessions of Nat Turner*, or, for that matter, for the author of *Lie Down in Darkness* or *Set This House on Fire* to have written at all. To begin with, it is, quite in the classic sense, a comedy: a mode of composition not normally associated with Styron, even though the darkest stretches of his fiction have always been shot through with timely and redeeming comic effects. Again, the play was conceived (as Styron himself notes in the interview printed in this collection) as a satire, suggesting even further an opening up of the interior, particularized, frenetic worlds of those novels supersaturated with tragedy and apocalypse, to a more palpable and universal realm: to an art, in short, that works through common exposure, rather than private disclosure. And most surprising of all is Styron's apparent departure from those "biases, sympathies, apprehensions"[1] that have sustained critics (predominantly urban and eastern, and often more acerbic and capricious than accurate) in their mechanical slapping on of the pre-pasted labels "southern" and "regional" writer.

I say "on the surface," for while the play must, almost by definition, be different from the novels, it is at the same time very much like them. Despite Styron's shift in genre and mode, despite his excursion into obvious satire, despite his rigorous exclusion of southern problems—aren't such, really, *all* our problems now?—the play balances the novels' passion, intensity and irony, takes on (in a way deceptively simple for the textured novelist Styron is) many of their patterns and overviews, and catches its hero up (as other of Styron's heroes are caught up) in the "ghastly struggle just to assert [his] humanness, to get over the barriers to understanding, to clear [his] personality of obsessions."[2] Styron has not relaxed his probings into the human condition, and he still ponders why (to paraphrase Hoffman) the human creature potentially capable of rising to dignity, even nobility, is "often the victim of accident and absurdity." But he has relaxed his tone and technique: moved out the furniture and fixtures of his novels—the solemnity, rhetoric, and lyricism—and left us with basic confrontations in a nearly naked room. One might almost believe that the superior exhaustion Styron experienced after the completion of *Nat Turner* demanded such relaxation, a new perspective, even, to emphasize the commonality rather than the eccentricity of human beings. And that instead of ripping and tearing back to expose the rawness of humanity's common wounds, Styron decided to probe them with the scalpel of the satirist, to make clean, direct incisions into human motives and actions.

The simile (if a trifle purple) is apposite to *In the Clap Shack*, for it is a play about disease—gonorrhea or "the clap" in particular—though Styron takes this common garden variety of venereal infection as the physical, solid center only, moving out through expanding and widening circles to operate on social, moral, psychological, even metaphysical disease. In a way that will not be strange to readers of *The Long March*, the urological ward of the naval hospital is a microcosm, peopled (as most American novels and plays about the war are conventionally peopled) with Negro, Pole, Jew, WASP, Irishman, Italian, southerner and northerner, officer and enlisted man, who share in their enforced isolation, in their taint, in their ostracism from the world outside, a kind of vulnerability that paradoxically unites and separates them.

Such a theme might appear unpromising for comic satire, especially since the play makes clear from the outset that its comedy is not to move via black, grotesque, or nihilistic routes. Somewhat eclectically, but with a fine intuitive sense for drama, Styron maneuvers freely among farce, set gags, and *shticks*, the comedy of situation, manners, humors even, in order to sustain the initial tone, to keep the pace up and the action fluid; yet no one of these devices can be singled out as the salient base of his comic method. For they all ultimately cohere in what I would call the comedy of dislocation or discontinuity: a type of dramatic irony dependent upon inversions of certain premises that must be accepted before the range of the satire and the thematic treatment of disease can be fitted together.

The first of these inversions evolves in a direct way from the ethics of illness: the very conception itself a parody of the normal. The venereal patients on the ward are viewed by their superiors— Dr. Glanz, the chief urologist, and Captain Budwinkle, the hospital commandant—as morally recalcitrant, antisocial beings; and their unfortunate but innocuous and totally human indiscretions are condemned as acts of "corrupt," "depraved," "licentious" voluptuaries. Enamored as each officer is with his professionalism, and the importance of his mission (one administrative, the other, supposedly, curative), neither the martinet Budwinkle nor the autocratic Glanz (who persists in speaking of himself in the first person plural) gives more than a mere nod to the most obvious of absolute truths: that the war is responsible for the conditions on the ward.

Glanz, with his strange, vintage puritanism—strange only until it is exposed as something more—and Budwinkle, with his idée fixe on efficiency and loyalty both assume that any displays of emotion or feeling are signs of moral weakness and turpitude: conduct unbecoming a man and a marine. These prejudices extend to the sexual act itself and would make any marine who refuses to remain monkish in the performance of his duty—who, that is, falls prey to natural drives (and contracts VD)—a near criminal, at least by service standards. Reduced from its specious premises to its absurd conclusion, the argument suggests a man must keep himself incorruptible and inviolate for the heroic mission before him—so in the end he will be in tip-top condition to fight and kill and die.

A ludicrous instance of such endemic logic at work comes in a brief "bit" during the first act, when a minor character, McDaniel, reads a letter he has received from Rhonda Fleming's "personal secretary":

Dear Davy: Like all screen stars, Miss Fleming receives hundreds of fan letters every day, and she could not possibly answer them herself. But you write her so often that she's terribly impressed, and she wanted me to send you this personal message. She thinks marines like you are the finest, cleanest, bravest boys in America, and she hopes you'll be thinking of her when you go overseas and slap that Jap. (CS, 1. 2)

And later, when Glanz and Budwinkle are grilling the young southerner Wallace Magruder about the "betrayal" of his fiancée (Magruder, drunk and lustful one summer night when his betrothed was away, "had relations" with a middle-aged cotton mill worker), the captain pays lip service to those Boy Scout virtues that equate moral with physical health:

I may be dense, Magruder. Obtuse. Stupid even. Feel free to correct me if I don't make sense. But one of the important aspects of love between man and woman is *fidelity*, is it not? Decks clean fore and aft, and all squared away amidships? (*Pauses*) I won't blow the whistle on you for having premarital relations, although that to my mind is a poisonous business. What I truly can't abide —and I want you to hear it loud and clear—is the idea that you betrayed this girl during her summer vacation! (CS, 2. 2)

As a satirist interested in going beyond the mere attitudinizing of his characters, Styron is not concerned with extensive or profound analyses of this discouraging sort of thinking. Both the movie star and Budwinkle may be honest and aboveboard in their moral stance ("clean fore and aft and all squared away amidships"), may not be posturing at all, but the demands of both are exigent—and possibly dangerous. They are a foil to the way human beings really act. The important point, however, is that neither belief is "realistic" in the context of the times or in view of the tempers of men. War, Styron suggests from the very beginning of the play, breeds its own ineluctable illness—the cry of the dying Chalkey that opens the first act, "Pearl! Pearl!" is the name of his sister, but (hardly fortuitously) the name of the harbor as well—inverting, subsequently, all values of normalcy and health. And with illness as the norm, all "healthy" standards become suspect.

The second of these major inversions develops from the ethos of the war itself. It is 1943. As men are dying on the battlefield, so they are dying on the ward. Chalkey has pyelonephritis complicated by galloping hypertension; Schwartz has a fatal renal tuberculosis. But more than metaphorical, the stench of death is literal, for the Negro Clark in the late ulcerative stages of granuloma emits a "rancid, pungent odor" from his bed that every now and again elicits nauseous shudders from fellow patients and doctor alike. It is onto this "thoroughly discouraging and corrupt scene" (as Glanz calls it) that Styron thrusts Magruder. Diagnosed for syphilis because of a three plus on his Wassermann and Kahn tests, Magruder is received admiringly by the men (he is an "ass *and* tit man," Dedario tells Stancik) and, since the syphilitic can anticipate blindness, paralysis, and insanity—a point that Glanz makes cheerfully plain in his several interviews with the young marine—even as something of a hero.

Magruder, a would-be writer who is innocent and hypersensitive as well as hypochrondriac, at first reacts with incredulity at the diagnosis. He has had sexual relations with only two women in his life—his fiancée and the factory worker—and never experienced any of the earlier indications of syphilis. But worked over by Glanz (in an attempt to reconstruct the patient's "sexual profile") and plagued by his own heightened romantic sense of doom, he soon overreacts. Mere disbelief becomes depression, then despair, and finally fear. A mild hypochondriac to begin with, Magruder whips himself into morbid melancholy and anxiety, is driven almost insane by Glanz's suggestion that the foulness and pollution have been transmitted to his fiancée, and, in the extreme terror of his neurotic imagination, sees himself as a walking corpse and the ward as a "charnel house."

Once it is understood how Styron must, for most of the play, enforce Magruder's brooding in order finally to affirm the vitality and comedy of life over the fact and horror of death—the charnel house atmosphere of the ward, though imagined by Magruder, is no less real for him; and indeed the world outside is already one huge, grim, universal charnel house—the slow raking of his hero over the coals becomes a thematic and dramatic necessity. For one thing it prepares for the comic catharsis galvanized by Styron's twist in plot: the discovery that Magruder's chronic trench mouth,

[231]

not syphilis, was responsible for the high positive readings on his Wassermann and Kahn. For another it resolves (in a catharsis of another sort) the agon between Magruder and Glanz which, too comically and casually, has built up over the long two acts; it allows Magruder's stifled rage and helplessness in the face of medical and military authority to burst full-blown into violence and to free him of past and present obsessions. As Magruder, in his final speech, says to Schwartz:

> I guess I am lucky. I guess anyone who gets out of here is lucky. You know, even going to the brig and all—a court-martial, prison, *anything* after this—I couldn't care less, really. It'll seem like being set free. . . . And you know another thing, Schwartz? Whatever else, I think I've gotten rid of my hypochondria. Breathe on me, Schwartz! . . . Fantastic. The breath of a babe! It was like a zephyr! (CS, 3. 3)

In the broadest way, however, Magruder's initiation and revelation together become the simple denial of the omnipresent death force wrought by war. With so many lines of life unlived, his true struggle is to overcome the absurd choices of death outlined calmly and logically by Lineweaver (the chief male nurse on the ward and a kind of choric voice) who tells him after the negative Wassermann report has come back: "You'll live to die a hero on a wonderful Pacific beach somewhere. That's a lot better, isn't it, than ending up with the blind staggers, or in the booby hatch? And if you really die with enough dash and style, they might even give you the Navy Cross." No less true for being absurd and more hopeless for appearing inescapable, the alternatives are annihilated, by Magruder at least, in his willfull, passionate, foolish, spontaneous, and very human aggression against Glanz. Practically, the bullying and humbling of the urologist is quixotic; but it might be the compulsive act of anyone who believes—and Styron seems to share the belief with his hero—that man's energies should be directed to the pursuit of living rather than the avoidance of dying: to the choices of life rather than of deaths.

Styron's attempt to invert these insidious, preconceived premises about illness and war is the groundwork for his satire. But his attack is not centered solely on men like Glanz and Budwinkle—

mere cogs in the machinery set in motion by more virulent and dangerous minds—but on all those who suffer from destructive and self-destructive obsessions. I do not mean to apply this generalization rigidly. At the most unsophisticated (though perhaps funniest) level of the comedy, Styron introduces foils like Dedario and Stancik—happy warriors and habitual offenders who are regularly in and out with the "clap" and who have spent most of the war at short arm inspections, "skinning it back, squeezing it, milking it down." These characterizations show how comparatively benign a good, solid, healthy obsession with sex can be. For Styron the fact of disease is unfortunate but irrelevant, a matter of fate and chance. Certainly disease per se is not being satirized and is even disposed horizontally through the play in a hierarchy of gravity. Dedario and Stancik's gonorrhea is of minor consequence placed side by side with Schwartz's renal tuberculosis or Clark's nephritis, though potentially more serious (penicillin has not yet replaced sulfadiazine) than Magruder's trench mouth. What *is* being satirized is tied more directly to the play's concentric movement: one originating with varieties of physical illness, but becoming either destructive or self-destructive as the obsession with disease is transformed into the disease of obsession.

Budwinkle's obsession, for example, is too obvious and too patent (though nonetheless dangerous) to demand any but the broadest strokes. It is that of the prototypic administrator—eternally the same in or out of uniform—whose concern over the incidence and treatment of VD is unrelated to the health and welfare of the men and is focused solely on the administrative problems they present. A Navy captain—"imperious, patrician of carriage, aloof and proud," as Styron characterizes him—he is determined to set the hospital administratively shipshape and to run it on the order of a seagoing vessel. "One of my first and most urgent duties on assuming this command," he tells Glanz on a tour of the ward, "is to get an accurate bearing on our venereal situation. To get a clear view from the poop deck, that is, so we can navigate the rocks and shoals . . . we'd better batten down all ports and hatches and man the fire stations." Budwinkle's total lack of empathy with the VD patients—he finds their morals repugnant and their presence (as the presence of patients in a hospital thoughtlessly tends to be) the chief stumbling block to perfect administration—is further aggravated by his mechanism:

> A splendid lab, Dr. Glanz, perfectly splendid. Great little gadgets! I especially am taken by those Kraft-Stekel monoprecipitators. . . . I'll bet they set the Navy back a pretty penny. . . . It is too bad, however, Doctor, that you don't have a Banghart twin-speed pressure pump for reverse catheterization. They're damned useful in a pinch. (CS, 1. 1)

This grim and bathetic fascination of Budwinkle's with things —an automaton's substitution for interest in people—resonates in act 2, when Glanz explains to him the wire recorder used for taking down the men's "sexual profiles." The machine is not freighted with the heavy symbolism it carries in a play like *Krapp's Last Tape*, but it is perhaps symbolic enough. As one of the smaller machines spawned by the grander mass machine—one of the "incalculable technological benefits" derived from war, as Glanz tells the captain—it ultimately functions as a replacement for the characters and personalities of the men themselves, who are taken by their superiors for little more than machines anyway. (Magruder, incidentally, is standing at strict attention outside the doctor's office while the explanation is going forward.) Implicit in Glanz's methods, greeted by Budwinkle with approbation, is the idea that in the last analysis a man can actually *become* his recording, fixed, exact, impersonal: "As you well know, sir, most venereal patients are inveterate liars, and the machine helps bend them in the direction of the truth. A patient will . . . choose his words more carefully . . . if he knows that his statements are . . . subject to scrutiny ex post facto." Such a technological tour de force could make the viability of the human mind and its freedom obsolete indeed!

Styron turns Budwinkle's indifference toward the men (except as VD cases and serial numbers) and his lack of sympathy or empathy with them into something appalling and ridiculous. But compared to Glanz's obliquity, his moral smugness and officiousness are straightforward. One expects scant humanity from the obsessive administrator, but one imagines the case to be quite different with a doctor of Glanz's training and experience. Normally it would be, I suppose, were it not that Glanz himself is psychologically ill. He is, to put it fairly directly, a megalomaniac, though the fact does not emerge until well toward the end of the play and is further complicated by his weird and novel "audiolagnia." For most of the play we think of him as a mere monomaniac. Styron has stacked the deck against Glanz, made him the whipping boy for what is deceitful and dangerous at any time and in any place. The satire against his toadying, egotism, blustering pomposity, spurious benignity, phony and patronizing solicitousness, against his gathering and culling of "sexual profiles," against his amateurish psychoanalyzing and mumbo jumbo, and finally against his sadism is unrelieved. Budwinkle at least shows a kind of stupid wonder and curiosity in the things going on about him; Glanz displays not so much as a flicker of humanity.

Though I imagine most people will find Glanz's "humors" and actions ludicrous and laughable long before they interpret them as dangerous, Styron's line with him may seem unusually severe for a comic satirist to take. Like any imaginative satirist, however, who in the end is interested in truth—or even in truths that admit of ambiguities—Styron does not care whether the means suffer incredible distortions. (Dr. Johnson, one remembers, remarked of *Gulliver's Travels* that once you got the idea for big men and little men the rest was easy.) Glanz must be pernicious *and* absurd because both qualities uncomfortably go hand in glove with men who desire to play god in all matters including life and death. And one of the "big" questions Styron is asking in the course of the play—a question to which Glanz is but the mark of punctuation—is up to what point will we sheepishly submit and knuckle under to authority, up to what point will we allow those of supposed intelligence, integrity, diligence, and concern to exercise control over us? It is, in another way, the same question asked in *Nat Turner*.

One could almost excuse Glanz his personality and idiosyncracies, ignore his eonistic practices in privately auditioning the recorded "sexual profiles," even feel some pathos at his being a megalomaniac, did not his grandest delusion unite what might otherwise have been disparate and ineffectual aberrations into a syndrome that actually blinds him to his power to destroy, rather than to save life. "I am a *healer!* I have taken the Hippocratic oath," Glanz howls while Magruder pins him to the chair. To which Magruder retorts: "You're not a healer, Glanz! You're a ghoul! You feed off the very dregs of death!" If Styron feels the need to spell out the incipient destructiveness of such an obsession, it is to keep this most forceful irony of the play from becoming lost in the violence of its climax. For, though perhaps less melodramatically than Magruder sees it, Glanz is a kind of parasite whose own illness unfortunately finds its "objective correlative" on the VD ward. Like VD itself, Glanz's psychological disease is antisocial, infectious, possibly even fatal.

It is not difficult to see the satirist's dilemma in suiting this problem to comedy, for the play could just as easily have tipped over into tragedy. Glanz's "infallible" diagnosis of Magruder as a syphilitic might have driven him, were he other than he is, into madness and suicide. Healers, naturally, must have sickness about them before they can heal; ironically, their raison d'être is predicated on it. And a mind as twisted and perverse as Glanz's must, in order to continually reaffirm its existence, take the rationalizing, self-fulfilling, logically insane step of believing disease exists even though there is the remotest chance it does not. The patient, as Magruder discovers, is a loser both ways:

MAGRUDER (*Very loud now*) You could have—*told* me!

GLANZ (*Slightly rattled by his tone*) Told you what?

MAGRUDER (*His words very precise and measured in his rage, which is barely controlled now*) Told me what you just told me now.

GLANZ We don't quite understand—

MAGRUDER (*Frankly aggressive now, heedless of his subordinate position*) Then I'll try to *make* you understand. If what you say is true you could have given me some *hope*. You could have told me that I *might* have had some other disease. Latent trench mouth. Athlete's foot! Ringworm! Something else! Anything! You could have been less goddamned certain that I was going to *die* full of paresis and locomotor ataxia!

GLANZ (*Alarmed by Magruder's tone here, rises from his chair*) Mind your tone, Magruder. We're in authority here! The reason we failed to give you such information is because it is our firm policy never falsely to arouse a patient's expectations, his hopes—

MAGRUDER (*Fully exercised now, he advances in a fury on the doctor, circling the corner of his desk*) Hope! What do you know about hope and expectations, you wretched son of a bitch! Don't talk to me about hope and expectations! . . . Don't give me any more of this "we" shit, either! You're not Congress, or some goddamned corporation, or the King of Sweden! You're a loathesome little functionary with a dirty mind and a stethoscope, and, goddamn you, from now on I insist you say *I*—like niggers, Jews and syphilitics! (CS, 3. 2)

Absurd as it might be to suggest that Styron is serving up the warmed-over admonition of "physician, heal thyself"—I don't believe for a moment, that is, that the author has an abiding grievance against the AMA in general or urologists in particular—the universal implications of this entire violent, though comic exchange (the heavy and villain *is* given a physical and mental drubbing) tangentially works off the precept. Ideally, the remedy for any matter of ills should originate with those with knowledge and power to cure them; yet our truckling to both or either too often obviates the measures necessary for the cure. Indeed, authority uses our very weakness and submission, our ignorance and innocence to sustain its own delusions and obsessions. Most of us, in our day-to-day confrontations, are powerless to strike out as directly and satisfyingly, and in this case symbolically, as Magruder or to reach any moral or psychological equivalence to even his Pyrrhic victory. Magruder's catharsis, which delivers him from the fear of death and affirms his faith in life (the bleak anticipation of a court martial and probable imprisonment notwithstanding) is won through Glanz's defeat and humiliation. Yet because this works for Magruder does not mean it will work for anyone else in quite the same way. Ironically, Magruder is able to heal himself *despite* "hope and expectations"—had he been given them earlier he would not have been able to sound his depths or experience the revitalizing changes—and Styron, no utopian, will not commit himself to the shallow fantasy and optimism that claims "hope and expectations" will sustain life when life is not there to begin with.

Too much else in the play controverts the idea. The most striking instances are the cases of Schwartz and Clark. Clark dies, and

Schwartz, dying, will die: the Negro harboring to the end hate
and anti-Semitism, the Jew holding on to tolerance and charity
and forgiveness as if holding on to life itself. Styron's selection of
these two apparently antipodal types runs the risk of plummeting
into cliché and turning representatives of long-suffering minor-
ities into caricatures; I imagine the play might be attacked on
this very point. The assumption is perhaps viable given the rapid
gloss of a theatrical production; but whether true or false, such
an assumption must account for the qualifications and extensions
of the characters, however close to types or stereotypes they might
first seem.

Schwartz, to be sure, is more fully drawn than Clark; simply
by virtue of being on stage longer and always in dialogue with
Magruder he is a rounder character. We know little else about the
southern Negro except his monolithic hatred of Jews, and we
know why he hates them: not (as Magruder tries to elicit from
him) because they crucified Christ, but because they "crucified
niggers,"—the point of departure for Clark's harangue about a
Jewish businessman in a small Tennessee town who reclaimed
all the appliances and furniture from Clark's father because he
was unable to meet payments. On the other hand, we know that
Schwartz's wife is going to fat; that he likes poetry (he considers
"Crossing the Bar" the acme of poetic inspiration), has dreams of
managing a pet shop after the war, reads self-improving ethnic
tracts like *Tolerance for Others: or How to Develop Human Compassion*, and (in the face of an ulcer complicating his renal TB)
delights in browsing through a Jewish cookbook called *Mazeltov*.

There is a great deal that is homespun and humane, pathetic,
compassionate and comic about Schwartz and much that is odious
and contemptible about Clark. Yet though the Negro is—in
Schwartz's words—"evil" and "no good" and has elevated his hate
of whitey and Jews to a kind of metaphysical disease, he, of all
the others on the ward, has the truest, if grimmest, sense of reality: a visionary fatalism that comprehends the ultimate link
among the men. And while no one else dares name it, Clark will:
"I *do* stink and I *is* black, and I is po' as Job's turkey, and I isn't
got any kinfolk to mou'n me to my grave. But one thing I does

know is dat dere ain't no difference between a dead nigger and a dead Jew-boy when dey is both food for de worms. *Equal!*" Clark's fatalism, inspired by a searing, outraged sense of inequality and injustice and fed by his obsessional hatred is amplified with multiplying ironies in a later scene in which the Negro tries to explain to Magruder why he "likes" him and not Schwartz:

> CLARK Because you is a *Southren* boy. I is Southren too. Born and reared in Bolivar, Tennessee. Us Southren boys got to stick together. Born together. Die together. Dat's *equality.* . . . You an' me—us Southren boys—us *knows* we gwine die. Jew-boy, he gwine die, too. He jus' skeered to own up to de nachel-born truth. . . .
>
> MAGRUDER (*There is an edge of compassion in his voice, as if he were trying to cope with or understand the irrationality of this Negro*) Can't you see how wrong and stupid it is of you to feel this way? It's a tough spot we're all in here. We're all in a terrible situation. Why don't you try to like Schwartz too, Lorenzo? It won't do any of us any good if you keep on storing up this unreasonable hatred. Hatred for someone who's done you not the slightest bit of harm.
>
> CLARK (*Feebly but with passion*) I'll like de Jew boy. I *will* like him! I'll like him on de day dat de Lawd make roses bloom in a pig's asshole. (CS, 2. 1)

As suspicious as he was of Magruder's appeal to "hope and expectations" of life when life is not there, so Styron is here distrustful of the appeal to reason when reason is not, cannot be there. As it should not be. Clark and his race had very little to be reasonable or rational about thirty years ago. His irrational hatred which grows uglier and more obsessional before he dies and in its last-ditch effort even succeeds in momentarily turning Schwartz and Magruder against each other—can only be purged through some sort of miracle.

Styron's comedy, however, does not toady to miracles; the edge of satire is honed until the very end. For a further irony is that neither compassion nor pacification can counter Clark's kind of implacable, irrational hatred—as the times showed too well. (The zeitgeist as a matter of fact makes its own grisly advent in the form of a yellow "S" for syphilitic on Magruder's robe: an analogy with the yellow star that the European Jews were forced to display and one that does not escape Magruder or Schwartz.) We are caught up short in our sympathies with Schwartz's trying to reach Clark in extremis as soon as we realize that this attempt at connecting, at understanding and pacifying is a weakness in itself—I would go so far as to say a disease in itself: the terrible and fatal rationalization of many who were swept away in the holocaust:

> Wally, as I got up and looked at him, looking at that fuckin' agony on his face, and watching him breathe in this tortured way, I said to myself, "Well, he's dying. . . ." Then I said to myself, "This hatred of his, it's only because of the hatred that we in turn—we whose skins are white—have poured out on *him*." I thought I should ask Lorenzo to forgive me—to forgive us—for all we've done to him. . . . And then I said, "Don't you understand, Lorenzo? Can't you forgive me?" And . . . I heard him say, "Forgiveness." And he . . . said again, "Forgiveness. Dat do grab my black ass. . . ." Wally, I was desperate! He was . . . dying right in front of my eyes. I felt that I just *couldn't* let him go with this hatred all bottled up inside him. . . . Then I . . . said: "Lorenzo, we mustn't live and die with this awful hate inside us. We must be brothers and love one another." Then at last I said, "I love you, Lorenzo. I love you as a brother. Please allow yourself to love me in return. . . ." And finally he spoke—so faint and weak—they must have been almost the last words he said. And you know what they were? . . . He said, "Yes, I'll love you . . . *Yes*, I'll love you! I will love you, Jew-boy. I will love you when the Lord makes roses bloom in a pig's asshole." (CS, 3. 2)

These dying words effectively foul the net of Judeo-Christian virtues that Schwartz casts out hoping to snare Clark's forgiveness and love. Schwartz has the right impulse toward love, but makes the wrong appeal for it; Clark has the proper hold on his hate, but the wrong outlet for it. As scapegoats of the ages, in degree and kind, both the Jew and the Negro are in some respects equal,[3] but their responses to persecution and slavery have been almost directly opposed: the one, even up until Nazi Germany, meeting these with suffering, the other with rebellion and revolution. Schwartz's grand but futile attempt at expunging in seconds hundreds of years of an inhuman and unbearable condition works out of a heritage that few southern Negroes would have then understood, just as Clark's last gasp of blasphemous contempt works out of one that would have been mystifying to most northeastern Jews. Thus, more than merely dynamiting the cliché of the deathbed scene, Styron is also piecing together fragments of ailing sensibilities that can never be whole again until the disease fostering hate and suffering—born and nurtured by the same institutions that created a Glanz and a Budwinkle—is eradicated.

I fear, however, that *In the Clap Shack* offers no remedy for this most persistent and recurrent disease. It is not a satire accommodating "hope and expectations," though it does manage tentatively to affirm the perdurability of man's spirit. The affirmation is found in Magruder's discovery—born out of wrath and indignation, a chastened sensitivity and sense of justice—that equality among men should not be gauged through suffering or disease or death, but through the joy and freedom in living. This is why, perhaps, in his farewell to Schwartz, he can inhale the dying man's fetid breath as "the breath of a babe . . . a zephyr." And why, too, this exaltation of his newly realized freedom hearkens back to a line from Wallace Stevens that he quoted earlier in the play, unconscious then of its ultimate connotation: "The body dies; the body's beauty lives." This would indeed be a strange message to take away from a charnel house had not Styron resurrected from the tragic fact of death the human comedy and purpose of life.

Notes

1. See the interview with William Styron in this collection.

2. This and the following quote are taken from Frederick J. Hoffman's article "William Styron: The Metaphysical Hurt," first printed in *The Art of Southern Fiction: A Study of Some Modern Novelists* (Carbondale, Ill., 1967), p. 145.

3. Schwartz's name symbolically links him with Clark in blackness.

JACKSON R. BRYER

William Styron: A Bibliography

This bibliography updates and supplements previous listings by Harold W. Schneider (*Critique*, Summer 1960), David D. Galloway (*The Absurd Hero in American Fiction*), August J. Nigro (*William Styron*, ed. by Melvin J. Friedman and Nigro; Configuration Critique, no. 11), and Jackson R. Bryer and Marc Newman (*William Styron's "The Confessions of Nat Turner"—A Critical Handbook*, ed. by Friedman and Irving Malin). It is closest in scope to the last named compilation, and thus any acknowledgments of assistance remain essentially the same. The book review section could not have been nearly as complete without the cooperation of the Publicity Department of Random House. Reviews of particularly noteworthy substance are marked with an asterisk. We have been unable to find any reviews of *The Long March*. In a few instances, where a review or article is only partially concerned with Styron, I have listed the page numbers of the full piece first and then, in brackets, listed the page or pages on Styron. I owe a debt of thanks to my colleague Lewis Lawson for his advice and assistance during several stages of this project. Marc Newman's collaboration on the bibliography from which this present list is adapted was of great value. Susan Robinson and Mrs. Joanne Giza gave generously of their time and energies in helping with the research.

I. Works by Styron

A. NOVELS

Lie Down in Darkness. Indianapolis: Bobbs-Merrill, 1951; London: Hamish Hamilton, 1952.
The Long March. New York: Random House, 1956; New York: Vintage, 1962.

Set This House on Fire. New York: Random House, 1960; London: Hamish Hamilton, 1961.

The Confessions of Nat Turner. New York: Random House, 1967; London: Jonathan Cape, 1968.

B. PLAY

In the Clap Shack. New York: Random House, 1973.

C. SHORT FICTION

"Autumn." In *One and Twenty: Duke Narrative and Verse, 1924–1945,* edited by William M. Blackburn. Durham, N.C.: Duke University Press, 1945. Pp. 36–53.

"The Long Dark Road." *In One and Twenty: Duke Narrative and Verse, 1924–1945,* edited by Blackburn (see above). Pp. 266–280. Reprinted in *William Styron's "The Confessions of Nat Turner"—A Critical Handbook,* edited by Melvin J. Friedman and Irving Malin. Belmont, Calif.: Wadsworth, 1970. Pp. 117–125.

"A Moment in Trieste." In *American Vanguard,* edited by Don Wolfe. Ithaca, N.Y.: Cornell University Press, 1948. Pp. 241–247. Reprinted in *New Voices: American Writing Today,* edited by Don Wolfe. Garden City, N.Y.: Doubleday, 1953.

"The Enormous Window." In *1950 American Vanguard,* edited by Charles I. Glicksberg. New York: School for Social Research, 1950. Pp. 71–89.

"The Long March." *In Discovery No. 1,* edited by John W. Aldridge and Vance Bourjaily. New York: Pocket Books, 1953. Pp. 221–283. Collected as LM. Reprinted in *The Best Short Stories of World War II: An American Anthology,* edited by Charles Fenton. New York: Viking Press, 1957. Pp. 361–421.

"The McCabes." *Paris Review* 22 (Autumn–Winter 1959–1960): 12–28. Incorporated into SHF.

"Works in Progress." *Esquire* 60 (July 1963): 50–51, 105. Incorporated into NT.

"Runaway." *Partisan Review* 32 (Fall 1966): 574–582.

"Virginia: 1831." *Paris Review* 9 (Winter 1966): 13–45. Incorporated into NT.

"The Confessions of Nat Turner." *Harper's* 235 (September 1967): 51–102. Incorporated into NT.

"Novel's Climax: The Night of the Honed Axes." *Life* 63 (13 October 1967): 54–60. Incorporated into NT.

"Marriott, the Marine." *Esquire* 76 (September 1971): 101–104, 196, 198, 200, 202, 204, 207, 208, 210.

D. ARTICLES

"Letters to an Editor." *Paris Review* 1 (Spring 1953): 9–16.

"Prevalence of Wonders." *Nation* 176 (2 May 1953): 370–371.

"The Paris Review." *Harper's Bazaar* 87 (August 1953): 122, 173.

"What's Wrong with the American Novel?" *American Scholar* 24 (Autumn 1955): 464–503. [Round table discussion with Ralph Ellison, Hiram Haydn, and others.]

"If You Write for Television . . . ." *New Republic* 146 (6 April 1959): 16.

Introduction to *Best Short Stories from "The Paris Review."* New York: E. P. Dutton, 1959. Pp. 9–16.

"Mrs. Aadland's Little Girl, Beverly." *Esquire* (November 1961): 142, 189–191. Reprinted in *First Person Singular: Essays for the Sixties*, edited by Herbert Gold. New York: Dial Press, 1963. Pp. 209–216. Reprinted in *Esquire's World of Humor.* New York: Esquire, 1964. P. 210 [as "True Confessions"].

"The Death-in-Life of Benjamin Reid." *Esquire* 57 (February 1962): 114, 141–145. Reprinted in *An Approach to Literature*, edited by Cleanth Brooks, John Thibaut Purser, and Robert Penn Warren. 4th ed. New York: Appleton-Century-Crofts, 1964. Pp. 496–503.

"As He Lay Dead, A Bitter Grief." *Life* 53 (20 July 1962): 39–42.

"Aftermath of Benjamin Reid." *Esquire* 58 (November 1962): 79.

"Writers under Twenty-five." In *Under Twenty-five: Duke Nar-*

rative and Verse, 1945–1962, edited by William M. Blackburn.
Durham, N.C.: Duke University Press, 1963. Pp. 3–8.

"Two Writers Talk It Over." *Esquire* 60 (July 1963): 57–59.
[Discussion with James Jones.]

"This Quiet Dust." *Harper's* 230 (April 1965): 135–146. Re-
printed in *Best Magazine Articles of the Year 1966,* edited by
Gerald Walker. New York: Crown Publishers, 1966, Pp. 1–18.
Reprinted in *William Styron's "The Confessions of Nat Turner"*
—A Critical Handbook, edited by Friedman and Malin (See 1,
C above). Pp. 18–35.

"Truth and Nat Turner: An Exchange—William Styron Replies." *Nation* 206 (22 April 1968): 544–547.

"Oldest America." *McCalls* 95 (July 1968): 94, 123.

"Symposium: Violence in Literature." *American Scholar* 37
(Summer 1968): 482–496. [Round table with Robert Penn
Warren, Theodore Solotaroff, and Robert Coles.]

"In the Jungle." *New York Review of Books* 11 (26 September
1968): 11–13.

"My Generation." *Esquire* 70 (October 1968): 123–124.

"On Creativity." *Playboy* 15 (December 1968). [Styron's statement appears on p. 138.]

"The Uses of Historical Fiction." *Southern Literary Journal* 1
(Spring 1969): 57–90. [Discussion with Ralph Ellison, Robert Penn Warren, C. Vann Woodward, and Styron.]

"Kuznetsov's Confession." *New York Times,* 14 September 1969,
sec. 4, p. 13. [Letter to the editor clarifying Styron's position
on Kuznetsov's defection.]

"A Letter from William Styron." *Barat Review* 6 (Spring/Sum-
mer 1971): 5.

E. BOOK AND RECORD REVIEWS

"New Editions." *New York Review of Books* 1 (Special Issue
1963): 43. [*Slave and Citizen: The Negro in the Americas* by
Frank Tannenbaum.]

"Overcome." *New York Review of Books* 1 (26 September 1963):
18–19. [*American Negro Slave Revolts* by Herbert Aptheker.]

"An Elegy for F. Scott Fitzgerald." *New York Review of Books* 1 (28 November 1963): 1–3. [*The Letters of F. Scott Fitzgerald*, edited by Andrew Turnbull.]

"The Habit." *New York Review of Books* 1 (26 December 1963): 13–14. [*The Consumers Union Report on Smoking and the Public Interest*, edited by Ruth and Edward Brecher.]

"A Southern Conscience." *New York Review of Books* 2 (2 April 1964): 3. [*A Southern Prophecy* by Lewis H. Blair.]

"Tootsie Rolls." *New York Review of Books* 2 (14 May 1964): 8–9. [*Candy* by Terry Southern and Mason Hoffenberg.]

"MacArthur." *New York Review of Books* 2 (8 October 1964): 3–5. [*Reminiscences* by Douglas MacArthur.]

"John Fitzgerald Kennedy ... as we remember him." *High Fidelity* 16 (January 1966): 38. ["John Fitzgerald Kennedy ... as we remember him" by Charles Kuralt: Columbia Recording L2L:1017.]

"The Vice That Has No Name." *Harper's* 236 (February 1968): 97–100. [*Light on Dark Corners* ... by B. G. Jefferis and J. L. Nichols.]

"The Shade of Thomas Wolfe." *Harper's* 236 (April 1968): 96, 98–104. [*Thomas Wolfe* by Andrew Turnbull.]

"A Timeless, Walled Yaddo for Gifted Misfit." *New York Times Book Review*, 25 April 1971, pp. 1, 10, 12. [*The Joint* by James Blake.]

"That Extraordinary Company of Writers Ironically Known as the Lost Generation." *New York Times Book Review*, 6 May 1973, pp. 8, 10, 12, 14. [*A Second Flowering* by Malcolm Cowley.]

II. Works about Styron

A. BOOKS

Aldridge, John W. "The Society of Three Novels." In his *In Search of Heresy*. New York: McGraw-Hill, 1956. Pp. 126–148. [LDD.]

———. "William Styron and the Derivative Imagination." In

his *Time to Murder and Create: The Contemporary Novel in Crisis*. New York: David McKay, 1966. Pp. 30–51. [SHF.]

Allen, Walter. *The Modern Novel in Britain and the United States*. New York: E. P. Dutton, 1964. Pp. 305–307. [LDD.]

Baumbach, Jonathan. "Paradise Lost: *Lie Down in Darkness* by William Styron." In his *The Landscape of Nightmare: Studies in the Contemporary Novel*. New York: New York University Press, 1965. Pp. 123–137.

Bradbury, John M. *Renaissance in the South: A Critical History of the Literature, 1920–1960*. Chapel Hill: University of North Carolina Press, 1963. Pp. 122–123 and passim. [LDD and SHF.]

Bryant, Jerry H. *The Open Decision—The Contemporary American Novel and Its Intellectual Background*. New York: Free Press, 1970. Pp. 264–268. [SHF.]

Butor, Michel. Préface to *La proie des flammes*. Translated by M.-E. Coindreau. Paris: Gallimard, 1963. Pp. vii–xx.

Chapsal, Madeleine. *Quinze écrivains*. Paris: Julliard, 1963. Pp. 173–181.

Clarke, John H., ed. *William Styron's "Nat Turner": Ten Black Writers Respond*. Boston: Beacon Press, 1968.

Core, George, ed. *Southern Fiction Today: Renascence and Beyond*. Athens: University of Georgia Press, 1969.

Davis, Robert Gorham. "The American Individualist Tradition: Bellow and Styron." In *The Creative Present: Notes on Contemporary Fiction*, edited by Nona Balakian and Charles Simmons. Garden City, N.Y.: Doubleday, 1963. Pp. 111–141.

Detweiler, Robert. "William Styron and the Courage to Be." In his *Four Spiritual Crises in Mid-Century American Fiction*. Gainesville: University of Florida Press, 1964. Pp. 6–13.

Duberman, Martin. "William Styron's *Nat Turner* and *Ten Black Writers Respond*." In his *The Uncompleted Past*. New York: Random House, 1969. Pp. 203–222. [Reprinted reviews plus new "second thoughts" on both pieces.]

Finkelstein, Sidney. "Cold War, Religious Revival, and Family Alienation: William Styron, J. D. Salinger, and Edward Albee." In his *Existentialism and Alienation in American Lit-*

erature. New York: International Publishers, 1965. Pp. 211–242.

Fossum, Robert H. *William Styron: A Critical Essay*. Grand Rapids, Mich.: Eerdmans, 1968.

Friedman, Melvin J. "William Styron." In *The Politics of Twentieth-Century Novelists*, edited by George A. Panichas. New York: Hawthorn Books, 1971. Pp. 335–350.

——, and Malin, Irving, eds. *William Styron's "The Confessions of Nat Turner—A Critical Handbook*. Belmont, Calif.: Wadsworth, 1970.

——, and Nigro, August J., eds. *Configuration critique de William Styron*. Paris: Minard, 1967 .

Fuller, Edmund. *Books with Men behind Them*. New York: Random House, 1962. Pp. 9–10.

Galloway, David D. "The Absurd Man as Tragic Hero" and "A William Styron Checklist." In his *The Absurd Hero in American Fiction*. Austin: University of Texas Press, 1966. Pp. 51–81 and 203–210.

Geismar, Maxwell. "William Styron: The End of Innocence." In his *American Moderns: From Rebellion to Conformity*. New York: Hill and Wang, 1958. Pp. 239–250.

Genovese, Eugene D. "William Styron before the People's Court." In his *In Red and Black—Marxian Explorations in Southern and Afro-American History*. New York: Pantheon, 1968. Pp. 200–217.

Gossett, Louise Y. "The Cost of Freedom: William Styron." In her *Violence in Recent Southern Fiction*. Durham, N.C.: Duke University Press, 1965. Pp. 117–130.

Hartt, Julian. *The Lost Image of Man*. Baton Rouge: Louisiana State University Press, 1963. Pp. 60–63, 130.

Hassan, Ihab. "Encounter with Necessity: Three Novels by Styron, Swados, and Mailer." In his *Radical Innocence: Studies in the Contemporary American Novel*. Princeton, N.J.: Princeton University Press, 1961. Pp. 124–152. [LDD.] Reprinted in *On Contemporary Literature*, edited by Richard Kostelanetz. New York: Avon, 1964. Pp. 597–606; and in *William Styron's*

"The Confessions of Nat Turner"—A Critical Handbook, edited by Friedman and Malin (see above). Pp. 141–148.

Hoffman, Frederick J. "The Sense of Place." In *South: Modern Southern Literature in Its Cultural Setting*, edited by Louis D. Rubin, Jr., and Robert D. Jacobs. Garden City, N.Y.: Doubleday Dolphin, 1961. Pp. 76–94. [LDD.]

————. "William Styron: The Metaphysical Hurt." In his *The Art of Southern Fiction: A Study of Some Modern Novelists*. Carbondale: Southern Illinois University Press, 1967. Pp. 144–161. Reprinted in *Configuration critique de William Styron*, edited by Friedman and Nigro (see above). Pp. 33–56 (in French); and in *William Styron's "The Confessions of Nat Turner"—A Critical Handbook*, edited by Friedman and Malin (see above). Pp. 126–141.

Kazin, Alfred. "The Alone Generation." In his *Contemporaries*. Boston: Little, Brown, 1962. Pp. 214–216.

Kort, Wesley A. "*The Confessions of Nat Turner* and the Dynamic Revolution." In his *Shriven Selves—Religious Problems in Recent American Fiction*. Philadelphia: Fortress Press, 1972. Pp. 116–140.

Kuehl, John. Appendix to his *Write and Rewrite—A Study of the Creative Process*. New York: Meredith Press, 1967. Pp. 294–308. *Write and Rewrite* was also published under the title *Creative Writing & Rewriting* by Appleton-Century-Crofts. [Facsimile of Styron's holograph of chap. 1 of *LM* and the published version.]

Lawson, Lewis A. "William Styron (1925–)." In *A Bibliographical Guide to the Study of Southern Literature*, edited by Louis D. Rubin, Jr. Baton Rouge: Louisiana State University Press, 1969. Pp. 300–302. [Selective and unannotated list of secondary materials.]

Ludwig, Jack. *Recent American Novelists*. Minneapolis: University of Minnesota Press, 1962. Pp. 31–34.

Mackin, Cooper R. *William Styron*. Austin, Tex.: Steck-Vaughn, 1969.

Mailer, Norman. *Advertisements for Myself*. New York: New American Library, 1960. Pp. 415–416.

Matthiessen, Peter, and Plimpton, George. "William Styron." In *Writers at Work: The "Paris Review" Interviews*, edited by Malcolm Cowley. New York: Viking Press, 1959. Pp. 267–282.

Meeker, Richard K. "The Youngest Generation of Southern Fiction Writers." In *Southern Writers: Appraisals in Our Time*, edited by R. C. Simonini, Jr. Charlottesville: University of Virginia Press, 1961. Pp. 162–191.

Mohrt, Michel. *Le nouveau roman Américain*. Paris: Gallimard, 1955. Pp. 171–174.

Mudrick, Marvin. "Mailer and Styron." In his *On Culture and Literature*. New York: Horizon Press, 1970. Pp. 176–199.

O'Connor, William Van. "John Updike and William Styron: The Burden of Talent." In *Contemporary American Novelists*, edited by Harry T. Moore. Carbondale: Southern Illinois University Press, 1964. Pp. 205–221.

Pearce, Richard. *William Styron*. Minneapolis: University of Minnesota Press, 1971.

Podhoretz, Norman. "The Gloom of Philip Roth." In his *Doings and Undoings*. New York: Farrar, Straus, 1964. Pp. 236–243.

Ratner, Marc L. *William Styron*. New York: Twayne, 1972.

Rubin, Louis D., Jr. *The Curious Death of the Novel: Essays in American Literature*. Baton Rouge: Louisiana State University Press, 1967. Pp. 4, 9, 10, 20–22, 146–147, 277, 280, 286, 292.

———. "William Styron: Notes on a Southern Writer in Our Time." In his *The Faraway Country: Writers of the Modern South*. Seattle: University of Washington Press, 1963. Pp. 185–230.

———; Porter, Katherine Anne; O'Connor, Flannery; Gordon, Caroline; and Jones, Madison. *Recent Southern Fiction*. Macon, Ga.: Wesleyan College, 1960.

Stevenson, David L. "Novelists of Distinction." In *The Creative Present*, edited by Nona Balakian and Charles Simmons. Garden City, N.Y.: Doubleday, 1963. Pp. 195–212.

———. "William Styron and the Fiction of the Fifties." In *Recent American Fiction: Some Critical Views*, edited by Joseph L. Waldmeir. Boston: Houghton Mifflin, 1963. Pp. 265–274.

Cambon, Glauco. "Faulkner fa scoula." *La fiera letteraria*, 7 March 1954, p. 5.

Cannon, Patricia R. "Nat Turner: God, Man, or Beast?" *Barat Review* 6 (Spring/Summer 1971): 25–28.

Canzoneri, Robert, and Stegner, Page. "An Interview with William Styron." *Per/Se* 1 (Summer 1966): 37–44.

Carver, Wayne. "The Grand Inquisitor's Long March." *Denver Quarterly* 1 (Summer 1966): 37–64. [LM and Dostoevski's *The Legend of the Grand Inquisitor*.]

Chapsal, Madeleine. "Entretien." *L'express*, no. 560 (8 March 1962): 26–27. [Interview.]

Cheyer, A. H. "WLB Biography: William Styron." *Wilson Library Bulletin* 36 (April 1962): 691.

Cooke, Michael. "Nat Turner: Another Response." *Yale Review* 58 (Winter 1969): 295–301. [Review of Clarke's *William Styron's "Nat Turner."*]

Core, George. "*The Confessions of Nat Turner* and the Burden of the Past." *Southern Literary Journal* 2 (Spring 1970): 117–134.

———."*Nat Turner* and the Final Reckoning of Things." *Southern Review* 4 (Summer 1968): 745–751.

Cunliffe, Marcus. "Black Culture and White America." *Encounter* 34 (January 1970): 22–35 [29–31].

Curtis, Bruce. "Fiction, Myth, and History in William Styron's *Nat Turner*." *University College Quarterly* 16 (January 1971): 27–32.

Davis, John Roderick. "Kuznetsov's Dilemma." *New York Times*, 27 August 1969, p. 42. [Letter to the editor on WS's recommendation that K not defect.]

Davis, Robert Gorham. "Styron and the Students." *Critique* 3 (Summer 1960): 37–46.

Dempsey, David. "Talk with William Styron." *New York Times Book Review*, 9 September 1951, p. 27.

Doar, Harriet. "Interview with William Styron." *Red Clay Reader*, 1964, pp. 26–30.

Dommergues, Pierre. L'ambiguité de l'innocence." *Langues modernes* 59 (March–April 1965): 54–59.

Duberman, Martin. "Historical Fictions." *New York Times Book Review*, 11 August 1968, pp. 1, 26–27. [Review of Clarke's *William Styron's "Nat Turner."*]

Duffer, Ken. "Now Nat Turner as He Might Have Written It." *Winston-Salem* (N.C.) *Journal and Sentinel*, 17 December 1967, p. 6-D. [Review of Daniel Panger's *Ol' Prophet Nat.*]

Durden, Robert F. "William Styron and His Black Critics." *South Atlantic Quarterly* 68 (Spring 1969): 181–187. [Review of Clarke's *William Styron's "Nat Turner."*]

Emmanuel, Pierre. "L'histoire d'une solitude." *Preuves*, no. 217 (April 1969): 17–20.

Fauchereau, Serge. "Oncle Nat et Oncle Tom." *La quinzaine littéraire* 70 (15 April 1969): 5–6.

Fosburgh, Lacey. "Styron and Miller Defend Yevtushenko against Charges in British Press of Hypocrisy." *New York Times*, 25 November 1968, p. 15.

Foster, Richard. "An Orgy of Commerce: William Styron's *Set This House on Fire.*" *Critique* 3 (Summer 1960): 59–70.

Fraisse, Simone. "Une tragedie de notre temps: *La Proise des Flammes* de William Styron." *Esprit*, October 1963, pp. 483–488.

Franklin, Jimme L. "*Nat Turner* and Black History." *Indian Journal of American Studies* 1 (November 1971): 1–6.

Fremont-Smith, Eliot. "Nat Turner I: The Controversy." *New York Times*, 1 August 1968, p. 29. [Review of Clarke's *Willim Styron's "Nat Turner."*]

———. "Nat Turner II: What Myth Will Serve?" *New York Times*, 2 August 1968, p. 31. [Review of Clarke's *William Styron's "Nat Turner."*]

Friedman, Joseph. "Non-Conformity and the Writer." *Venture* 20 (Winter 1957): 23–31.

Friedman, Melvin J. "The Cracked Vase." *Romance Notes* 7 (Spring 1966): 127–129.

———. "William Styron: An Interim Appraisal." *English Journal* 50 (March 1961): 149–158, 192. Reprinted in *William Styron's "The Confessions of Nat Turner"—A Critical Handbook*, edited by Friedman and Malin (see 2, A above) and, revised, as Preface to *Configuration critique de William Styron*, edited by Friedman and Nigro (see 2, A above).

Fuentes, Carlos. "Unslavish Fidelity." *Times Literary Supplement* (London), 16 May 1968, p. 505.

Galloway, David D. "The Absurd Man as Tragic Hero: The Novels of William Styron." *Texas Studies in Literature and Language* 6 (Winter 1965): 512–534. Reprinted in his *The Absurd Hero in American Fiction* (see 2, A above).

Geismar, Maxwell. "The American Short Story Today." *Studies on the Left* 4 (Spring 1964): 21–27.

Genovese, Eugene D. "An Exchange on 'Nat Turner.'" *New York Review of Books* 11 (7 November 1968): 34–36.

————. "The Nat Turner Case." *New York Review of Books* 11 (12 September 1968): 34–37. [Review of Clarke's *William Styron's "Nat Turner."*]

Gilman, Richard. "Nat Turner Revisited." *New Republic* 158 (27 April 1968): 23–32. Reprinted in *William Styron's "The Confessions of Nat Turner"—A Critical Handbook*, edited by Friedman and Malin (see 2, A above).

Gresset, Michel. "*Les confessions de Nat Turner*: l'histoire récle et le roman—un sociodrame Américain." *Preuves*, no. 217 (April 1969): 3–5 .

————. "Sur William Styron." *Mercure de France* 350 (February 1964): 297–303.

————. "William Styron." *La nouvelle revue Française* 204 (December 1969): 898–907.

Gross, Seymour L., and Bender, Eileen. "History and Politics, and Literature: The Myth of Nat Turner." *American Quarterly* 23 (October 1971): 486–518.

H., E. P. "On Author." *Saturday Review of Literature* 34 (15 September 1951): 12.

Hamilton, Charles V. "Nat Turner Reconsidered: The Fiction and the Reality." *Saturday Review* 51 (22 June 1968): 22–23. [Review of Clarke's *William Styron's "Nat Turner."*]

Harding, Vincent. "An Exchange on 'Nat Turner.'" *New York Review of Books* 11 (7 November 1968): 31–33.

Hassan, Ihab. "The Character of Post-War Fiction in America." *English Journal* 51 (January 1962): 1–8.

———. "The Novel of Outrage: A Minority Voice in Postwar American Fiction." *American Scholar* 34 (Spring 1965): 239–253 [243–244].

Hays, Peter L. "The Nature of Rebellion in *The Long March*." *Critique* 7 (Winter 1965–1966): 70–74.

Hazard, E. P. "Eight Fiction Finds." *Saturday Review of Literature* 35 (16 February 1952): 17.

———. "William Styron." *Saturday Review of Literature* 34 (15 September 1951): 12.

Holder, Alan. "Styron's Slave: *The Confessions of Nat Turner*." *South Atlantic Quarterly* 68 (Spring 1969): 167–180.

"Howe and Styron to Write Book Column for *Harper's*." *New York Times*, 26 October 1967, p. 40.

Hutchens, John K. "William Styron." *New York Herald Tribune Book Review*, 9 September 1951, p. 2.

Johansson, Eric. "Lettres: les sortiléges de la mauvaise conscience." *Démocratie*, 27 June 1963, p. 10.

Juin, Hubert. "Rencontre avec William Styron." *Lettres Françaises*, 1–8 March 1962, p. 5.

Kazin, Alfred. "The Alone Generation." *Harper's* (special supplement) 219 (October 1959): 127–131. Reprinted in his *Contemporaries* (see 2, A above).

Kihss, Peter. "Pulitzer to Styron Novel; No Prize Given for Drama." *New York Times*, 7 May 1968, pp. 1, 34.

Klotz, Marvin. "The Triumph Over Time: Narrative Form in William Faulkner and William Styron." *Mississippi Quarterly* 17 (Winter 1963–1964): 9–20.

Kostelanetz, Richard. "The Bad Criticism of This Age." *Minnesota Review* 4 (Spring 1964): 389–414.

Las Vergnas, Raymond. "Étoiles Anglo-Américaines: Nathanael West, William Styron, Robert Penn Warren, Carson McCullers, V. Sackville-West." *Les annales*, August 1962, p. 33.

Lawson, John Howard. "William Styron: Darkness and Fire in the Modern Novel." *Mainstream* 13 (October 1960): 9–18. [SHF.]

Lawson, Lewis. "Cass Kinsolving: Kierkegaardian Man of Despair." *Wisconsin Studies in Contemporary Literature* 3 (Fall 1962): 54–66.

Le Clec'h, Guy. "Un 'grand' de la nouvelle vague américaine: William Styron." *Figaro littéraire*, 24 February 1962, p. 3 [Interview centered on SHF.]

————. "Pour les noirs Américains la 'Confession de Nat Turner' n'est que celle de William Styron." *Figaro littéraire*, 3 March 1969, p. 24.

Leo, John. "Some Negroes Accuse Styron of Distorting Nat Turner's Life." *New York Times*, 1 February 1968, p. 34.

Lewis, R. W. B., and Woodward, C. Vann. "Slavery in the First Person." *Yale Alumni Magazine* 31 (November 1967): 33–39. [Interview about NT.] Reprinted in *William Styron's "The Confessions of Nat Turner"—A Critical Handbook*, edited by Friedman and Malin (see 2, A above).

Lichtenstein, G. "The Exiles." *New Statesman and Nation* 55 (6 September 1958): 320.

Lukas, J. Anthony. " 'Om,' Ginsberg's Hindu Chant, Fails to Charm a Judge in Chicago." *New York Times*, 13 December 1969, p. 19. [WS as witness at trial of the so-called Chicago 7.]

Macbeath, Innis. "Miller Defends Yevtushenko." *Times* (London), 26 November 1968, p. 5.

McNamara, Eugene. "The Post-Modern American Novel." *Queen's Quarterly* 69 (Summer 1962): 265–275.

————. "William Styron's *Long March:* Absurdity and Authority." *Western Humanities Review* 15 (Summer 1961): 267–272.

Mailer, Norman. "Norman Mailer vs. Nine Writers." *Esquire* 60 July 1963): 63–69, 105.

Markos, Donald W. "Margaret Whitehead in *The Confessions of Nat Turner.*" *Studies in the Novel* 4 (Spring 1972): 52–59.

Mason, Robert. "Teacher Guided, Publisher Fired Him—Encouragement and a Kick Made Bill Styron a Writer." *Norfolk Virginian-Pilot*, 9 September 1951, sec. 5, p. 5. [Detailed biographical sketch, based on interview with WS's father.]

Matthiessen, Peter, and Plimpton, George. "William Styron."

Paris Review 5 (Spring 1954): 42–47. [Interview.] Reprinted in *Writers at Work*, edited by Cowley (see 2, A above).

Mellen, Joan. "Polemics—William Styron: The Absence of Social Definition." *Novel* 4 (Winter 1971): 158–170.

Meras, Phyllis. "The Author." *Saturday Review* 50 (7 October 1967): 30.

Mizener, Arthur. "Some People of Our Time." *New York Times Book Review*, 5 June 1960, pp. 5, 26.

Mohrt, Michel. "Interview de William Styron." *Nouveau candide*, no. 70 (29 August 1962): 70.

————. "Michel Mohrt présente la première révélation du roman Américain depuis la guerre: j'ai vécu avec William Styron la dolce vita." *Arts*, no. 786 (7–13 September 1960): 3.

————. "Les trois obsessions de William Styron: le péché, le désespoir, le désir d'évasion." *Arts*, no. 858 (28 February–8 March 1962): 3.

Monaghan, Charles. "Portrait of a Man Reading." *Book World* (*Washington* [D.C.] *Post*), 27 October 1968, p. 8. [Interview.]

Moore, L. Hugh. "Robert Penn Warren, William Styron, and the Use of Greek Myth." *Critique* 8 (Winter 1965–1966): 75–87.

Morse, J. Mitchell. "Social Relevance, Literary Judgment, and the New Right; or, The Inadvertent Confessions of William Styron." *College English* 30 (May 1969): 605–616 [614–615: NT].

"Movies." *Newsweek* 63 (9 March 1964): 59. [Influence of movies on WS's technique.]

Moyano, Maria Clara. "Speaking Volumes—The Confessions of William Styron." *Book World* (*Washington* [D.C.] *Post*), 1 October 1967, p. 6.

Mudrick, Marvin. "Mailer and Styron: Guests of the Establishment." *Hudson Review* 17 (Autumn 1964): 346–366.

Mullen, Jean S. "Styron's Nat Turner: A Search for Humanity." *Barat Review* 6 (Spring/Summer 1971): 6–11.

"Nat Turner Saga to Be Filmed." *Plain Dealer* (Cleveland), 18 February 1968, p. 5-G.

Newcomb, Horace. "William Styron and the Act of Memory: *The Confesesions of Nat Turner.*" *Chicago Review* 20, no. 1 (1968): 86–94.

Nigro, August. "*The Long March:* The Expansive Hero in a Closed World." *Critique* 9, no. 3 (1967): 103–112.

Noggle, Burt. "Variety and Ambiguity." *Mississippi Quarterly* 17 (Winter 1963–1964): 33.

Nolte, William H. "Styron's Meditation on Saviors." *Southwest Review* 58 (Autumn 1973): 338–348.

Normand, J. "L'homme mystifié: les héros de Bellow, Albee, Styron, et Mailer." *Études Anglaises* 22 (October–December 1969): 370–385 [378–381].

"Notes on People." *New York Times,* 21 December 1971, p. 43. [WS has completed his first play, *In the Clap Shack.*]

Nye, Russel. "Le roman Américain contemporain." *Revue des lettres modernes* 8 (Spring 1961): 3–16.

O'Connell, Shaun. "Expense of Spirit: The Vision of William Styron." *Critique* 8 (Winter 1965–1966): 20–33.

————. "Styron's Nat Turner. . . ." *Nation* 205 (16 October 1967): 373–374.

O'Rourke, Elizabeth. Review of *Best Short Stories from "The Paris Review.*" *Best Sellers* 19 (1 November 1959): 259.

Phillips, John. "Styron Unlocked." *Vogue* 150 (December 1967): 216–217, 267–271, 278.

Pickens, Donald K. "Uncle Tom Becomes Nat Turner: A Commentary on Two American Heroes." *Negro American Literature Forum* 3 (Summer 1969): 45–48.

Pinsker, Sanford. "Christ as Revolutionary/Revolutionary as Christ: The Hero in Bernard Malamud's *The Fixer* and William Styron's *The Confessions of Nat Turner.*" *Barat Review* 6 (Spring/Summer 1971): 29–37 [33–37].

Plimpton, George. "William Styron: A Shared Ordeal." *New York Times Book Review*, 8 October 1967, pp. 2, 3, 30, 32, 34.

Ragan, Sam. "Southern Accent." *Raleigh* (N.C.) *News and Observer*, 16 September 1951, sec. 4, p. 5. [WS and the reception of LDD.]

Ratner, Marc L. "Rebellion of Wrath and Laughter: Styron's *Set*

This House on Fire." *Southern Review* 7 (Autumn 1971): 1007–1020.

————. "The Rebel Purged: Styron's *The Long March.*" *Arlington Quarterly* 2 (Autumn 1969): 27–42.

————. "Styron's Rebel." *American Quarterly* 21 (Fall 1969): 595–608.

Raymont, Henry. "Italian Poet Gets $10,000 Prize: Styron Is Cited for 'Nat Turner.'" *New York Times*, 14 March 1970, p. 28. [WS awarded Howells Medal.]

————. "P.E.N. Congress May Discuss Censorship of Soviet Writers." *New York Times*, 12 August 1969, p. 36. [WS quoted on plight of Soviet writers.]

Robb, Kenneth A. "William Styron's Don Juan." *Critique* 8 (Winter 1965–1966), 34–46.

Roberts, Steven V. "Over the 'Nat Turner' Screenplay Subsides [*sic*]." *New York Times*, 31 March 1969, p. 28. [On controversy about screen version.]

Rosenthal, Jean. "William Styron." *Informations et documents* no. 158 (15 March 1962): 24.

Roth, Philip. "Writing American Fiction." *Commentary* 31 (March 1961): 223–233 [232].

Rubin, Louis D., Jr. "Notes on the Literary Scene: Their (Southerners' Own Language." *Harper's* 230 (April 1965): 173–175.

Sachs, Viola. "Contemporary American Fiction and Some Nineteeth Century Patterns." *Kwartalnik neofilogizny* 13 (First Quarter 1966): 3–29.

Saint-Phalle, Thérese de. "William Styron (heritier littéraire de Faulkner): 'je ne veux pas être appelé un écrivain du sud.'" *Figaro littéraire*, 1–7 July 1965, p. 16.

Salisbury, Harrison E. "Kuznetsov Backs Soviet on China." *New York Times*, 24 August 1969, p. 20. [Kuznetsov replies to WS's statement that he shouldn't have defected.]

Salomon, Michel. "Interview avec William Styron." *Magazine littéraire* 27 (March 1969): 24–25.

Schneider, Harold W. "Two Bibliographies: Saul Bellow, William Styron." *Critique* 3 (Summer 1960): 71–91.

Shepard, Richard F. "Stage and Literary Names Enlist for Candidates." *New York Times*, 14 August 1968, p. 40 [WS as co-sponsor of fund-raising party for McCarthy.]

Sitkoff, Harvard, and Wreszin, Michael. "Whose Nat Turner: William Styron vs. the Black Intellectuals." *Midstream* 14 (November 1968): 10–20.

Stevenson, David L. "The Activists." *Daedalus* 92 (Spring 1963): 238–249.

————. "Styron and the Fiction of the Fifties." *Critique* 3 (Summer 1960): 47–58. Reprinted in *Recent American Fiction*, edited by Waldmeir (see 2, A above).

Sullivan, Walter. "The Decline of Regionalism in Southern Fiction." *Georgia Review* 18 (Fall 1964): 300–308 [306, 307].

Sussman, Robert. "The Case against William Styron's *Nat Turner*." *Yale Literary Magazine* 137 (September 1968): 20–23.

Swanson, William J. "Religious Implications in *The Confessions of Nat Turner*." *Cimarron Review*, no. 12 (July 1970): 57–66.

Talese, Gay. "Looking for Hemingway." *Esquire* 60 (July 1963): 44–47.

Taylor, Robert. "The Controversions of William Styron." *Washington* (D.C.) *Post*, 11 May 1969, p. 5-B. [Interview on NT reprinted from *Boston Globe*.]

"Teacher Is Backed in Stand on Pledge." *New York Times*, 23 February 1970, p. 24. [WS as signer of statement supporting Roxbury, Conn., teacher who refused to say Pledge of Allegiance with her class.]

Thelwell, Michael. "Arguments: The Turner Thesis." *Partisan Review* 35 (Summer 1968): 403–412; reply by Robert Coles, pp. 412–414.

————. "An Exchange on 'Nat Turner.'" *New York Review of Books* 11 (7 November 1968): 34.

————. "Mr. William Styron and the Rev. Turner." *Massachusetts Review* 9 (Winter 1968): 7–29. Reprinted in *William Styron's "Nat Turner,"* edited by Clarke (see 2, A above).

Thomas, Emory E. "Ten Views of the Man Who Would Not Die." *Saturday Review* 51 (17 August 1968): 23–24. [Review of Clarke's *William Styron's "Nat Turner."*]

Thorp, Willard. "The Southern Mode." *South Atlantic Quarterly* 63 (Autumn 1964): 576–582 [578–579].

"The Times Diary." *Times* (London), 2 April 1969, p. 10. [On controversy over filming of NT.]

Times Literary Supplement (London), 5 August 1955, pp. II–III.

Tischler, Nancy M. "*The Confessions of Nat Turner:* A Symposium—Introduction." *Barat Review* 6 (Spring/Summer 1971): 3–4.

——. "Negro Literature and Classic Form." *Contemporary Literature* 10 (Summer 1969): 352–365. [NT and *Invisible Man.*]

Tragle, Henry Irving. "Styron and His Sources." *Massachusetts Review* 11 (Winter 1970): 134–153.

Tyrmand, Leopold. "Yevtushenko's Career." *New York Times*, 8 December 1968, sec. 4, p. 13. [Letter to the the editor in response to WS's defense of Yevtushenko.]

Urang, Gunnar. "The Broader Vision: William Styron's *Set This House on Fire.*" *Critique* 8 (Winter 1965–1966): 47 –69.

Via, Dan O., Jr. "Law and Grace in Styron's *Set This House on Fire.*" *Journal of Religion* 51 (April 1971): 125–136.

"W. S. Writes PW about His New Novel." *Publisher's Weekly* 177 (30 May 1961): 54–55.

Waldmeir, Joseph. "Quest without Faith." *Nation* 193 (18 November 1961): 390–396.

Warren, Robert Penn. "William Styron." *Book of-the-Month-Club News*, October 1967, pp. 6–7, 14.

Weiler, A. H. "Styron Charges 'Black Pressure' on Turner Film." *New York Times*, 28 January 1970, p. 48. [Interview.]

Wells, Anna Mary. "An Exchange on 'Nat Turner.'" *New York Review of Books* 11 (7 November 1968): 31.

White, John. "The Novelist as Historian: William Styron and American Negro Slavery." *Journal of American Studies* 4 (February 1971): 233–245.

Whitman, Alden. "Styron Discloses Protest in Soviet—Criticized Jailing of Writers during Visit to Moscow." *New York Times*, 1 November 1968, p. 21. [Interview.]

————. "William Styron Examines the Negro Upheaval." *New York Times*, 5 August 1967, p. 13.

Whitney, Blair. "Nat Turner's Mysticism." *Barat Review* 6 (Spring/Summer 1971): 21–24.

Wicker, Tom. "In the Nation: What Sense in Censorship?" *New York Times*, 3 April 1969, p. 42. [On censoring NT as racist.]

Wiemann, Renate. "William Styron: *Lie Down in Darkness*." *Die Neueren Sprachen* 19 (July 1970): 321–332.

Winner, Anthony. "Adjustment, Tragic Humanism, and Italy." *Studi Americani* 7 (1961): 311–361.

C. DOCTORAL DISSERTATIONS

Baumbach, Jonathan. "The Theme of Guilt and Redemption in the Post Second World War Novel." Stanford University, 1961.

Corodimas, Peter N. "Guilt and Redemption in the Novels of William Styron." Ohio State University, 1971.

Galloway, David D. "The Absurd Hero in Contemporary Fiction: The Works of John Updike, William Styron, Saul Bellow, and J. D. Salinger." University of Buffalo, 1962.

Hux, Samuel H. "American Myth and Existential Vision: The Indigenous Existentialism of Mailer, Bellow, Styron, and Ellison." University of Connecticut, 1966.

Kime, Benna K. "A Critical Study of the Technique of William Styron." Tulane University, 1971.

Luttrell, William. "Tragic and Comic Modes in Twentieth Century American Literature: William Styron and Joseph Heller." Bowling Green State University, 1969.

Mewshaw, Michael F. "Thematic and Stylistic Problems in the Work of William Styron." University of Virginia, 1970.

Morgan, Henry G., Jr. "The World as Prison: A Study of the Novels of William Styron." University of Colorado, 1972.

Nelson, Doris L. "The Contemporary American Family Novel: A Study in Metaphor." University of Southern California, 1970.

Nigro, August. "William Styron and the Adamic Tradition." University of Maryland, 1964.

O'Connell, Shaun V. "The Contexts of William Styron's *The Confessions of Nat Turner.*" University of Massachusetts, 1970.

Ownbey, Ray W. "To Choose Being: The Function of Order and Disorder in William Styron's Fiction." University of Utah, 1972.

Scott, James B. "The Individual and Society: Norman Mailer versus William Styron." Syracuse University, 1964.

Swanson, William J. "William Styron: Eloquent Protestant." Northern Colorado University, 1972.

D. BOOK REVIEWS

Lie Down in Darkness

Aldridge, John W. "In a Place Where Love Is a Stranger." *New York Times Book Review*, 9 September 1951, p. 5.

Bedell, W. D. "William Styron—Bitter Story Hits Home." *Houston Post*, 9 September 1951, sec. 1, p. 22.

Breit, Harvey. "Dissolution of a Family." *Atlantic Monthly* 188 (October 1951): 78–80.

Byam, Milton S. *Library Journal* 76 (15 September 1951): 1423–1424.

Cady, Ernest. "Books—Impressive First Novel Surmounts Handicap of Overworked Theme." *Columbus* (Ohio) *Dispatch*, 9 September 1951, p. 7-F.

Chapin, Ruth. "Twilight of the South." *Christian Science Monitor*, 4 October 1951, p. 11.

Cowley, Malcolm. "The Faulkner Pattern." *New Republic* 125 (8 October 1951): 19–20.

Crume, Paul. "Strong Novel of Virginia Tragedy." *Dallas Morning News*, 9 September 1951, sec. 6, p. 7.

"Dark Misery." *Newsweek* 38 (10 September 1951): 106–107.

Davis, Robert Gorham. "A Grasp of Moral Realities." *American Scholar* 21 (Winter 1951–1952): 114, 116.

Derleth, August. "Idea Is Good But It Needs a Little Editing." *Chicago Sunday Tribune Magazine of Books*, 9 September 1951, p. 3.

Downing, Francis. "The Young: A Lost Generation." *Commonweal* 54 (5 October 1951): 620.

Elwood, Irene. "Family Has Everything, Loses All." *Los Angeles Times*, 16 September 1951, sec. 4, p. 5.

Geismar, Maxwell. "Domestic Tragedy in Virginia." *Saturday Review of Literature* 34 (15 September 1951): 12–13.

Govan, Christine Noble. "Story of Weak Family Is Plea for More Maturity in Adults." *Chattanooga Times*, 16 September 1951, p. 19.

Grove, Lee. "Memorable First Novel Demolishes a Family." *Washington* (D.C.) *Post*, 9 September 1951, p. 6-B.

Heth, Edward Harris. "A Torrential New Talent." *Milwaukee Journal*, 16 September 1951, sec. 5, p. 5.

Janeway, Elizabeth. "Private Emotions Privately Felt." *New Leader* 35 (21 January 1952): 25.

Jones, Carter Brooke. "Work of Virginia's William Styron Hailed as Extraordinary First Novel." *Washington* (D.C.) *Sunday Star*, 9 September 1951, p. 3-C.

Jones, Howard Mumford. "A Rich, Moving Novel Introduces a Young Writer of Great Talent." *New York Herald Tribune Book Review*, 9 September 1951, p. 3.

Kelley, James E. "Promising First Novel—Violence of Love and Hate." *Denver Post*, 9 September 1951, p. 6-E.

Kirby, John Pendy. *Virginia Quarterly Review* 28 (Winter 1952): 129–130.

L[aycock], E[dward] A. "An Exciting Discovery—William Styron Writes Magnificent First Novel about a Tragic Family." *Boston Sunday Globe*, 9 September 1951, p. 27-A.

Mason, Robert. "Story of the Spirit Is Rich in Poetry and Insight—William Styron of Newport News, 26, Is Suddenly a Major Novelist." *Norfolk Virginian-Pilot*, 9 September 1951, sec. 5, p. 4.

New Yorker 27 (29 September 1951): 118–119.

O'Brien, Alfred, Jr. "Lie Down in Darkness." *Commonweal* 55 (19 October 1951): 43–44.

O'Leary, Theodore M. "Styron's Remarkable First Novel." *Kansas City* (Mo.) *Star*, 29 September 1951, p. 16.

Pasley, Gertrude. "Unhappy People." *Newark* (N.J.) *Sunday News*, 16 September 1951, sec. 4, p. 88.

Prescott, Orville. "Books of the Times." *New York Times*, 10 September 1951, p. 19.

Ragan, Marjorie. "A New Southern Author Shows Literary Promise." *Raleigh* (N.C.) *News and Observer*, 16 September 1951, sec. 4, p. 5.

Rubin, Louis D., Jr. "What to Do About Chaos." *Hopkins Review* 5 (Fall 1951): 65–68.

S., A. *Canadian Forum* 31 (January 1952): 239.

Scott, Eleanor M. *Providence* (R.I.) *Sunday Journal*, 9 September 1951, sec. 6, p. 8.

Scott, J. D. "New Novels." *New Statesman and Nation* 43 (19 April 1952): 472–473.

Sessler, Betty. *Richmond* (Va.) *Times-Dispatch*, 16 September 1951, p. 8-Ā.

Sherman, John K. "First Novel Stamps Young Writer as Great." *Minneapolis Sunday Tribune*, 30 September 1951, feature-news section, p. 6.

Smith, Harrison, "Young Writer Depicts Trials of Human Soul." *Buffalo* (N.Y.) *Evening News*, 8 September 1951, magazine section, p. 7. See also *Charlotte* (N.C.) *Observer*, 9 September 1951, p. 14-D; *Philadelphia Sunday Bulletin*, 9 September 1951, magazine section, p. 6.

Snyder, Marjorie B. "Love, Hate, Passion All in His Book." *Boston Sunday Herald*, 9 September 1951, sec. 1, p. 6.

Stix, Frederick W. *Cincinnati Enquirer*, 9 September 1951, sec. 3, p. 13.

Swados, Harvey. "First Novel." *Nation* 272 (24 November 1951): 453.

"The Unbeautiful and Damned." *Time* 58 (10 September 1951): 106, 108.

Wallace, Margaret. "Of a Nobel Laureate and Other Novelists." *Independent Woman* 30 (November 1951): 325.

Ziegner, Edward. "Here's a First, Not a Last, We Hope." *Indianapolis News*, 8 September 1951, p. 2.

Set This House on Fire

Adams, Phoebe. *Atlantic Monthly* 206 (July 1960): 97–98.

Baro, Gene. "Styron's New Novel: Search for the Meaning of Evil." *New York Herald Tribune Book Review*, 5 June 1960, pp. 1, 12.

Betts, Doris. "Serious Violent Novel." *Houston Post*, 12 June 1960, Houston Now section, p. 36.

Borklund, Elmer. "Fiction of Violence and Pain." *Commentary* 30 (November 1960): 452–454.

Bourg, Gene. "Italy Is Scene of American Drama." *New Orleans Times-Picayune*, 19 June 1960, sec. 2, p. 13.

Bradley, Van Allen. "Second Styron Novel Close to a Masterpiece." *Chicago Daily News*, 4 June 1960, p. 13.

Breit, Harvey. "A Second Novel." *Partisan Review* 28 (Summer 1960): 561–563.

Bryden, Ronald. "Near Amalfi." *Spectator*, no. 6921 (17 February 1961), pp. 232–233.

Cheney, Frances Neel. "Rich, Sensitive Prose—Eye for Detail." *Nashville Banner*, 3 June 1960, p. 24.

Covici, Pascal, Jr. "Powerful Vision for Our Time." *Dallas Morning News*, 5 June 1960, sec. 5, p. 6.

Creed, Howard. "Styron Doesn't Set Reviewer on Fire." *Birmingham* (Ala.) *News*, 21 August 1960, p. 8-E.

Culligan, Glendy. "Styron Returns—Jury Still Hung." *Washington* (D.C.) *Post*, 5 June 1960, p. 6-E.

Cunningham, Bill. *San Antonio Express and News*, 10 July 1960, p. 5-G.

*Curley, Thomas F. "The Quarrel with Time in American Fiction." *American Scholar* 29 (Autumn 1960): 552–560.

Dahms, Joseph G. *America* 103 (18 June 1960): 380–381.

Daniels, N. A. "The Identity of Opposites." *San Francisco People's World*, 9 July 1960, p. 6.

Dawkins, Cecil. "Our Man in Italy—A Study of Evil and Its Expiation." *Milwaukee Journal*, 5 June 1960, sec. 5, p. 4.

Dwight, Ogden G. "In 'Set This House on Fire' Styron Has Quite a Blaze." *Des Moines* (Iowa) *Register*, 3 July 1960, p. 11-G.

"Empty Soul Blues." *Time* 74 (6 June 1960): 98.

*Fenton, Charles A. "William Styron and the Age of the Slob." *South Atlantic Quarterly* 59 (Autumn 1960): 469–476.

Fuller, Edmund. "A Picture of Hell by a Writer of Maturing Vision." *Chicago Sunday Tribune Magazine of Books*, 5 June 1960, p. 3.

Gentry, Curt. "Styron's Superb Third Novel." *San Francisco Sunday Chronicle*, 5 June 1960, This World section, p. 22.

Griffin, Lloyd W. *Library Journal* 85 (15 June 1960): 2458.

Hayes, E. Nelson. "Novels by Styron and Fifield." *Providence* (R.I.) *Journal*, 5 June 1960, p. 20-W.

Hicks, Granville. "After the Fury, a Time of Peace." *Saturday Review of Literature* 43 (4 June 1960): 13.

Highet, Gilbert. *Book-of-the-Month-Club News*, June 1960, p. 7.

Hill, Susan. *Time and Tide* 42 (24 February 1961): 285.

Hollander, John. *Yale Review* 50 (Fall 1960): 152–153.

Hunter, Anna C. "Styron Fulfills Promise with Explosive New Novel." *Savannah* (Ga.) *Morning News*, 5 June 1960, magazine section, p. 14.

Hutchens, John K. *New York Herald Tribune*, 3 June 1960, p. 11.

Jones, Carter B. "Mr. Styron's New Novel Is a Disappointment." *Washington* (D.C.) *Sunday Star*, 5 June 1960, p. 11-C.

"Just Out: A Kind of Tenderness." *Newsweek* 55 (6 June 1960): 117–118.

Kaufman, Clarence. "Second Styron Novel Proof of Major Talent." *Lincoln* (Neb.) *Sunday Journal and Star*, 5 June 1960, p. 12-B.

Kenney, Herbert, Jr. "Moralizing Binge Spoils Styron Talent." *Indianapolis News*, 6 August 1960, p. 2.

Kirsch, Robert R. "Styron's 'House' Nears Greatness." *Los Angeles Times*, 5 June 1960, p. 7-C.

Kohn, Sherwood. "Styron . . . an heir of Camus?" *Louisville* (Ky.) *Times*, 15 June 1960, p. 11.

L., E. A. "American Spoiled Boy—Styron's Third Novel Shocking, Powerful Picture of Degradation." *Boston Sunday Globe*, 5 June 1960, p. 7-A.

L., E. H. "New Book Plenty Hot—It Deserves to Burn." *Salt Lake City Tribune*, 14 August 1960, p. 15-W.

Layton, Mike. "Critics Predictions Fulfilled by Styron." *Olympia* (Wash.) *Sunday Olympian*, 12 June 1960, p. 22.

Lea, George. "New Novel Won't Set House on Fire." *Chicago Sun-Times*, 10 July 1960, sec. 3, p. 5.

"Life, Death of Sadistic Millionaire." *Miami Herald*, 12 June 1960, p. 14-J.

Lindau, Betsy. *Asheville* (N.C.) *Citizen-Times*, 5 June 1960, p. 3-D.

Lowman, Ann. "Too Much Retrospect Mars Styron's Second." *Columbus* (Ohio) *Sunday Dispatch*, 26 June 1960, TAB section, p. 12.

McDermott, Stephanie. "Arty People Flounder in Own Morass." *St. Louis Globe Democrat*, 5 June 1960, p. 4-F.

McManis, John. *Detroit News*, 5 June 1960, p. 3-F.

Malcolm, Donald. "False Alarms." *New Yorker* 36 (4 June 1960): 152–154.

Mason, Robert. "Characters Clash in Heroic Conflict." *Virginian Pilot and Portsmouth Star*, 5 June 1960, p. 8-F.

Miller, Nolan. *Antioch Review* 20 (Summer 1960): 256.

Mizener, Arthur. "Some People of Our Time." *New York Times Book Review*, 5 June 1960, pp. 5, 26.

Monaghan, Charles. "Styronic Manner." *Commonweal* 72 (22 July 1960): 380.

Mooney, Harry, Jr. "Styron Raises Issues, Faces Them Squarely, but Novel Is Seriously Marred by Author's Undisciplined Rhetoric." *Pittsburgh Press*, 5 June 1960, sec. 5, p. 14.

Murray, James G. *Critic* 19 (August–September 1960): 37.

"Must Books." *Kirkus* 28 (15 April 1960): 333.

Newberry, Mike. "Shock of Recognition." *Mainstream* 13 (September 1960): 61–63.

New Mexico Quarterly 30 (Winter 1960–1961): 412.

Nichols, Luther. "Styron's Literary Shock Treatment." *San Francisco Examiner*, 29 May 1960, Highlight section, p. 6.

O'Leary, Theodore M. "All the Elements of Greatness." *Kansas City* (Mo.) *Star*, 4 June 1960, p. 18.

Peckham, Stanton. "Styron's Second Novel Fulfills Promise." *Denver Sunday Post*, 5 June 1960, Roundup section, p. 9.

Perkin, Robert L. "Important Fiction." *Denver Rocky Mountain News*, 26 June 1960, p. 14-A.

Pickrel, Paul. "Heroic Proportions." *Harper's* 221 (July 1960): 93.

Prescott, Orville. *New York Times*, 3 June 1960, p. 29.

Price, Emerson. "Magnificent Novel Portrays Man Trapped by His Own Folly." *Cleveland Press*, 7 June 1960, p. 28.

Price, R. G. *Punch* 240 (15 March 1961): 441–442.

Ragan, Marjorie. "A Brilliant Fire of Tragedy." *Raleigh* (N.C.) *News and Observer*, 5 June 1960, sec. 3, p. 5.

Rogers, W. G. "Killing in Italy Theme of New Styron Novel." *Cleveland Plain Dealer*, 12 June 1960, p. 8-H.

*Rothberg, Abraham. "Styron's Appointment in Sambuco." *New Leader* 43 (4–11 July 1960): 24–27.

*Rubin, Louis D., Jr. "An Artist in Bonds." *Sewanee Review* 69 (Winter 1961): 174–179.

———. *Baltimore Evening Sun*, 3 June 1960, p. 30.

Scott, Paul. *New Statesman and Nation* 61 (17 February 1961): 270–271.

Sherman, John K. "Melodrama of Good and Evil Probes Human Undercurrents." *Minneapolis Tribune*, 12 June 1960, p. 6-E.

Sinclair, Reid B. "Prodigious Effort by a Virginian." *Richmond* (Va.) *Times Dispatch*, 26 June 1960, p. 10-L.

Southern, Terry. *Nation* 192 (19 November 1960): 382.

Virginia Quarterly Review 36 (Autumn 1960): civ.

Watts, Harold H. "Assembly of Horrors." *St. Louis Post-Dispatch*, 19 June 1960, p. 4-B.

"What Happened at Sambuco." *London Times Literary Supplement*, 17 February 1961, p. 101.

The Confessions of Nat Turner

America 117 (25 November 1967): 666.

America 118 (24 February 1968): 269.

Ancrum, Calhoun. "Novel by Styron Gets Rave Notices." *Charleston* (S.C.) *News Courier*, 31 December 1967, p. 2-D.

Barkham, John. "Sixty Whites Were Killed in 1831 Slave Riots." *Youngstown* (Ohio) *Vindicator*, 8 October 1967, p. 2-B. See also *Woodland* (Calif.) *Democrat*, 18 October 1967; *Lewiston* (Idaho) *Tribune*, 15 October 1967; *Albany* (N.Y.) *Times-Union*, 8 October 1967.

Bernstein, Victor. "Black Power, 1831." *Hadassah Magazine*, November 1967, pp. 16, 37.

Billings, Claude. "Confessions Bares Negro Slave Revolt." *Indianapolis Star*, 17 December 1967, sec. 8, p. 7.

Birlchaui, John. "Nat Turner's Rampage Told." *Tucson* (Ariz.) *Daily Citizen*, 2 December 1967, Ole magazine, p. 7.

Booklist 64 (1 December 1967): 425.

Bradley, Van Allen. "Styron Tells Slave's Saga." *Memphis Commercial Appeal*, 15 October 1967, sec. 5, p. 6. See also *Birmingham* (Ala.) *News*, 15 October 1967.

Brown, Cecil M. *Negro Digest* 17 (February 1968): 51–52, 89–91.

Bryden, Ronald. "Slave Rising." *New Statesman* 75 (3 May 1968): 586–587.

Buckmaster, Henrietta. "Racism, 1831: The Fire Last Time." *Christian Science Monitor*, 12 October 1967, p. 5.

Bunke, Joan. "Styron Novel Is Powerful as Fiction and Sermon." *Des Moines* (Iowa) *Register*, 15 October 1967, p. 7-T.

Callanan, Kathleen B. "Curl Up and Read." *Seventeen*, January 1968, p. 116.

Chicago American, 8 October 1967, sec. 3, p. 5.

Choice 5 (March 1968): 54.

Clemons, Joel. "Author Dramatizes Event Masterfully." *Charleston* (S.C.) *News Courier*, 31 December 1967, p. 2-D.

* Coles, Robert. "Blacklash." *Partisan Review* 35 (Winter 1968): 128–133.

Collier, Peter. "Saga of Rebellion." *Progressive*, December 1967, pp. 41–42.

"Confessions of Nat Turner Condemned as Racist Book." *Los Angeles Free Press*, 29 March 1968, p. 8.

*Cooke, Michael. "Nat Turner's Revolt." *Yale Review* 57 (Winter 1968): 273–278.

*Core, George. *"Nat Turner* and the Final Reckoning of Things." *Southern Review*, n.s. 4 (July 1968): 745–751.

Cunningham, Dick. "Styron Writes of Negro with Inside-Out View." *Minneapolis Tribune*, 8 October 1967, p. 6-E.

Currie, Edward. "Author William Styron—Era's Clarion." *Denver Rocky Mountain News*, 22 October 1967, Startime section, p. 19.

Delany, Lloyd Tom. "A Psychologist Looks at *The Confessions of Nat Turner.*" *Psychology Today* 1 (January 1968): 11–14.

Driver, Tom F. "Black Consciousness through a White Scrim." *Motive* 27 (February 1968): 56–58.

*Duberman, Martin. *Village Voice*, 14 December 1967, pp. 8–9, 16.

Duffer, Ken. "Nat Turner: Slave to a Terrible Vision." *Winston-Salem* (N.C.) *Journal Sentinel*, 8 October 1967, p. 6-D.

Fadiman, Clifton. *Book-of-the-Month-Club News*, October 1967, pp. 2–5.

Ferguson, Charles A. "Styron Revises Story of Slave Revolt of 1831." *New Orleans Times-Picayune*, 29 October 1967, p. 12.

Fremont-Smith, Eliot. "A Sword Is Sharpened." *New York Times*, 3 October 1967, p. 45.

————. " 'The Confessions of Nat Turner'—II." *New York Times*, 4 October 1967, p. 45.

*Friedman, Melvin J. *"The Confessions of Nat Turner:* The Convergence of 'Nonfiction Novel' and 'Meditation on History.' " *Journal of Popular Culture* 1 (Fall 1967): 166–175. See also *The University of Wisconsin at Milwaukee Magazine*, Spring 1968, pp. 3–7 (abridged).

Fuller, Edmund. "Power and Eloquence in New Styron Novel." *Wall Street Journal*, 4 October 1967, p. 16.

*Gilman, Richard. "Nat Turner Revisited." *New Republic* 158 (27 April 1968): 23–26, 28, 32.

Goodheart, Eugene. "When Slaves Revolt." *Midstream* 14 (January 1968): 69–72.

Greenwood, Walter B. "Nat Turner's Revolt a Tragic Comment

on Slavery's Evils." *Buffalo* (N.Y.) *Evening News*, 14 October 1967, p. 12-B.

Griffin, Lloyd W. *Library Journal* 92 (1 October 1967): 3448–3449.

Grimes, Roy. "Books and Things—*The Confessions of Nat Turner*." *Victoria* (B.C.) *Advocate*, 15 October 1967, p. 10.

H., S. "Novel of Slave Revolt Eloquent." *San Antonio Express*, 8 October 1967, p. 3-H.

Hall, Joan Joffe. "Jehovah's Rebel Slave." *Houston Post*, 22 October 1967, Spotlight section, p. 12.

* Harnack, Curtis. "The Quidities of Detail." *Kenyon Review* 30 (Winter 1968): 125–132.

Heise, Kenan. *Extension* 62 (December 1967): 54.

Herman, Dick. "Is Grim Message of Slavery Just Beginning to Be Felt?" *Lincoln* (Neb.) *Journal and Star*, 15 October 1967, p. 15-F.

Hicks, Granville. "Race Riot, 1831." *Saturday Review* 50 (7 October 1967): 29–31.

———. "Five for Year's End." *Saturday Review* 50 (30 December 1967): 19.

Hicks, Walter J. "The Futile Insurrection." *Baltimore Sunday Sun*, 15 October 1967, p. 5-D.

Hogan, William. "William Styron's American Tragedy." *San Francisco Chronicle*, 9 October 1967, p. 43.

———. "Further Thoughts on the Styron Novel." *San Francisco Chronicle*, 10 October 1967, p. 39.

Hurt, Richard L. "Slavery's Quiet Resistance." *Boston Globe*, 8 October 1967, p. 43-A.

"The Idea of Hope." *Time* 90 (13 October 1967): 110, 113.

Ingle, H. L. "Meditation on History." *Chattanooga Times*, 12 November 1967, p. 30.

* Kauffmann, Stanley. "Styron's Unwritten Novel." *Hudson Review* 20 (Winter 1967–1968): 675–679.

* Kazin, Alfred. "Instinct for Tragedy: A Message in Black and White." *Book World*, 8 October 1967, pp. 1, 22.

Kincaid, Anne. *Library Journal* 92 (15 November 1967): 4274.

Kirkus 35 (1 August 1967): 905.

Kirsch, Robert. "The Virginia Slave Revolt." *Los Angeles Times*, 8 October 1967, p. 36.

Krupat, Arnold. "The Shock of Nat Turner." *Catholic World* 206 (February 1968): 226–228.

LaHaye, Judson. *Best Sellers* 27 (1 November 1967): 308.

Layton, Mike. "A Negro Slave Revolt and What It Tells Us." *Olympia* (Wash.) *Sunday Olympian*, 28 October 1967, p. 27.

Lehan, Richard. *Contemporary Literature* 9 (Autumn 1968): 540–542.

Lewis, Claude. "Slavery, Murder, and God." *Philadelphia Sunday Bulletin*, 15 October 1967, Books and Art section, p. 3.

Long, James. *Portland Oregon Journal*, 11 November 1967, p. 6-J.

McCormick, Jay. "An American Tragedy—Lessons That the Gallows Failed to Teach." *Detroit News*, 8 October 1967, p. 3-E.

McGroaty, Rev. Joseph G. " 'Nat Turner': A Racial Tract for Our Times." *Tablet* 60 (16 November 1967): 13.

McNeill, Robert. *Presbyterian Survey* 58 (February 1968): 26–27.

McPherson, James Lowell. "America's Slave Revolt." *Dissent* 15 (January–February 1968): 86–89.

Mason, Robert. "A Brilliant 'Meditation on History'—Nat Turner, from Birth to Rebellion." *Virginian Pilot and Portsmouth Star*, 8 October 1967, p. 6-C.

Meyer, June. "Spokesmen for the Blacks." *Nation* 205 (4 December 1967): 597.

Miller, William Lee. "The Meditations of William Styron." *Reporter* 37 (16 November 1967): 42–46.

Moody, Minnie Hite. "Documentary Novel Is Pegged to 1831 Revolt." *Columbus* (Ohio) *Dispatch*, 22 October 1967, TAB section, p. 14.

Murray, Albert. "A Troublesome Property." *New Leader* 10 (4 December 1967): 18–20.

"Nat Turner's No Longer Unknown—1831 Insurrection Gets a Timely Revival in 'Confessions.' " *Grand Rapids* (Mich.) *Press*, 8 October 1967, p. 39.

Nolte, William H. "Fact Novel of Revolt in Hot Summer of 1831." *St. Louis Sunday Post-Dispatch*, 8 October 1967, p. 4-D.

Parker, Roy, Jr. "Styron's 'Nat Turner'—Fact Transmuted into Art." *Raleigh* (N.C.) *News and Observer*, 30 October 1967, sec. 3, p. 3.

Penne, Leo. "Out from the Vicious Circle." *Seattle Post-Intelligencer*, 22 October 1967, Northwest Today section, p. 4.

Platt, Gerald M. "A Sociologist Looks at *The Confessions of Nat Turner*." *Psychology Today* 1 (January 1968): 14–15.

Q., G. "Revolt of Negro Slaves Echoes over the Years." *Waco* (Tex.) *Tribune-Herald*, 5 November 1967, p. 13-D.

*Rahv, Phillip. "Through the Midst of Jerusalem." *New York Review of Books* 9 (26 October 1967): 6, 8, 10.

Redding, Saunders. "A Fateful Lightning in the Southern Sky." *Providence* (R.I.) *Journal*, 29 October 1967, p. 18-W.

Richter, David H. *Chicago Literary Review*, October 1967, pp. 1, 10–11.

Robertson, Don. "One View: Styron Is a Brave Failure." *Cleveland Plain Dealer*, 15 October 1967, p. 8-H.

Rubin, Louis D., Jr. "Books—Eloquent Story of a Slave Rebellion." *Washington* (D.C.) *Sunday Star*, 8 October 1967, p. 14-G.

*———. "William Styron and Human Bondage: *The Confessions of Nat Turner*." *Hollins Critic* 4 (December 1967): 1–12.

Schaap, Dick. "Framework for Confessions." *San Francisco Sunday Examiner and Chronicle*, 15 October 1967, This World section, pp. 39, 46.

Schlucter, Paul. "Soul Torment." *Christian Century* 85 (21 February 1968): 234–235.

Schroth, Raymond A. "Nat Turner's Sword." *America* 117 (14 October 1967): 416.

Schwartz, Joseph. "Negro Revolt of 1831 Flares Again in a 'Big' Novel of Fall." *Milwaukee Journal*, 8 October 1967, sec. 5, p. 4.

Shaw, Russell. *The Sign*. 47 (January 1968): 63.

*Sheed, Wilfrid. "The Slave Who Became a Man." *New York Times Book Review*, 8 October 1967, pp. 1–3, 30, 32, 34.

Sherman, John K. "Portrays Negro View—Novel Illuminates History of Slavery." *Minneapolis Star*, 10 October 1967, p. 4-E.

Smith, Miles A. "Slave Revolt of 1831 Is Recounted." *Indianapolis*

News, 21 October 1967, p. 30. See also *St. Louis Globe Democrat*, 21 October 1967, p. 5-F.

Sokolov, Raymond A. "Into the Mind of Nat Turner." *Newsweek* 70 (16 October 1967): 65–69.

Steiner, George. "Books—The Fire Last Time." *New Yorker* 43 (25 November 1967): 236.

Thomas, Sidney. "Slave Broke His Chains." *Atlanta Journal-Constitution*, 12 November 1967, p. 10-D.

*Thompson, John. "Rise and Slay!" *Commentary* 44 (November 1967): 81–85.

Tucker, Martin. *Commonweal* 87 (22 December 1967): 338–339.

Turney, Charles. "Virginian's Novel Seeks 'Meditation on History.'" *Richmond* (Va.) *Times-Dispatch*, 15 October 1967, p. 5-F.

"Unslavish Fidelity: The Confessions of William Styron." *London Times Literary Supplement*, 9 May 1968, p. 480.

Virginia Quarterly Review 44 (Winter 1968): viii.

W., B. "The Negro Fury: A Vital Insight." *Long Beach* (Calif.) *Independent Press-Telegram*, 18 November 1967, p. 6-A.

Wade, Gerald. "The Only Effective U.S. Negro Revolt." *Omaha* (Neb.) *World-Herald*, 29 October 1967, p. 36-I.

Weber, R. B. "Styron's Power Creates a Real Being." *Louisville* (Ky.) *Times*, 13 October 1967, p. 11-A.

Weeks, Edward. *Atlantic* 220 (November 1967): 130.

Winfrey, Lee. "When a Negro Slave Rebelled." *Detroit Free Press*, 8 October 1967, p. 5-B.

Wolff, Geoffrey A. "Slavery Intersects Present." *Washington* (D.C.) *Post*, 24 October 1967, p. 16-A.

*Woodward, C. Vann. "Confessions of a Rebel: 1831." *New Republic* 157 (7 Octobber 1967): 25–28.

Wright, Giles E. "Life of Real Slave Treated in Top Novel." *Los Angeles Herald Examiner*, 8 October 1967, p. 4-J.

Yardley, Jonathan. "Mr. Styron's Monumental 'Meditation on History.'" *Greensboro* (N.C.) *Daily News*, 8 October 1967, p. 3-D.

JACKSON R. BRYER

In the Clap Shack

Brockway, Jody. *Theatre Crafts* 6 (June 1973): 44.

Leon, Phillip W. "Styron Publishes First Play." *Nashville Tennessean*, 2 September 1973, p. 10-E.

Publishers Weekly 203 (7 May 1973): 63.

Spearman, William. *Chapel Hill* (N.C.) *Weekly*, 8 July 1973, p. 4-C.

Washington (D.C.) *Post*, 15 July 1973, *Book World*, p. 15.

Notes on Contributors

ROBERT K. MORRIS, Professor of English at the City College of the City University of New York, is the author of *The Novels of Anthony Powell*, *The Consolations of Ambiguity: An Essay on the Novels of Anthony Burgess*, *Continuance and Change: The Contemporary British Novel Sequence*, and *Paradoxes of Order*, as well as a number of reviews and articles on contemporary British and American literature. He is at work on a book-length critique of Anthony Powell's "A Dance to the Music of Time."

IRVING MALIN, Professor of English at the City College of the City University of New York, is the author of *William Faulkner: An Interpretation*, *New American Gothic*, *Jews and Americans*, *Saul Bellow's Fiction*, *Isaac Bashevis Singer*, and *Nathanael West's Novels*. He has edited critical collections of essays on Bellow, Singer, *In Cold Blood*, contemporary American Jewish literature, as well as a casebook (with Melvin J. Friedman) on *The Confessions of Nat Turner*.

EILEEN BENDER, a Kent Fellow, is presently working on her Ph.D. dissertation, a critical study of Joyce Carol Oates, at the University of Notre Dame.

JACKSON R. BRYER, Professor of English at the University of Maryland, is the author of *The Critical Reputation of F. Scott Fitzgerald*, editor of *Sixteen Modern American Authors: A Survey of Research and Criticism*, and coeditor of *Dear Scott/Dear Max: The Fitzgerald-Perkins Correspondence*, *F. Scott Fitzgerald in His Own Time: A Miscellany*, and F. Scott Fitzgerald's *Basil and Josephine Stories*. He is the head of the American Literature Section of the MLA Bibliography and coeditor of *Resources for American Literary Study*.

[278]

GEORGE CORE, formerly senior editor of the University of Georgia Press, is now editor of the *Sewanee Review*. He is also the author of the forthcoming study *The Literalists of the Imagination: Southern New Critics and the Profession of Letters*, the editor of two books, and the coeditor of two others. His articles and reviews have appeared in the *Southern Review*, the *Southern Literary Journal*, the *Michigan Quarterly Review*, and other periodicals.

JAN B. GORDON, currently Professor of English at the University of Singapore, spent 1967–1968 as a Leverhulme Fellow to the University of Warwick, United Kingdom. His essays on Victorian and modern literature have appeared in the *Southern Review*, *Criticism*, the *Journal of Arts and Aesthetics Criticism*, *Kenyon Review*, *Victorian Studies*, and *Commonweal*. He is coeditor of a forthcoming collection of essays on the nineties and is presently at work on a book dealing with modes of reconstituting the family as a theme in Victorian fiction.

SEYMOUR L. GROSS, Burke O'Neil Professor of American Literature at the University of Detroit, is the author of *Images of the Negro in American Literature* (with John E. Hardy), *Survey of American Literature* (with Milton Stern), and some sixty articles on American and British literature.

NORMAN KELVIN, Professor of English at the City College of the City University of New York, is the author of *A Troubled Eden: Nature and Society in the Works of George Meredith, E. M. Forster*, and numerous articles on British and American literature. He is at present preparing a comprehensive edition of the letters of William Morris with the assistance of a grant from the Guggenheim Foundation.

JOHN O. LYONS, Professor of English at the University of Wisconsin–Madison, is the author of *The College Novel in America*, *Studying Poetry* (an anthology), and a number of articles on Joyce and contemporary American literature. In recent years he has been a Fulbright lecturer in Iraq, Iran, and Turkey and is presently engaged in a study of the emergence of self-consciousness in various forms of literature.

ROBERT PHILLIPS, writer, editor, and anthologist, is the author of *Inner Weather* (poems), *The Land of Lost Content* (short stories), *Aspects of Alice* (a critical anthology), *The Confessional Poets*, *Moonstruck* (an anthology of poetry about the moon), and *Denton Welch*. He has taught literature at Syracuse University and writing at the New School, and his essays and reviews have appeared in the *New York Times Book Review*, the *Saturday Review*, *Commonweal*, *Centennial Review*, and elsewhere. He is a former editor of the literary journal *Modern Poetry Studies* and vice-president at Grey Advertising in New York City.

LOUIS D. RUBIN, JR., Professor of English at the University of North Carolina, is one of the most distinguished contemporary critics of American literature. Among his many books are *The Faraway Country*, *The Writer in the South*, and *The Teller in the Tale*. He is coeditor of the *Southern Literary Journal* and most recently the editor of *Thomas Wolfe* and *The Comic Tradition in American Literature*.